EVERY TOWN IS A SPORTS TOWN

EVERY TOWN IS A SPORTS TOWN

Business Leadership at ESPN,
from the Mailroom to the Boardroom

GEORGE BODENHEIMER
with *Donald T. Phillips*

GRAND CENTRAL
PUBLISHING

NEW YORK   BOSTON

Grand Central Publishing
Hachette Book Group
1290 Avenue of the Americas
New York, NY 10104

www.HachetteBookGroup.com

Printed in the United States of America

RRD-C

First Edition: May 2015
10 9 8 7 6 5 4 3 2 1

Grand Central Publishing is a division of Hachette Book Group, Inc.
The Grand Central Publishing name and logo is a trademark of Hachette Book Group, Inc.

The Hachette Speakers Bureau provides a wide range of authors for speaking events. To find out more, go to www.hachettespeakersbureau.com or call (866) 376-6591.

The publisher is not responsible for websites (or their content) that are not owned by the publisher.

Library of Congress Cataloging-in-Publication Data has been applied for.

ISBN 978-1-4555-8609-7

This book is dedicated to my family. First and
foremost, to my wife, Ann, whose love,
support, and friendship mean everything to me.
And to Vivian, Julian, Kate, George, James,
and Rob. Also, Tatters and Dottie.

Contents

Author's Note

All royalties the author receives will be donated to the V Foundation for Cancer Research.

The V Foundation was created by legendary Coach Jim Valvano and ESPN in 1993. Since then, a total of more than $130 million in research grants has been awarded. One hundred percent of direct cash contributions go directly to cancer researchers to fund their studies.

If you would like to make a donation or learn more about the V Foundation for Cancer Research, please visit www.jimmyv.org.

"Don't Give Up...Don't Ever Give Up."

EVERY TOWN IS
A SPORTS TOWN

I started at ESPN in 1979. Eighteen months later, they hired this guy named George Bodenheimer out of Denison University. One of his responsibilities was to pick me up at the airport and drive me places.

Back then, George was an aspiring marketing guy. But he was young, impatient, and at the bottom of the totem pole. One day he said, "Dick! Am I really going to have a career here? All I do is drive you around!"

When George was in his early twenties, I could tell he had what it took to be successful. The way he looked you in the eye. The way he shook your hand. The way he made you feel. He had all the qualities you would want in a leader—and he was likable.

So I said to him: "George, relax, baby! Something about you has 'winner' written all over it. You're Awesome—with a capital A. You're a three-S man: Super, Scintillating, Sensational! You are a prime-time performer—flat out! And by the way, this whole ESPN thing is going to succeed. You're going to have a great career. There's no doubt in my mind!"

George stayed with ESPN. He used to be my driver and then he became my boss. But he always treated me the same—great! And he never forgot where he came from. We formed a friendship that has lasted over thirty years.

Dick Vitale

I was Dickie V's regular driver when I started at ESPN in January 1981. He was coming into Bristol regularly and I would pick him up at the Hartford airport. Often, we'd drive to a diner and get something to eat. Then I'd take him to the only hotel anywhere near ESPN's offices, the Holiday Inn in Plainville, Connecticut (where all the original ESPN Christmas parties took place).

At that time, Dick was one of the company's top on-air talents, growing in stature, and well respected. But only a couple of years earlier, in 1979, he'd been unceremoniously fired as head coach of the Detroit Pistons (Dick called it "getting the ziggy"). Recognizing both his personality and his upside potential, ESPN quickly gave him a shot as a broadcaster—and Dick Vitale did the very first national basketball game that ever aired on ESPN (a DePaul victory over Wisconsin).

During those forty-five-minute drives to and from the airport, Dick and I would talk about all kinds of things. He took an immediate interest in me and my career, which I deeply appreciated. We became good friends.

I was just a kid and in my very first job out of college. I was green, unsure of my career path, and a driver. But Dickie V treated me like royalty. I'm proud to say that our friendship has lasted more than thirty years.

George Bodenheimer

Two-Minute Interview

My job interview with ESPN was fast, really fast. The place was buzzing and everybody seemed like they had too much to do. When ushered into the HR director's office, I found him sitting at his desk looking over my résumé. He didn't get up, didn't look up, and I wasn't offered a seat. So I just stood there for a moment—a nervous kid dressed in a coat and tie.

"Okay," he finally said, "based on this résumé you'd be qualified to be a driver, which is what we call our mailroom guys. They deliver mail around to the buildings and drive people to and from the airport. We might have an opening in about a week. The job pays $8,000 a year. You wouldn't mind shoveling snow, would you?"

"No, sir. I wouldn't mind," I said.

"All right, thanks for coming in. We'll let you know."

And that was it. The interview lasted two minutes, and it was only five minutes from the time I walked through ESPN's front door before I was back out in the parking lot.

As I started the sixty-mile drive from Bristol back home to Greenwich, Connecticut, I kept reliving the interview in my mind. Eight thousand dollars was less than one-quarter of the starting salary offered

ESPN Broadcast Center, 1979. *ESPN Images*

by big companies (such as U.S. Steel, International Paper, Xerox, and Procter & Gamble), which were recruiting at Denison. I didn't know what I was going to do. It had now been nine months since graduation, I was bartending part-time, and I was still living at home. My parents, Julian and Vivian Bodenheimer, knew I was anxious to begin a career, but they didn't put too much pressure on me. Rather, they were supportive, just like a family should be.

Dad was a retail store manager, Mom a banker. They raised my sister, Sue, and me to always treat others with respect. The worst thing my father could ever say to me when I was a kid was that I had disappointed him. And in those rare instances, it almost always had something to do with how I had interacted with people. "Always treat others the way you would want to be treated." That was the rule in our household. It was the Golden Rule and it was lived every day.

My dream was to work somewhere in a field related to sports or perhaps in the entertainment business, which I thought would be rewarding and fun. Along those lines, Dad helped me write letters to each of the twenty-six major-league baseball teams inquiring about a job. "You need me in your office," I wrote in each letter. But we received twenty-five "no-thank-you" responses and one "come-on-down-for-an-interview" reply.

The one interview was with Bill Giles of the Philadelphia Phillies, who was also a graduate of Denison University. Clearly, that connection was the reason I received the invitation. Mr. Giles was friendly and encouraging, but he didn't offer me a job. "Baseball front offices are generally small, and many are family-run operations," he said. "You should fire up your letter-writing campaign by reaching out to minor-league franchises." Then he gave me a Philadelphia Phillies necktie (commemorating the team's World Series victory that year) and wished me luck.

After I came up empty looking for jobs at major sports arenas, such as Madison Square Garden and the New Orleans Superdome, my dad suggested I go see his old friend Bud Lamoreaux, a longtime CBS producer. "If you want to get involved in sports *television*," said Bud, "I would seriously consider cable. As a matter of fact, there's this new twenty-four-hour sports network called ESPN you might want to check out. It's Connecticut-based—they're in Bristol. I know a couple of guys up there and can probably get you an introduction. Why don't you write to them and mention my name?"

I knew nothing about the cable television industry. Actually, we didn't even have cable in our house and I had never heard of ESPN. But I wanted a job and certainly wasn't going to miss an opportunity for an interview with anybody. So I dashed off a letter and, a week or so later, I was invited up to Bristol and it resulted in that two-minute interview.

As I pulled up to our house, I agonized about what I was going to tell my dad. Gee, I wasn't offered a job, but with my degree in economics they said I'd be qualified to work in the mailroom. Something might come up next week, but it'll only pay $8,000 a year. They'll let me know. Oh, and by the way, would I mind shoveling snow?

Shoot!

When I got home I laid it out for Dad, and he could see my concern. "Let's go out for a beer and talk about it," he said. So we went to a famous old restaurant in the Cos Cob section of Greenwich called The Clam Box where we had a beer, some chowder, and a father-son conversation.

"Do you think sports television is an industry you'd like to work in?" Dad asked.

"Yes, I think it is," I said.

"Okay, then if ESPN offers you a job, you'll be making a career decision, not a money decision, won't you?"

I paused, took another sip of beer, and looked back at my father.

"Forget about the pay and the duties," he continued. "If they make you an offer, you should probably take it. It'll get your foot in the door and you can go from there."

After listening to my dad, it really seemed like an easy decision. I loved sports, I *was* interested in television, and it *would* be a way for me to start a career. A week later, the call came and I was offered the job. Starting salary was $8,300 a year. I took it.

I moved north right away and rented a room ten miles from Bristol at the YMCA in New Britain. I showed up for my first day at work wearing a coat and tie. That was on my dad's advice and, since he was on a roll, I followed it.

No sooner had I set foot in the mailroom than my new boss said, "Hey, you! Take these videotapes over to communications, then come back and haul this small tree over to the legal department."

I didn't know where communications was and I didn't ask. I ditched my coat and tie, picked up the box of videotapes, and just took off. Officially, I was ESPN Employee #150.

If You're a Sports Fan

Outside, the building wasn't finished. Five dozen employees were working in three trailers. There was no running water. They had to trudge through the mud to use outside Porta-Potties. Inside, the studio was still under construction. The set was being held up by loose two-by-fours. Much of the audio and video equipment had been installed only a few hours earlier. The paint was still wet.

It was Friday, September 7, 1979, and as the clock counted down toward 7 p.m., ESPN prepared for its very first broadcast. People were scurrying around taking care of last-minute details. Extension cords were being plugged in. Technicians were making their final checks and praying everything would work. A guy was washing windows. At 6:59 p.m., people crowded into the control room. ESPN's founder, Bill Rasmussen, paced back and forth.

Finally, the producer yelled, "Good luck, everybody. Take one and roll theme."

A video of cheering sports fans appeared on the monitor. Lee Leonard, in a voice-over, said: "If you're a fan, *if* you're a fan, what you'll see in the next minutes, hours, and days to follow may convince you you've gone to sports heaven. [Video switched to a blue sky with white clouds.] Beyond that blue horizon is a limitless world of sports. And right now, you're standing on the edge of tomorrow: sports twenty-four hours a day, seven days a week with ESPN, the total sports cable network. [Then a musical build and a jingle (ESPN's first theme song) is heard, while new video of scenes from softball, wrestling, golf, boxing, and football runs.]"

♪♫♪♪ Pick us up and catch our act, 'cause we're the one worth watchin'.
Total sports and entertainment, we're the one worth watchin'.
Come alive without a doubt, you'll see the best, we'll work it out, with total sports and entertainment.
Everything worth seein'. Everything worth seein'.
Total sports entertainment.
E—S—P—N.
Everything worth seein'. ♪♫♪♪

The producer yelled, "Cue Lee," and the monitor closed in on a sportscaster sitting alone on the set. "Hi. I'm Lee Leonard welcoming you to Bristol, Connecticut—110 miles from New York City. Why Bristol? Because here in Bristol is where all of the sports action is happening as of right now.

"And we're just minutes away from the first event on the ESPN schedule. That's the 1979 NCAA college football preview. And then we're going to follow that with a doubleheader of games—two of the professional slow-pitch softball World Series games will be seen tonight. Now, softball is one of those rare sports that everybody knows something about. Why? 'Cause we all play it on Sunday when we drink a little beer."

―――――――

That modest broadcast may not seem particularly innovative or revolutionary, but it's worth noting that it occurred long before twenty-four-hour news, twenty-four-hour weather, twenty-four-hour music, and twenty-four-hour everything became the staples we now enjoy on television. ESPN went on the air, in fact, at the dawn of a technological revolution. Towns across America were just getting wired for cable television. People were arguing about whether or not this new medium had any chance of succeeding. And the entire idea of a twenty-four-hour sports network was considered ridiculous.

Back then, nearly all Americans watched television from a signal that was broadcast over the air by one of the big three networks—NBC, CBS, or ABC. The top brass at these three major corporations (based in New York City) took a close look at ESPN's first few broadcasts and shook their heads. "It's just a bunch of tape-delay reruns!" they said. "Nothing to worry about. They're just a niche. They'll never make it." The truth is that to them, ESPN was a bad idea, the dumbest thing they'd ever heard of, a laughingstock.

There was one person, however, who didn't worry about what the network executives thought. Bill Rasmussen was a huge sports fan who had guts, optimism, and a vision for the future. After being fired as communications director and play-by-play announcer for the New England Whalers of the old World Hockey Association, Bill (working in tandem with his son, Scott) innocently started looking for a way to broadcast basketball games from the University of Connecticut across the state. While he knew next to nothing about cable television, he had a hunch that it could be a game changer.

In his research, Bill learned that cable TV consisted of a big ground-based "dish" capable of receiving signals from satellite transponders orbiting twenty-three thousand miles above the earth. Bill also found out that there were only fourteen million homes receiving cable TV (less than 20 percent of television viewers in the United States). With that kind of distribution capability and the low number of subscribers, there was clearly upside potential. But then Bill found out that it was less expensive, on an hourly basis, to lease satellite time for a full twenty-four hours than it was for only five or six hours. And that's when the big idea hit him. "We can broadcast sports across the nation twenty-four hours a day!" he realized. "That's what we'll do!"

And that's what he did, naming his new enterprise the ESP Network (*ESP* stood for "Entertainment and Sports"). Soon after, a graphic design artist said it would look better if it just read ESPN, so the logo was changed.

In order to make his revolutionary new idea a success, Bill Rasmussen fell back on his hockey experience and performed an amazing "hat trick." He felt he had to pull off three big-time deals. First, he needed a contract with RCA to lease time on a satellite transponder. Second, in order to have enough games to fill up a twenty-four-hour day, he had to have a multiyear agreement with the NCAA for the rights to telecast college sporting events. And third, he set his sights on securing an advertising deal with Anheuser-Busch. It would be a kind of three-legged stool—without any one leg, the whole thing would fall flat. Pulling off his hat trick wasn't going to be easy, but Rasmussen was a natural-born salesman. He could do it.

As it turned out, RCA was eager for customers. They had an underused satellite and plenty of transponder sites available. It would cost $35,000 a month, but Bill didn't have anywhere near that much money. So RCA offered him an easy payment program and, in July 1978, he put the entire amount on one of his credit cards.

One down.

After persuading Getty Oil to purchase a majority stake in ESPN (which provided much-needed cash to get the network off the ground), Bill now had the credibility to negotiate seriously with the National Collegiate Athletic Association. Early on, he had received NCAA approval to broadcast UConn men's basketball, men's soccer, and women's basketball for three years. But now, after many meetings and lengthy negotiations, they settled on a two-year deal to televise a minimum of 230 games per year featuring eighteen different NCAA sports.

To fill airtime, Bill planned to broadcast the same games multiple times. Although ESPN would not be allowed to televise live football, it would be able to rerun games from tape. The fifty-six-page NCAA/ESPN "cornerstone" contract, as Rasmussen liked to call it, was signed on March 14, 1979.

ESPN Founder Bill Rasmussen on the cover of *Connecticut Magazine*, September 1979. Connecticut Magazine

Two down.

Originally, Bill planned to charge cable operators one cent a day for ESPN's service. But he reconsidered that and decided to try to become the cable industry's first advertisement-supported network. Selling advertising time to generate all revenue was, of course, the traditional business model for network television. And while some budding cable networks accepted corporate sponsorship money to help make ends meet, none had significant advertising sales. Knowing that sports reaches beer drinkers, Bill pitched his new network to Anheuser-Busch and offered to let them in on the ground floor. Some forward-thinking executives there realized the idea could really pay off and, in May 1979, they purchased $1.4 million of advertising on ESPN. At the time, it was a record advertising deal for cable television.

Three down.

Bill Rasmussen's hat trick was complete.

———

ESPN's first offices were located on the upper floor of the United Cable building in Plainville, Connecticut (the space was kindly offered by cable system manager Jim Dovey). And even before Rasmussen had the cash infusion from Getty, he set his sights on acquiring property to construct ESPN's own place of business. He soon spotted some undeveloped land in the next town over from Plainville. Bristol was a real working-class community in the heart of Connecticut's manufacturing corridor. Its largest business, a General Motors ball bearings plant, dated back to World War II and employed about three thousand people. The vacant property that interested Bill was surrounded mostly by green pastures dotted with a few small single-story buildings housing such things as a truck stop diner, a lawn mower repair shop, and a junkyard/scrap metal business. After persuading the City of Bristol to sell him one acre for only $18,000, Rasmussen began construction of ESPN's new headquarters.

By the time of its first broadcast, the new cable network employed approximately seventy-five people. Brought in well before the launch to run the day-to-day operations were a couple of veteran television executives from NBC. Chester R. "Chet" Simmons (who had helped develop ABC's *Wide World of Sports* and later became president of NBC Sports) agreed to become ESPN's president, and his colleague Allan B. "Scotty" Connal (who had started as a page in the NBC mailroom and grew to become an Emmy Award–winning producer) became our executive vice president, operations and production. Coming in on their heels from NBC were on-air talents Lee Leonard and Jim Simpson. Scotty Connal made personal phone calls and hired a number of experienced sports veterans, including Bill Fitts, a former NBC and CBS producer. Bill mentored many of ESPN's young producers and was instrumental in developing the company's early remote production capability. Scotty also hired George Grande (a CBS reporter doing pre- and postgame interviews for NFL games) and Dick Vitale. "Dick, I want you to come work for my new company, ESPN," Scotty said in his call to Vitale. "ESPN?" replied Dick. "What is ESPN? Sounds like a disease!"

Also coming in to join the ESPN first team were some regional and local young talent that included Chris Berman (a Brown graduate and weekend television sportscaster in Hartford), Bob Ley (a graduate of Seton Hall working at Suburban Cablevision in New Jersey), Tom Mees (a sports director in Tallahassee, Florida), and technician Chuck Pagano (who was working on an electrical engineering degree from the University of Hartford and had worked as a rock-and-roll disk jockey).

Pagano's colleague Bill Lamb (a local technical director from New Haven) started at ESPN after receiving a call the night of the very first ESPN broadcast asking him to come over and relieve Pagano, who had no backup. Twenty-seven-year-old Steve Bornstein (producer for Ohio State football games on local cable) came on board as a programming coordinator.

In contrast with experienced hands at the major broadcast networks who viewed ESPN as a bad idea or a joke, these new-hire young people thought that a twenty-four-hour sports network actually seemed like a *good idea* and offered real opportunity.

Right after Lee Leonard made his opening remarks for ESPN, he turned the program over to his colleague George Grande by saying, "Now, here's another innovation on ESPN, and it's going to be a big part of our future: The *SportsCenter* with George Grande." That statement was telling, because *innovation* became embedded in ESPN's culture, part of our DNA, and *SportsCenter* would soon become the network's backbone.

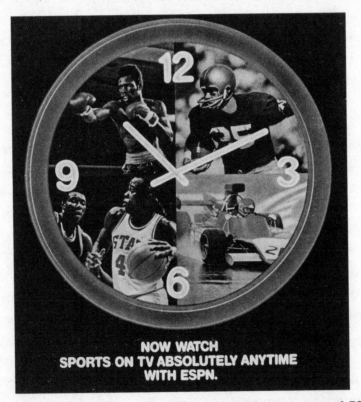

An early print advertisement (1981) capturing the essence of ESPN's appeal: twenty-four-hour sports. *ESPN Images*

The rest of that first night's broadcast has become fodder for sports trivia buffs. The first result reported was Chris Evert's victory over Billie Jean King at the U.S. Open. The first live interview was from Denver with the University of Colorado head football coach Chuck Fairbanks. Due to a technical problem, the entire interview was done in silence with video only. After audio was restored, it was replayed later in that first half hour of *SportsCenter*. Later that night, the first-ever live sporting event to air on ESPN was a slow-pitch softball World Series game featuring the Milwaukee Schlitzes versus the Kentucky Bourbons—sponsored by Budweiser!

Few people (an estimated thirty thousand viewers) were in a position to see ESPN's first show. We were just a cable start-up that was not widely distributed. We were flying by the seat of our pants and no one knew if we were going to make it. However modest, though, it was a beginning.

When Lee Leonard turned that first program over to George Grande, the camera showed George sitting alone behind the first *SportsCenter* desk. "Thanks, Lee," he said. "And welcome, everyone, to the ESPN *SportsCenter*. From this very desk in the coming weeks and months, we'll be filling you in on the pulse of sporting activity, not only around the country, but around the world, as well.

"If it takes an interview, we'll do it.

"If it takes play-by-play, we'll do it.

"If it takes commentary, we'll do that, too."

With those words that very first night, George Grande essentially articulated ESPN's mission, which was to do whatever it took to serve sports fans. That thought wasn't plastered all over the walls of our unfinished building. It wasn't something people talked about every day. But it drove everything ESPN did in those early years. Everything.

George Grande and Lee Leonard on the original *SportsCenter* set, 1979.   *ESPN Images*

All In

"You! Have you ever run camera?"

It was 4 p.m. I was sitting alone in the videotape library. A producer had burst through the door and was pointing at me.

"No, I haven't," I responded.

"No problem! Come with me!"

He led me down to the television studio where Jim Simpson was sitting behind a desk about to start his college football show. "We're short on people," the producer said to me. "Put this headset on and stand behind this camera. If Simpson shifts in his chair, move the camera a little bit to follow him."

I did the entire half-hour show moving the camera about a quarter of an inch left or right as needed. I'm proud to say I never missed a beat. That's the way it was in those early years. We were often scrambling and everybody did what we could to help out. *[In my entire thirty-plus-year career with ESPN, it was the only time I was ever behind the camera.]*

After a few months driving and working in the mailroom, I had been promoted to the videotape library. It was simple enough work. If a producer needed tape from, say, the 1975 World Series, we'd pull it and sign it out. There were no computers or digital video files back then. We kept paper records and worked with index cards and shelves of videotapes. The library was staffed twenty-four hours a day and, at various times, I worked all three eight-hour shifts, including the late one from midnight to 8 a.m. During those wee morning hours, there were just a handful of people in the building, each doing our own thing. Still, we managed to find each other. Chuck Pagano and I would screen hockey games together, Chris Berman would drop by to pick up some videotapes, or we would all just shoot the breeze in the hallways during breaks.

By the time I started at ESPN in January 1981, we'd only been on the air for a year and four months, but we were growing so fast that our physical space had a hard time keeping up. We now had several buildings, we were short on parking, people doubled up on desks, and whenever we needed more room we simply brought in another trailer. Oh, those trailers! Ten people (like Rosa Gatti, Chris LaPlaca, Mike Soltys, and the communications staff) crammed into them, all using folding tables as desks, all sharing one phone, using a single IBM typewriter that froze up during the cold winter months. When I delivered mail to them, the wind rushed in from the open door and would blow loose papers all over the place—and I'd hear: "For crying out loud, George, shut the damn door!"

The buildings were very plain, there were no fancy offices, and after a while the trailers became a point of pride. We were working continuously, so there was no time to even think about amenities. Besides, we were always so short on money that on paydays, everybody rushed to the bank to deposit our checks in case they bounced.

In making three "sweeps" a day to deliver mail (or anything else that needed to be delivered), I discovered quickly that ESPN was not a hierarchical place and that there was little formality. That was also obvious when I shuttled our executives and on-air talent to and from the airport. On a good day, the trip from Bristol to Bradley

International took at least forty-five minutes, and I had them all to myself. I took full advantage of that time by asking lots of questions. "What do you do? What do you like about it? What's happening in your area?" I not only learned about all the opportunities that ESPN offered, I developed a lot of personal relationships. Being a driver in the mailroom allowed me to get to know everybody at ESPN—and it taught me that there is opportunity in every job.

During my very first week at ESPN, I delivered mail to Scotty Connal, who had been my hockey coach when I was in junior high school. He smiled and said, "Hi, George! I heard you'd been hired. Welcome to the company."

Scotty, along with Chet Simmons, set the tone for how ESPN operated in those days, and for what ESPN was to become. They were a unique leadership duo, described by some as Mr. Inside and Mr. Outside. Chet was a brilliant visionary who understood the sports broadcasting industry and ESPN's potential role in it. He knew virtually everybody in the business and jumped into the tank headfirst to forge deals and acquire new sports programming for the fledgling network. Chet Simmons was Mr. Outside.

Scotty was not only brilliant in how he handled production and operations, he was a gifted "people person" who always focused on inclusion as opposed to exclusion. He made everybody feel good about themselves and inspired us all to go the extra mile. Scotty Connal was Mr. Inside.

While each was an excellent leader in his own right, together they made a powerful and collaborative team. Both walked the floor every day. Both made it a point to learn every employee's name and get to know each of us personally. Every time someone new was brought on board, one or the other of them personally escorted that person around and introduced them to everybody else. Chet and Scotty set the tone for our company in those early days. They cared about us and we cared about them. It was a reciprocal relationship. It was a team.

Of particular importance back then was the strategy of hiring a lot of young people and giving them the opportunity to grow and advance. It was a good policy, because young people have a higher energy level, are more inclined to take risks, and are not encumbered by the traditional ways of doing things. Of course, at a time when money was very important to ESPN, you could also pay them less. Chet and Scotty started us in entry-level positions by design. The mailroom was just one of the many places they put guys like me. There were young people all over ESPN—in production, in programming, in engineering, in communications, in finance, you name it. We were being tested to see how we would handle starting at the bottom. Were we adaptable to a new environment? Were we hard workers? Were we self-starters? Were we bright enough to do a job we'd never been trained for? Could we work with others? Could we be part of a team?

Many years later, I learned that Chet and Scotty met with all the department heads every Monday morning over coffee. In this "Monday Morning Quarterback Club," as they liked to call it, the group would review the list of young people in every department. If a person showed aptitude for programming, or production, or marketing and sales, he or she was moved to one of those areas. Those who had ambition and demonstrated the ability to learn were put in positions of growth. Those who didn't fell by the wayside.

One Monday morning, my boss said some good things about me. "Okay," replied Chet, "time to give young George the true test. Put him on Vitale." Endlessly gregarious, Dick Vitale was a full-court press. He was always going a hundred miles an hour—here, there, and everywhere. Not many people could handle his energy level. When he'd come into Bristol before the weekend shows, I'd pick him up at the airport, drive him wherever he needed to go, and get him back in time to catch his return flight. I guess I passed the test, because I was Dick's driver until being promoted to the tape library.

The one and only Dick Vitale. *ESPN Images*

As an impressionable young man, I learned a lot from Dick Vitale, Chet Simmons, Scotty Connal, George Grande, and the other professionals at ESPN. Most of them had left good-paying careers to come to a risky start-up that many experts said never had a chance of succeeding. We had no limos, no fancy food, no fresh-cut flowers, and a dirt-surface parking lot that became a muddy quagmire when it rained. But our early leaders went with their guts, and I learned from them that taking risks is okay and that you shouldn't be afraid to pursue something you love to do. Their passion for sports was their personal motivation and, like jolts of electricity, it surged into the rest of us and fueled the company. When we were all just making it up as we went along, the sheer force of Scotty Connal's personality, for instance, gave everybody confidence that ESPN was going to be a success. He had the experience, he had the confidence, and he was one of the most optimistic people I ever met. If Scotty said we were going to make it, then we were going to make it.

Of course, the truth is that all of us at ESPN were sports fans. In fact, we were pinching ourselves that we were getting paid to do this kind of work. Early on, we knew we had a product. The question was: How do we make it work? ESPN had an untested business model, because there were no precedents upon which to base one. We would have to develop an effective model through trial and experimentation, and that would take time. Our mantra became, "Let's try it and see what happens." We were in the ultimate sports TV innovation lab in bucolic Bristol, Connecticut. At that time of my life, nothing could have been more exciting.

Okay, so we had an untested business plan, no profits, and could not see a light at the end of the tunnel. What, then, kept the company going? First, we were all optimistic that sports fans were going to like what we were doing. Second, the early esprit de corps generated at ESPN made a big difference. We were all in this thing together—and we were either all going to make it together or we were all going to be out of a job together. It was just that simple.

So we operated as a family. Everybody knew everybody else. If other employees needed help, they got help. If they needed support, they were supported. ESPN truly felt like a family to me, and that was a pretty compelling concept for a young man in his first job out of college. "Keep your priorities straight," Scotty used to say. "Family comes first."

It was a collegial, powerful atmosphere. Actually, it was a culture—a can-do culture. And we created it with two powerful motivators: (1) our informal mission to serve sports fans, and (2) our passion for sports.

ESPN's early culture had all the positive elements of people working together in a common endeavor. We respected each other. We told each other the truth, even when it hurt—and that required both honesty and integrity. We had that old New England lunch-pail work ethic. We tried new things and made many mistakes. But it was okay to make mistakes as long as they were honest mistakes.

Because we didn't know if we were going to have two nickels to rub together, and we didn't know if we were going to make it as a company, taking ourselves too seriously would have been a big mistake. So we decided to have fun. After all, sports *are* entertainment. So after working hard all day or all night, we often went out together and tipped a few—sometimes at the White Birch, a favorite local watering hole just up the street. Once in a while we'd line up shot glasses of Jack Daniel's or Southern Comfort and pound them down all at once. We didn't always do those shooters (usually when celebrating a significant success), but they made for some great memories.

Just about every Friday night, there would be a party to celebrate something—a new assignment, a birthday, whatever excuse we could come up with. Frequently, we ended up at Scotty's house on the lake—and almost everybody working at ESPN showed up. We did everything together back then. I remember one New Year's Eve sitting in Bob Ley's kitchen drinking beer and planning our futures together. But while we all had our fun, we were also dedicated to quality, which led to ESPN's unofficial motto: "We take our sports seriously, but we don't take ourselves too seriously."

In those early years, ESPN's culture was our strategic advantage. It bred and fed on success. Every small achievement energized us—every new program, every positive review, and every fan letter that praised what we were doing. We viewed ourselves as the ultimate underdogs, so we took that extra step and did more than was required, whether it was re-editing the last segment of *SportsCenter* at 2 a.m. to get it right for fans waking up with us that morning, or making the extra sales call on a Friday afternoon after a week's worth of sales calls. To use a poker expression, we were "all in." ESPN's culture served to enable people with passion. And people with passion over-deliver—time and time again.

Because there was no it's-not-my-job mentality at ESPN, I often pitched in to help in other areas. It not only seemed like the right thing to do, I usually had a lot of fun doing it. For instance, John Wildhack (a young producer back in 1981) invited me to go to Totowa, New Jersey, and assist in a production of *Top Rank Boxing*, which was one of ESPN's early staples. All I did was "pull cable" for the production team, which included running errands, moving equipment around, and doing whatever I was asked to do. Essentially, I was a gopher. And because management wasn't going to pay for a mailroom driver's lodging, I slept on the floor of Wildhack's hotel room. One thing that impressed me was that the twenty-member production team was extraordinarily close. They spent all day together and had a kind of one-for-all-and-all-for-one group mentality.

Another time, I was asked to stage-manage a professional hockey game by our NHL producer, Bruce Connal (Scotty's oldest son and my high school friend). All I needed to do was stand in the penalty box with a red light and hold it over the boards while we were in commercial break. Pulling the light back meant we were on the air, and the referee, who took his cue from me, would drop the puck to continue the televised action. That was pretty much the complete extent of my responsibilities. No problem, I thought. This is great. I'm a big hockey fan. I'm rinkside for an NHL game. How could it get any better!

The first break occurred about two minutes into the game, and I dutifully held the red light over the boards. As soon as we went to commercial, I heard through my headset numerous people talking—and then a countdown: "Ten...nine...eight...seven...six..." I thought that was my cue, so when it got to zero, I pulled the light back, the referee dropped the puck on cue, and play resumed.

Suddenly, through my earpiece, I heard somebody shout, "They're back!" And then Bruce screamed: "Bodie! What the #%$&! are you doing?"

It turned out that the countdown I heard was not for me. It was an honest mistake, but I had still blown it. The end result was that when ESPN came back from a Budweiser commercial, the game was already in progress. It wasn't the end of the world, but from a production point of view I had screwed up—and it taught me a good lesson. Stage-managing a hockey game wasn't as easy as it sounded and every job at ESPN required preparation, skill, and performance.

One morning, after working a long night in the videotape library, I was walking out of the building and I heard a phone ring in a nearby office. We didn't have many secretaries or assistants back then, and, not seeing anybody around, I paused a moment to see if the phone was going to be answered. After all, it might have been a potential viewer, a rights holder, a cable operator, or an advertiser calling. And that wasn't just any phone ringing, it was ESPN's phone. So after three rings, I ran into the office and picked up the receiver.

"Hello, this is ESPN," I said. "How can I help you?"

Roberto "Remember the" Alomar

H ello, this is ESPN," I said. "How can I help you?"

"Hi. Can you tell me where the nearest bar or hotel is that carries ESPN? I want to watch my team play tonight."

"Well, sure we can. Where do you live?"

We often received calls like this after ESPN started televising the opening rounds of the NCAA Men's "March Madness" Basketball Tournament. That was certainly a programming risk that paid off. Of course, because it had never been done before, reactions in the industry varied between laughter and dismay. "What are you guys thinking? You want to televise the early rounds? Are you kidding me? Nobody is going to watch those!"

But we moved forward anyway and, in the process, pioneered an exciting production element now taken for granted—what we called the "whip-around" format. If there was a blowout, we left that game and switched to other more competitive games, often with only a minute or so left. Viewers were routinely treated to exciting buzzer-beater finishes one after another. Viewership for those early tournament games was surprisingly strong. College kids skipped classes. Die-hard fans stayed away from work. People without access to cable went to bars or took out rooms at hotels. That's when fans called us to ask where the nearest places were that carried ESPN. They wanted to watch their school's games.

Soon motel and bar owners got wise and started advertising on their marquees that they had ESPN. There turned out to be a big demand for the early rounds of the NCAA basketball tournament. In fact, it became one of our signature events. Not only did the fans like it, so did the college coaches, because they knew that if their team made the tournament, the next year ESPN would televise at least one of their regular-season games, which did a lot for recruiting and alumni relations.

In truth, college basketball was an early mainstay for ESPN. It was the first sport where we were able to televise some of the best events. In those days, we couldn't compete with the networks on weekends, but we could during the week when a Syracuse-Georgetown or Duke–North Carolina basketball game on ESPN would certainly attract sports fans. Our efforts back then were led by the programming team of Loren Matthews (former promotions director for the New York Mets) and Tom Odjakjian (former assistant commissioner of the Eastern College Athletic Conference). Together they took advantage of the fact that the Big East Conference, which was also founded in 1979, became an essential part of ESPN programming.

Eventually others clamored for more television coverage. Executives from the Big Ten, for instance, called Odjakjian and asked what night their games could be televised to receive the highest ratings. "That would be Monday night after the Big East game," Tom replied. After the conference agreed to that time slot, Matthews coined the phrase *Big Monday*. ESPN would feature a Big East game at 7 p.m., a Big Ten game at 9 p.m., and perhaps a Pac-10 game at 11 p.m. Big Monday turned out to be a phenomenal success, thriving for more than thirty-five years on ESPN. Eventually Tom and Loren found themselves at the epicenter of college basketball scheduling, where they had the

The 1987 Big East Championship Game, Georgetown vs. Syracuse, in Madison Square Garden.   *Thomas Maguire Jr. / ESPN Images*

opportunity to be creative. On one Presidents' Day, for example, they were able to schedule George Washington and James Madison to play each other!

In the early days, college basketball helped put ESPN on the map. And believe it or not, so did televising the relatively obscure (at the time) National Football League player draft. Chet Simmons saw college football fans as a built-in audience for it, so he met with NFL Commissioner Pete Rozelle and pitched the idea. Rozelle's immediate reaction was to laugh. "You gotta be kidding me," he said. "It's just a business meeting with team officials sitting around talking on the phone and shuffling papers. But if you want to do it, we'll work with you."

George Grande anchored our first NFL draft (held on April 29, 1980, in New York) while Bob Ley hosted back at the studio in Bristol. There was absolutely no formal production plan at first. The idea was just to try it and figure out the details later. In fact, Chet's instructions to George were: "Make it up as you go along. If it starts to *not work*, just get off the air." In preparation, Bob Ley worked on his folding card table at home with index cards on who would be the most likely players to be drafted and by which teams. And driven by the need to produce twenty-four hours of sports, George and Bob hosted pre-draft shows with profiles on the players and their schools.

The first telecast was held on a Tuesday morning at 8 and lasted the whole day. Similar to what we experienced around the NCAA basketball tournament, a lot of sports fans called in sick to work so they could tune in to ESPN's coverage—and we received good enough results and feedback to televise it the next year. Gradually, we added more production resources and on-air commentators to scrutinize a team's pick moments after the selection was made. One of those hired to help with our analysis was an unknown Mel Kiper Jr., a passionate fan who for years had followed the draft, the teams, and all the picks. One year, while interviewing Indianapolis Colts General Manager Bill Tobin, an ESPN reporter told him that Mel Kiper thought he had made a mistake in not taking Cal State quarterback (and future ESPN analyst) Trent Dilfer for his first pick. "Who the hell is Mel Kiper?" Tobin responded.

Football fans loved it and wanted more. Soon the league and all the teams became more involved, and as a result the draft grew and grew. Eventually, ratings came to rival those of a live football game, and the draft coverage became a three-night (Thursday, Friday, and Saturday) prime-time event. And then *every* professional sports league wanted its draft televised.

In those early days, ESPN aired a lot of different sports, and the truth is that we televised almost everything we could get our hands on. Mostly, we put on sporting events that nobody else was carrying, and certainly there was essentially no other outlet for some of these sports before ESPN came along. Some of our early programming included slow-pitch softball, college wrestling, college soccer, college hockey, Canadian football, Australian rules football, Davis Cup tennis, horse jumping, Irish bicycling, Irish Munster hurling, hunting, fishing, darts, and hydroplane racing.

Our programmers were risk takers, operating without the benefit of a lot of research. They did it as much on instinct and intuition as anything else, and more often than not their gut feelings paid off. For instance, because we did not have the rights to televise NCAA football games live, we would broadcast tape-delayed games. As a result, one of my jobs was to drive to the airport on Sunday mornings to pick up the videotapes from the weekend games that were flown in to Bradley International Airport. Then I'd hustle back to Bristol so the games could be aired throughout the day on Sunday. Overall, we'd show five college football games every week. A lot of industry types laughed at us. But surprise! Tape-delay college football became one of ESPN's most successful programs, another early staple of the network.

Because most of our early programming had never before been televised nationally, ESPN was not taken seriously. Johnny Carson and *Saturday Night Live* poked fun at us and the mainstream press ridiculed us. The traditional television industry, including all three of the major networks, still largely derided us. "You're talking about a tempest in a teapot," they said. "ESPN is not even in the same business."

But the most important audience—the sports fans—was beginning to take notice of what we were televising. And so did the commissioners, team owners, and coaches of sports leagues in the United States. Before long, ESPN quietly gained a number of important acquisitions. We signed agreements to telecast games from the NBA (National Basketball Association), the NHL (National Hockey League), WCT (World Championship Tennis), and NASCAR (National Association for Stock Car Auto Racing). Also, in what turned out to be ESPN's first live event produced overseas, we carried the World Cup Track and Field competition from Rome, Italy.

It seemed the more ESPN gave sports fans, the more they wanted. We began to realize that we were filling a need, and in trying to cobble together a twenty-four-hour sports lineup, we were mostly doing what made sense to us and then we'd listen to our viewers to see what they liked and what they didn't like.

One of the best examples of ESPN's trial-and-error strategy was *SportsCenter* itself, and how it developed with time. Chet Simmons absolutely believed from day one that the key to ESPN's success—its differentiator from any and all future competition—would be *SportsCenter*. One person who agreed with Chet was George Grande.

Because George had the most experience among the *SportsCenter* staff, he led the selection decisions for news content and "took care of the guys," as he liked to say. A great believer that "teams lead themselves," George Grande did not have the title of director, nor did he seek it. He wanted to let the younger announcers experience things on their own and learn from watching more seasoned pros like himself, Jim Simpson, and veteran radio play-by-play man Lou Palmer. In short, George wanted *SportsCenter* to be a team and run itself.

Back then, we generally produced three *SportsCenter*s a night—6 p.m., 11 p.m., and 2:30 a.m. Empty airtime was an ongoing worry, because the capability did not yet exist to obtain video for all the U.S. games played earlier in the day. So *SportsCenter* producers focused on what they could find. They were able, for instance, to videotape games that were carried by the local television channels in Hartford, which included all the New York and Boston teams. Highlights were plentiful for the Yankees, Mets, Giants, Jets, Knicks, Islanders, Rangers, Red Sox, Patriots, Celtics, Bruins, and, of course, the Hartford Whalers. When short on content, we would have some videotapes of the Phillies, Eagles, 76ers, and Flyers driven up from Philadelphia. For other national games, however, all we could do was have previous-day videos flown into the airport (similar to what we did with our college football games). So in a very real sense, at various times, *SportsCenter* then was yesterday's news today.

Traditionally, back in the day, sports news coverage aired at the end of local television news programs, usually following the weather report. Almost always, individual game highlights were kept at twenty to thirty seconds each. But *SportsCenter* was a game changer—and ESPN's producers and on-air talent rose to the occasion by creating an entirely new way of reporting sports news. Actually, along the way, they broke every rule for conventional sports highlights. Game clips, for instance, were extended to a full minute or two. The games were more fully analyzed, complete with more statistics and more insightful commentary. Essentially, each game highlight became a story in and of itself.

Highlights alone, of course, could not fill all of *SportsCenter*'s available time. So the on-air guys had to be willing to try a number of new and different things. That's when they decided to gather everybody together (on-air talent, producers, et cetera) and say, "Okay, the floor's open. Whoever has the best idea will carry the day." Then the team would sit and debate the merits of each new concept (sometimes passionately yelling and screaming at each other) and then go out and try the experiment. What worked best became the standard.

One important thing everybody settled on was to have the *SportsCenter* anchors both report from the studio *and* go into the field and generate stories. George Grande went to the World Series, Chris Berman to the Super Bowl, and Bob Ley to the Final Four, each with only a cameraman and a producer. No one told them they couldn't cover those major events with only three people. They could. And they did. Then they flew the tapes back to Bristol to air as soon as possible.

Somebody also had to determine exactly what constituted a news event worthy of being presented on *SportsCenter*. Sometimes it was one of the on-air talent who came up with an idea and secured an okay from George Grande or Scotty Connal. For instance, when President Carter was calling for an Olympic boycott of the Moscow summer games in 1980 due to the Soviet invasion of Afghanistan, *SportsCenter* producer Fred Muzzy came up with the idea to conduct a phone poll using two numbers, one for "yes" and one for "no." Surprisingly, the results were decidedly in favor of the boycott, and ESPN received a lot of national exposure regarding the poll. Fred received kudos for that idea, but it was just one of the many things he was famous for, including once producing *SportsCenter* covered in mud after falling in the parking lot and another time (as legend has it) producing the show from a phone booth while at the White Birch bar.

SportsCenter producers like Fred Muzzy were, by necessity, always keeping close track of the time during shows. Often, they might say something like: "We're ten minutes short, so talk about the National League East for about four minutes or talk about the pennant race for five minutes." If the on-air talent couldn't do it, they were dead. You had to be able to talk sports without a script.

George Grande wanted everybody to do their reporting extemporaneously and with enthusiasm, to present highlights to viewers as if the reporters were sitting next to them in the stadium watching the games live. Everybody had to do their homework, their own writing, and not rely on somebody else, because there *was nobody else.* *[SportsCenter anchors writing their own copy at ESPN became a real point of pride and a hallmark of the network.]* Young guys like Ley and Berman could handle it, in part, because they weren't locked in to past ways of doing things.

But one time George brought in an older, more experienced reporter, and his first question was, "Where's the prompter person?" "There is no prompter person," George replied. "We don't use teleprompters. We can't afford them." That fella couldn't ad-lib, so he and ESPN parted ways quickly.

In those days, the *SportsCenter* manual about how to do things wasn't long. Our young reporters and producers were experimenting, and sometimes stumbling. It was okay to make mistakes, but we had to talk about them so they were not repeated. "You were dealing with young people who were trying to do their best," recalled Grande. "You didn't want them to feel bad, because it would cause them to shut down. So I'd let things settle and deal with mistakes the next day. And I tried never to get personal or be antagonistic."

Gradually, the early *SportsCenter* team became more mature, more polished—and members were placed in the areas they liked best. Bob Ley liked college basketball, Tom Mees liked the NHL, Lou Palmer liked golf, George Grande liked baseball, and Chris Berman liked the NFL. Each got his own weekly show, and they took ownership of it by presenting their work with solid sports journalism and their own unique personalities. We didn't know it then, but allowing the reporters to truly be themselves, to be fans, would begin to build a brand for ESPN that would set us apart from our competition.

In the early days of *SportsCenter*, everybody was scrambling, just trying to stay on the air. "We were Lewis and Clark hoping to find the Pacific," recalled Chris Berman. "We knew we were going in the right direction. Were we sure we were going to make it? Not really."

Ironically, it would be the sheer force of Chris Berman's personality that would vault *SportsCenter* into the American stream of consciousness. He used to anchor the 2:30 morning show alone, sometimes with Tom Mees. One morning, alone, not knowing how many people might be watching, and perhaps a little bored, Berman spontaneously started making up nicknames for baseball players during highlights. By his own recollection, he first said either Frank Tanana "Daiquiri" or John Mayberry "RFD." Right away, the cameraman started laughing, which caused the television picture to shake. And the surprised producer screamed "What?" into Berman's earpiece.

Undeterred, Chris continued to give more players nicknames and, with time, the numbers started to add up. There was Tom "Leave It to" Seaver, Bruce "Eggs" Benedict, Jamie "Men at" Quirk, Ross "I Never Promised You a" Baumgarten, Ron "Born in the US" Cey, Dave Righetti "and Meatballs," Jose "Can You See" Cruz, Jesse "Belly Up to the" Barfield, Bert "Be Home" Blyleven, Roberto "Remember the" Alomar, and Glen "Mother" Hubbard, to name just a few.

No one had ever done anything like this before, and pretty soon it wasn't just the ESPN producer who was saying, "What?" Baseball fans all over the country had perked up. *"What did he say?"* People loved Berman's nicknames, and they started tuning in just to listen to him. "Gee, I hope he gives my favorite player a nickname," they said. Some baseball players even called ESPN and suggested nicknames for themselves. A few were angry that they hadn't yet been given one. After a while, Berman's nicknames became a national phenomenon. It seemed like everybody was quoting him.

Unbeknownst to any of us, Chris's nicknaming of baseball players was one of the early building blocks of an ESPN brand, part of which was having fun. Our brand took shape gradually because we were addressing the task at hand, which was to fill up twenty-four hours in a day with things we believed sports fans would like. As such, it is accurate to say that the ESPN brand developed because we were following our mission to serve sports fans.

ESPN's developing brand revolved around three things, all weighted equally (kind of like that three-legged stool, again): (1) a variety of sports (something for every fan); (2) a commitment to sports journalism (including in-depth highlights and storytelling); and (3) entertainment (laughing and having fun on the air).

Sports fans everywhere were beginning to discover ESPN. They were tuning in to watch sports, to be informed, and to be entertained. But we were still not making a profit. Our revenues were minuscule and our expenses massive. The truth is that we were bleeding money and most of the ESPN team was still not sure whether we were going to make it as a successful business. We did, however, experience a few early signs of validation that we were growing a loyal, if modest fan base.

When our crews arrived to broadcast a game, for instance, we were often short on personnel to set up our production equipment, which had to be tailored to each venue. One day, an on-site producer offered an ESPN hat to an electrician milling about in return for helping with our setup—and he accepted enthusiastically! That producer then suggested to other producers that the ESPN trucks start carrying a dozen or so hats for that very purpose. "What?" came the response. "They want our hats?"

The next thing we knew, some of our enterprising crew members started bootlegging ESPN T-shirts, hats, and sweatshirts. They bought the items wholesale, had the ESPN logos printed on, and sold them on site. And sports fans flocked to the trucks to buy them. Of course, that was before we had an organized merchandising program, so the guys were making some money on the side (which they sorely needed). But, hey, it helped promote our new network.

Another sign that ESPN's star was on the rise was the fact that fans began to steal the ESPN banners we put up at events. All television networks hang banners so that when they're shooting the game and pan to the sidelines or into the crowds, the network logo can be seen. After one game, Jim Simpson noted the thefts and mentioned it to one of our other sportscasters. "What?" came the reply. "They want our banners?"

One of the very first vivid, tangible signs ESPN received that we were touching a real nerve with sports fans involved Australian rules football (of which we ran the sprockets off). It's a very rugged sport where the players use no helmets or pads. And the referees, in their white coats, look more like pharmacists than referees. But it was a bit confusing for American fans, because this was the first time it had been shown regularly in the United States. So we put a graphic up on the screen that read: "Send us a postcard and we'll mail the rulebook to you."

From that one simple graphic, we received more than ten thousand postcards. And those of us in the mailroom had to lug all those cards to the marketing department for processing.

"*This* Is a Sports Town"

A l, I'm going to go interview for this job in Texas," I said. "I don't know much about it. Can you help me?"

I was sitting in the office of Al Wieder, vice president of affiliate marketing, clutching a cup of coffee. It was a Tuesday morning in the spring of 1982.

"What job, George?"

"The account executive job in Texas was posted on the company bulletin board. I applied for it and they want me to fly down for an interview."

"Sure, we can help you. Let's get you loaded up with some information. Then I'll make a call before your interview to grease the skids."

From my sales and marketing buddies, I learned that the term *affiliate* referred to a local cable operator, which meant that in this particular job, I'd be on the road selling ESPN, which was exactly what I wanted to do. After stage-managing *Top Rank Boxing*, helping out with an NHL hockey game, and pulling cable a time or two at basketball games, I decided that I was best suited for a career in sales and marketing rather than production and programming.

This wasn't the first time I had asked an ESPN executive for help.

Several months earlier, after making my career aspirations known, I'd received a nice handwritten note from the same executive letting me know there were no current openings, but inviting me to come by and see him to discuss it. That's the kind of culture that had been established at ESPN. If younger employees wanted to see the boss, they would be seen and would get support.

I had first learned to let people know what I wanted to do with my life when I was back in high school working at the Hess gas station in Riverside, Connecticut. Three of the twelve workers were managers and, when a manager job came open, I didn't get it. So I went to see the owner. "What's going on?" I asked. "I thought I was next in line."

"Well, George, I didn't know you wanted to be a manager," he said. After that, I made sure to let people know what my goals were, especially if they knew I was a credible employee who worked hard and deserved a shot. So I had been planning for a while to try for the first sales and marketing job that opened up—and that position in Texas was it.

Even though I had zero sales experience, I saw this upcoming interview as a great opportunity. On the flight down to Dallas, I read the half-dozen trade magazines Al had given me, hoping to pick up a few concepts and buzzwords so I could sound at least halfway intelligent. The interview lasted a couple of hours, included lunch, and went well. So I flew back to Bristol with high hopes. Greatly enhancing my chances of getting the job, I later learned, was the fact that I was the only person who applied for it!

The night after receiving a phone call telling me I had gotten the job, I ran into Chris Berman in the hall and told him the news. "Hey, Chris, I'm going to Dallas," I said.

"Wow, that's a real outpost for us," he replied. "What are you going to do there?"

"I'm not sure exactly, but I know I'll be selling ESPN to cable operators across the Southwest."

"Okay, George. Good luck, buddy."

A couple of weeks later, I packed up and moved to Arlington, Texas. ESPN's "Dallas office," as we called it, consisted of three people (a manager, an account executive, and an assistant) and was responsible for selling and distributing ESPN throughout the southwestern United States. While my official title was "account executive," I still felt like an ESPN "driver," only now I would be driving myself to all the cities and towns in a five-state area (Texas, Oklahoma, Arkansas, Louisiana, and Mississippi) hawking ESPN to every cable operator I could find.

As I began traveling around the southwestern United States, I carried a sense of optimism about our company combined with a lingering question over our long-term viability. The business plan that Getty had bought into called for a *cumulative* investment of $25 million and breakeven in three years. But that entire amount had been quickly spent and ESPN was losing approximately $25 million *per year*. Such financial pressure, among other things, had already caused Getty to shake up the senior leadership of ESPN.

Bill Rasmussen was out a little more than a year after the launch of ESPN and, in June 1982, President Chet Simmons was replaced by J. William "Bill" Grimes, a senior CBS Radio executive. Of course, these moves caused all sorts of internal rumors, primarily that we were on the verge of going out of business. People also felt that Rasmussen and Simmons leaving was the first sign of a big corporate mentality. But Scotty Connal helped temper the worry and unease.

Bill Grimes embraced our culture and often walked the halls of ESPN to get to know everyone, even though his main office was located in New York City. While it was only 110 miles away, that geographic distance resulted in the beginnings of a schism that eventually developed between Bristol and New York.

While I was saddened that ESPN's founder, Bill Rasmussen (the visionary with the passion and the original idea for ESPN), and our president, Chet Simmons (a very accomplished sports television executive), had both left the company, it became apparent that ESPN needed to continue to evolve. Soon our new leaders would take some important steps to ensure the success of our fledgling twenty-four-hour sports network.

Bill Grimes, for example, realized that Getty might sell ESPN if the financial situation didn't turn around. After all, we were just a small part of the Getty portfolio, whose primary focus, of course, was the far more profitable oil and gas industry. So McKinsey & Company was brought in to assess ESPN's future, and they quickly concluded that our initial business model wasn't working. In those days, ESPN's only revenue stream was from advertising, and *we actually paid the cable operators* to carry our channel. Grimes knew that had to change, because with only meager advertising revenue, ESPN couldn't possibly compete with the established networks to purchase sports rights. We simply had to have more income.

Grimes astutely hired McKinsey's lead consultant, Roger Werner, and together they developed a plan to flip ESPN's business model. Their idea was to charge the cable operators a small monthly fee for each home hooked up to cable: four cents a month, gradually increasing to twenty cents by 1985. After quickly receiving approval from Stuart Evey (Getty's vice president in charge of non-oil activities, who oversaw ESPN), they began laying the groundwork for implementation. The moment to strike came in the fall of 1982 when CBS pulled the plug on its fledgling arts and culture network, CBS Cable, after a little over a year in existence.

As cable company stocks plunged and news organizations questioned the future of the industry, Grimes and Werner made their pitch to the large operators. "Look, CBS Cable just went away," they said. "If you want ESPN as one of your channels, we have to be paid some sort of fee. Otherwise, we can't survive."

This new business model had never before been attempted by a cable network. And not surprisingly, most of the major cable operators were not very interested in paying us fees, however modest they might be. Less than half of them signed up at first, and the rest would have to be persuaded by Grimes and Werner's persistent salesmanship.

By 1983, there were only a handful of major cable operators in the United States, but there were thousands of smaller ones scattered all over the place. While Grimes and Werner handled the big boys, it fell to ESPN's affiliate sales force to persuade all the mom-and-pops to start paying ESPN's subscriber fee. And that's where I came in. I was a member of the group where the rubber met the road.

I started selling ESPN town-to-town almost immediately after arriving in Texas. I'd never before been in any of the five states for which I was responsible, but now I was seeing the backbone of America—and I truly loved it. Because of poor broadcast reception for local TV stations, cable television had its roots in rural communities and small towns, often starting there before it made its way to the big cities.

When I began my new job, although everyone had heard of ESPN, many cable systems did not carry us, and those that did were operating off the old business model. It wasn't until about four months after I moved to Texas that we began transitioning the change to subscriber fees. To the few who had ESPN, the earlier model was a very difficult bell to un-ring. "What do you mean you want us to pay *you*?" they said. "Right now, you're paying *us*. I don't understand."

I tried to make three sales calls a day—morning, noon, and afternoon. Although at this point I had received little formal sales training, I naturally figured that to be successful, I had to be organized, move quickly, and stay on time. At night, in local motels, I prepared myself. In order to be a student of the business, I read everything I could to enhance my technical knowledge of the cable industry, the television business, and the sales and marketing potential for a cable operator to carry ESPN. We were growing so fast, and things were changing so rapidly, that I had to be on a continual learning curve. I simply could not afford to have a potential customer tell me something about my own company or industry that I did not yet know. And every night, the last thing I did before going to bed was research who I would be calling on the next day—and then I'd tailor my pitch specifically to those particular cable operators. Overall, I had three simple rules that I reminded myself of every night: *(1) have a dialogue, not a monologue; (2) listen and learn; and (3) build personal relationships.*

On a typical sales call, I often found myself sitting on a wooden box in the back room having a cup of coffee or a sandwich with "Mom and Pop," the owners. I'd tell them all about ESPN and our programming—the sports we currently aired and the sports we were working on obtaining. "We have this twenty-four-hour sports network and you have a cable system," I'd say. "We'd like you to put it on. I know your customers will love it."

The reactions I received were often the same. "Gee, the idea of a twenty-four-hour sports channel is kind of nutty," they'd say. "But we'll carry it because, you know, George, *this is a sports town.*"

Wherever I was—Biloxi, Waco, Tulsa, Baton Rouge, Hot Springs, you name it—I was informed that I was in a "sports town." It might have been a passion for high school sports, or college, or professional, or all three depending on location. But over the years, I came to understand that every town in America considers itself a sports town.

Seeing the passion for sports on one hand, and the cable systems' need for quality programming on the other, I became increasingly optimistic about ESPN's future. Independent cable operators all over America were looking for product and, clearly, there was a desire for ours. They began to sign us up in droves, and we welcomed each of them with an on-air graphic like: "Tonight, we welcome Summit Cablevision, Buena Vista, Colorado; Arlington TeleCable, Arlington, Texas; and Frontier Color Cable, Fairbanks, Alaska. You believe in us. Thank you." ESPN's business partnership with these cable operators enabled all of us to succeed together and, as a result, the entire cable industry benefited.

Despite the encouraging growth, there was still the necessity of flipping ESPN's business model around. And that was my first indoctrination to a real business crisis. If we weren't successful in selling ESPN with a subscriber fee, there wasn't going to be any company—and that was real motivation. Through hard work and persistence, our affiliate sales force negotiated more than a thousand contracts across the country—and that put ESPN on the road to firm financial footing. I was far from the executive suite back then, and it was our corporate leadership that developed the new business model. Trust me, turning that model around wasn't easy. But I'm proud to say I was one of the foot soldiers who helped make it happen.

In 1984, a couple of major events significantly aided ESPN's growth. First, ABC (the American Broadcasting Company), one of the big three broadcast networks, acquired our company in two separate transactions (one with Getty and one with Getty-acquirer Texaco) for a total of about $230 million. Leonard Goldenson, chairman and founder of ABC, had a real vision for the future of cable networks. He recognized that cable was going to be big, and that its future would be one of targeted, highly focused networks, such as all sports, all history, all arts, all weather, all news, and so on. Long before his competitors, Goldenson (along with top lieutenant Herb Granath) began making strategic investments in the cable industry.

Because ESPN was starting to look like a viable business, and because ABC had a history steeped in sports, they went after us. Moreover, it is not an exaggeration to say that our new owner, through the iconic *Wide World of Sports*, actually paved the way for the creation and eventual success of a twenty-four-hour sports network like ours. In its early days, *Wide World* pioneered unusual sporting events not previously seen on television, such as cliff diving from Acapulco, barrel jumping from Slovenia, rodeo, demolition derby, and badminton.

Under the leadership of legendary producer Roone Arledge, ABC Sports eventually became the preeminent sports operation in American broadcasting with its coverage of such top-tier events as NFL *Monday Night Football*, the Olympics, the Indianapolis 500, and the British Open, to name a few. During its thirty-seven-year run (1961–98), *ABC's Wide World of Sports* entered the American stream of consciousness, even to the point that its opening segment's "the thrill of victory and the agony of defeat" became internationally known.

Although I was working in Texas at the time of the acquisition, I felt the reverberations, as did everybody else in the company. After all, ABC was an established broadcast network whose leader believed in the future of cable and in our company. Those of us at ESPN were ecstatic. We knew that Getty was looking to sell, and we'd heard an ominous rumor that Ted Turner of CNN, who had made several unsolicited offers for ESPN over the years, was making another run at us—and if successful, he was planning to cut a lot of jobs. Being acquired by ABC instead changed everything. It not only was a huge validation for us but also provided something of a scheduling boost, because we were able to obtain additional sports programming as a result of having a new parent company. Additionally, most of the ABC executives were indifferent to ESPN and, therefore, our culture was not affected. Essentially, we were left to run our own shop.

The second major event of 1984 that provided a boost to ESPN occurred when the NCAA rules limiting the televising of college football games were changed by a Supreme Court decision, which allowed ESPN to begin broadcasting Saturday night games. These broadcasts—the first live college football games shown on ESPN—improved the makeup of our viewing audience by delivering hard-to-reach, primarily male, upscale viewers. This resonated with advertisers, who began noticing our improved demographics.

Our ability to televise live college football was especially good news to Anheuser-Busch, which in 1980 had been given an exclusive contract (for beer companies) when they paid us $25 million for five years' worth of advertising. It was a great deal for Budweiser and, at first, a great deal for ESPN, because we very much needed the influx of revenue. With time, however, our growing popularity resulted in other beer companies banging on the door of ESPN's advertising department. Eventually, the exclusivity was ended, but not before we worked out a mutually advantageous deal with Anheuser-Busch, which was our first advertiser and to whom we were very loyal.

Print advertisement (1980) touting the Anheuser-Busch/ESPN deal. *ESPN Images*

At about this time, ESPN officially became cable's largest network, with a reach of nearly thirty million households. And because we had succeeded in changing the business model, we were finally turning a profit. Now our company at least had a chance to become a modest success. Eventually, charging subscriber fees would become the business standard among virtually all cable television programmers and, over time, would quite literally revolutionize the industry.

In those early days, it was our persistence and their desire for sports programming that led most of the mom-and-pops to agree to carry ESPN for a subscriber fee. But let me tell you, it wasn't easy.

Some cable operators got up in arms, refused to pay, and actually took us off the air. In one case, I ended up in a small-town Kansas high school gymnasium, where I had to debate a local cable owner in front of the whole town. He was a lawyer, he was polished, and he was about twenty-five years older than I was. I drove there with my ESPN colleague Randy Brown and, at one point, we passed through the town where the *In Cold Blood* murders took place, which I considered a very bad omen. I was so nervous that I had Randy pull over a couple of times so I could throw up. By the time we got to the gym, I had nothing in my stomach, I was ashen gray (as I was later told), and I couldn't remember all the points I wanted to get across.

The debate, in front of three or four hundred people, was the main event in town that night and lasted about an hour. While I must have looked like a real rookie, my opponent was an eloquent speaker and well prepared. But the truth is that it really didn't matter what either one of us said, because a farmer dressed in blue overalls in the back row stole the show. He interrupted the debate three times.

"I don't care about any of this crap!" he said. "I just want ESPN!" And each time he said it, the crowd cheered and applauded louder than it had the time before.

Well, that was it. I won the debate! But I can assure you it had nothing to do with my oratory skills.

Sure enough, the very next morning, my debate opponent put ESPN back on his cable lineup. The lesson I learned was that we had a product that fans really liked and wanted. We just had to make sure everybody knew about it.

Punch-Through Programming

I was ready for a change when a job came open in Chicago. It was a lateral—an account executive position in affiliate sales with responsibility for five states in the Midwest: Missouri, Ohio, Indiana, Illinois, and Michigan.

"Are you going to apply for that job, George?" one of my co-workers asked as we stood at the bulletin board together.

"I apply for that job every day," I replied.

I wasn't being flippant, and my friend knew what I meant. There were no part-time employees at ESPN. We worked hard. It was part of who we were. I was also interested in transferring around and moving up. Change is good, I figured, because I could be a better student of the business if I actually experienced it in various settings and in different parts of the country.

Although hard work was always part of my makeup, I now had additional motivation to build a career, because I was newly married. My wife, Ann, and I had met at a cable television convention in San Antonio. We were both from Connecticut and thought it would be an adventure to live and work in Chicago. So when I was offered the job, we headed north right away. But no sooner had Ann landed a job as a marketing assistant in Disney's local office in Chicago than I received a call from Bristol. "Hey, George, the manager position in Denver just opened up. It's yours. Pack your bags."

The next day, Ann (who was only in her second day on the job) resigned her position. "I'm so sorry," she said, "but my husband has just been transferred to Colorado." She knew this was a huge opportunity for me and she didn't think twice. That kind of support meant the world to me, and I knew I had a great wife. So three months after arriving in Chicago, we moved to Denver where I became part of ESPN's Rocky Mountain Region. Actually, as in Dallas, it was just a three-person office (including me). Only this time, I was heading it up.

During my change of jobs, ESPN also experienced a bit of a transition. On March 18, 1985, Albany, New York–based Capital Cities Communications announced a surprise $3.5 billion purchase of the much larger ABC (and with it, ESPN). In the year previous, ABC executives had pretty much left ESPN alone to run our business, with the notable exception of Bob Iger. Iger, who had come up through the ranks of ABC Sports, went out of his way to give ESPN some added value. And right out of the gate, we gained two prominent programming additions. First, we secured Thursday and Friday coverage of the U.S. Open, the British Open, and the PGA Championship, three of professional golf's four majors. Second, ESPN was able to broadcast a more extensive array of college football games, in part because of negotiating help from ABC.

At the head of CapCities were two pillars of the television industry, Tom Murphy and Dan Burke, both of whom espoused a "decentralized management" philosophy. The idea was that individual leaders were free to run their own departments and divisions as long as they made their numbers by staying on budget and always acting with integrity. So now that I was a new manager in Denver, I knew I was going to be expected to run my own shop without significant supervision from corporate headquarters.

Only twenty-seven years old and more than a little wet behind the ears, I took my new job very seriously. It quickly became apparent to me that people look at you differently when you're the manager. So I felt I had to live that role every day by dressing well, by being upbeat, by setting a good example with my work ethic, and by delivering results. Even though our office had only three people, we were ESPN's representatives to all the company's biggest customers because, at the time, Denver was the cable capital of the country. Every major operator was there, including industry leaders United Cable, TCI (Tele-Communications, Inc.), and ATC (American Television & Communications). My main goal was to meet all the executives in those companies and build personal relationships so that I could effectively represent ESPN's interests. But I knew we would have to earn that trust.

I met a lot of great people during those years, but one who stands out is Bill Daniels, a legend of the business. Often called "the father of cable television," Daniels started a cable brokerage operation and financed independent entrepreneurs in return for equity percentages. He amassed a personal fortune by envisioning what cable television could be, and then by taking action to make that vision a reality. He called his company Daniels & Associates and he had a plaque in the lobby that read: THE BEST IS GOOD ENOUGH FOR ME.

Fortunately, Bill Daniels took a liking to me and always made sure we had a chance to chat at every major social event in Denver. Many times, those occasions took place at his 19,500-square-foot mansion, which he named Cableland. It was wired with the most up-to-date technology and, at one point, featured a wall of sixty-four televisions, each tuned to a different cable channel. The Denver cable community was a real social scene back then. The industry felt like it was taking off, and everybody who was anybody in our industry showed up at a Bill Daniels–hosted event.

Cable networks that had helped establish and grow the industry, such as CNN, MTV, and USA, had done a superb job. But cable operators wanted to get to the next level and, as a result, the entire industry was clamoring for better programming, particularly from ESPN—because sports were so popular. Everybody grumbled that there was little to no first-run programming. There was nothing exclusive to cable like *Seinfeld*, or *The Cosby Show*, or *Saturday Night Live*. "Where is the *boom?*" the cable operators wanted to know. "Why don't we have something where a customer says: 'I have to get cable, because I must see *that* program'?"

John Sie, a top executive with TCI, came up with the term *punch-through* programming, and it became a kind of call to arms. Before long, cable operators were frequently asking me: "When is ESPN going to give us punch-through programming, George?" they asked. "When?"

Actually, ESPN was continually adding to its lineup. In addition to signing new sports contracts, we were developing new and innovative sports programming. A good example was *Scholastic Sports America*, which profiled high school athletes across the nation. Its 1986 debut featured a young Chris Fowler, who was only one year out of the University of Colorado when ESPN offered him the position. "I was doing the Jimmy Olsen cub reporter job at the NBC local station in Denver," Fowler remembered. "I was advised to stay put and work my way up the conventional way. But ESPN seemed committed and, besides, I liked the fact that it was a nontraditional way to get into the sport business. It also sounded like fun, so I took the job."

Fowler and the *Scholastic Sports America* team were on the road for the entire academic year producing one show a week. It was a very young crew who had both the energy and the will to do the work. Fowler was so young looking back then that he was mistaken at high schools for a student a couple of times and asked for his hall pass. Over the years, they profiled hundreds of young high school athletes, including future stars Emmitt Smith (football) and Alonzo Mourning (basketball). As head of the Denver office, I found *Scholastic Sports*

America to be a very good show, the kind of show that really made a difference. Whenever they did a segment in the Rocky Mountain Region, we made sure to let the local cable operators know so they could generate some good press.

Although shows like *Scholastic Sports America* were original and popular, they weren't the punch-through programming cable operators were looking for. The truth is, from a sports perspective, we knew what would really make them happy. They all wanted the National Football League, which at the time could only be viewed on the broadcast networks. If the cable industry could get the NFL, we thought—now, *that* would be punch-through programming.

ESPN had been coveting professional football since our inception. We started by airing games in the Canadian Football League (CFL), which served us well in those early years. And in the mid-1980s, ESPN did, indeed, set our sights on acquiring some sort of NFL coverage. At one point, we were working on an idea that would have moved *Monday Night Football* from ABC (our sister company) to ESPN. But that plan eventually collapsed of its own weight.

Meanwhile, from 1983 to 1985, ESPN (and ABC) televised games of the United States Football League (USFL), which was created, in part, by unhappiness over an eight-week NFL strike. A group that included Bill Daniels formed twelve teams in major markets across the country (nine in NFL cities). Surprisingly, the new league became an instant rival of the NFL by signing young college stars to multiyear, multi-million-dollar contracts. For example, Herschel Walker (the 1982 Heisman Trophy winner) skipped his senior year at the University of Georgia and was signed by the USFL's New Jersey Generals. At the time, his three-year, $4 million contract was the most lucrative deal ever signed.

After ESPN's former president, Chet Simmons, became the USFL's commissioner (at the behest of Bill Daniels), both ABC and ESPN agreed to broadcast USFL games for a combined $29 million over the first two years. ABC's package ($23 million) called for twenty-one games, including a Sunday afternoon game-of-the-week, one prime-time evening game, and coverage of the divisional play-offs and championship game. ESPN's more modest deal (at a cost of $6 million) gave us two prime-time games (on Saturdays and Mondays) every week of the season.

Unfortunately, the USFL lasted only three seasons. Its demise was caused by low attendance, conflicting agendas among the owners, and a number of very poor business decisions. The owners, for instance, expanded from twelve to eighteen teams after only twelve months, and by the end of the third year they had decided to go head-to-head with the NFL by moving the USFL's playing season from the spring/summer to the fall. To top it all off, the USFL decided to file a federal antitrust lawsuit against the NFL for monopolistic practices. (They actually won the case, but were awarded only $1 in damages, which were trebled to a grand total of $3.)

So after an interesting, at times exciting, three seasons, the USFL owners suspended play and released all their players. However, the USFL provided ESPN with a sizable boost. We were able to implement some new innovations, such as the very first sports telecast presented in stereo (Oakland Invaders at the Philadelphia Stars on June 20, 1983). In addition, our ratings saw a considerable upward spike and we were able to expand our business with major advertisers (such as Ford, American Motors, DuPont, GMC, Mattel, Michelin, Nissan, and Timex), which all provided valuable ongoing business relationships for the future.

By 1986, ESPN was clearly picking up momentum. We were now in thirty-nine million households and constantly adding new sports to our programming lineup. That year, for example, we televised eighty-four live auto races, most of which were NASCAR events. ESPN's coverage of NASCAR began in 1981, thanks largely to our head of programming, Steve Bornstein, who secured a deal with Bill France Jr. (Bill France Sr. had founded the association in 1947–48). Back in 1981, NASCAR was mostly a Southern sport in which the major networks had little interest. Because Bill believed that ESPN could provide exposure to grow his sport nationally, and because he always wanted his partners to do well, he sold us the rights for a very reasonable fee.

When ESPN started broadcasting its first NASCAR races, attendance at many of the tracks was sparse. But after we started broadcasting the events live, NASCAR fans took notice. Just as college basketball fans had done, they, too, started going to bars and renting hotel rooms that offered ESPN. Our flag-to-flag coverage naturally included interviewing the drivers, the owners, and their teams, promoting NASCAR like it had never been done before on a national scale. Soon NASCAR fans, who are among the most loyal and rabid of all sports fans, began demanding that their local cable operators carry ESPN. The truth is that NASCAR and ESPN grew together. Our television coverage provided them with a big nationwide publicity boost, and their fans generated more advertising revenue and subscriber demand for us.

In addition to the record number of NASCAR races we broadcast in 1986, ESPN also televised soccer's World Cup tournament live from Mexico, and we secured a new contract with the NHL that included broadcasting a record number of Stanley Cup play-off games. But more than anything else, it was ESPN's surprisingly successful coverage of the America's Cup yacht race in Australia that provided a true taste of the punch-through programming that cable operators everywhere were demanding.

Despite it being the oldest trophy in sports, unless they were serious sailors, most people hadn't even heard of the America's Cup until Dennis Conner of the San Diego Yacht Club lost it in the 1983 races off Newport, Rhode Island. Up until that time, the United States had held the cup for 132 consecutive years, dating back to the event's inaugural competition. But now Conner was competing to get it back and Americans everywhere were captivated by the challenge. "It's our cup!" was the prevailing attitude. "And we want it back!"

Because ESPN had televised a portion of the 1983 America's Cup, our top three executives at the time, Bill Grimes, Roger Werner, and Steve Bornstein, believed that a combination of American national pride and support for USA being the underdog visiting team would generate viewers. So they took a sizable risk and secured rights to broadcast all the 1986–87 races (some seventy hours of coverage).

Of course, when ESPN announced its plans, most critics yawned and said it would be like watching paint dry. Big-time advertisers, however, saw it differently. Because the America's Cup was yachting's premier event, sponsors quickly bought up all of ESPN's advertising time. As a result, from October 1986 to February 1987, American households were treated to live action-packed sailing in the middle of the night (U.S. time) from the picturesque Indian Ocean.

To produce our coverage of the event, ESPN's team included Geoff Mason, Jed Drake, and past America's Cup champion Gary Jobson. One of their innovations was to place miniature television cameras the size of lipstick containers (called Budweiser Yacht Cams) on Conner's yacht, which provided breathtaking television pictures from a variety of angles. Viewers were able to peer into the faces of the crews, including the athletic "grinders" hoisting sails under all sorts of difficult conditions—and that revealed them to viewers as highly skilled and conditioned athletes. The action and television pictures were mesmerizing.

The America's Cup turned out to be a groundbreaking success for ESPN, not to mention a ratings bonanza. The *New York Times* devoted a front-page story to the coverage, noting how people were hosting late-night and early-morning parties to watch the races, or gathering in bars to cheer on the American team. Johnny Carson and David Letterman, rather than lampooning us, acknowledged the excitement. Actually, ESPN's average rating for the America's Cup was 3.4, which translated to an audience of 1.4 million homes, seven times the usual audience for a late-night time slot. The final race earned a 4.5 rating

Action from the 1986–87 America's Cup.   *Dan Nerney / ESPN Images*

and peaked with a 27 percent share as record numbers of American viewers stayed up late into the night to witness Conner's *Stars and Stripes 87* win the best of seven series (four straight) against the Australian defender *Kookaburra III*.

The morning after that final race, I received a phone call from the president of one of Denver's biggest cable operators. He sounded quite serious and annoyed. "George, I've got a bone to pick with you," he said.

Now, it was not unusual for cable executives to call me with all sorts of complaints, so I braced myself and asked what the problem was. "George, I didn't get any sleep last night, because I was up watching sailing all night! *And it's your fault!*"

[The placement of miniature cameras on Dennis Conner's yacht was one of the earliest on-screen ESPN innovations. Others would include football's first-down yellow markers ("1st & Ten"), bottom line score scrolling, and baseball's "K Zone."]

Sunday Night Football

The unusual and innovative America's Cup coverage brought ESPN unprecedented critical acclaim. It boosted our position among media companies and secured for us a place on the national and international broadcasting maps. Surprisingly, the momentum from America's Cup coverage set the stage for securing our first National Football League contract.

When the USFL went away in 1985, so, of course, did ESPN's professional football programming from the United States (we still had Canadian football). While we never really stopped our efforts to acquire an NFL package, action began to heat up when we learned that the cable operators, themselves, had formed a consortium (called the Cable Football Network) to negotiate with the league and cut ESPN out altogether. That information really lit a fire under our management team, whose challenge now was to be nimble and quick enough to beat our own customers to the punch. Interestingly, this unexpected competition created some high intrigue among the cable industry players in Denver—and I found myself right in the middle of it.

The personal and professional relationships I had worked so hard to develop became invaluable during this time. On Sundays, virtually everybody in our industry attended the Broncos' games, and when I'd go from one suite to another to say hello, the possibility of acquiring an NFL television package was suddenly the only thing anybody wanted to talk about. Sometimes people volunteered information, but most of the time I peppered them with questions. "What operators are in the consortium?" "What package are they trying to get from the NFL? A full season? *Monday Night Football*? What?" "What's the pitch they'll be making to the league?" "Why would the NFL do business directly with the cable operators?" "How much money will it take to get a deal?" "How will the cable guys pay for the deal?"

At halftime of one game, an executive pulled me aside and showed me a written proposal the operators were going to make to the NFL. "You have to read it right here and now, George," he said. "You can't make any copies and you damn sure can't take it with you." This executive was doing me a favor because we had become friends. But it was this gesture, among others, that made it apparent to me that the cable operators were divided over the plan. Some were trying to get rights to the National Football League ahead of ESPN. Others were encouraging us to get there first. The reasons for the divergent thinking were almost purely financial. If the operators got the deal, they would have to pay tens of millions of dollars up front. On the flip side of the coin, if ESPN got the deal, *we* would have to figure out how to pay for it. There were really no easy choices. Either way, with the division among the cable operators, ESPN really had an opening to make something happen. But we had to move quickly.

During this time, I became a trusted lieutenant to our senior executives in trying to make a deal with the NFL to televise games on Sunday night. After all, Denver was the cable capital of the country, and I was in charge of ESPN's Denver office. So, by circumstance, I began interacting directly with people at the highest levels of our company. Essentially, I would gather intelligence from the front lines and report back to Bristol and New York. ESPN's president, Bill Grimes, along with our executive vice president, Roger Werner, spent many long hours negotiating personally with NFL Commissioner Pete Rozelle.

At one point, John Sie (who was leading the cable consortium) offered ESPN the chance to distribute *Sunday Night Football*, but the consortium would own the NFL contract. Tom Murphy and Dan Burke, however, immediately rejected that proposal. "Why have your best product owned by someone else?" they said. Ultimately, we were able to convince Rozelle and the NFL that ESPN could deliver the goods and that partnering with us was their best option. So we got the landmark deal and *Sunday Night Football* on ESPN came into being.

In 1987, it was unprecedented for the NFL to put their games on cable television. Not only was this their first cable contract, but they had never before played games on Sunday nights. Our package consisted of eight games in the second half of the regular season over each of the next three years. We also got four preseason games and the Pro Bowl. In return, ESPN agreed to pay the National Football League $153 million (an extraordinary amount at the time). When word of the deal got around internally, the prevailing sentiment at ESPN was a combination of euphoria and concern. "Great! We got the NFL! We've made it to the big time! But wait a minute! For $51 million a year? How the heck are we gonna pay for it?"

After a series of internal meetings, ESPN's executive management team decided to finance the rights fees by establishing a cable operator surcharge. Back then, such an idea was creative, innovative—and very risky because it had never before been tried. Clearly, ESPN's changing of the original business model back in 1982 to add subscriber fees had made this move possible. By 1987, ESPN was being paid twenty-seven cents per customer per month by cable operators to carry our network. We estimated that the surcharge would require an additional nine cents per subscriber per month if all the cable operators signed up for the new *Sunday Night Football* package. That would make

ESPN's new monthly rate thirty-six cents, which was a substantial increase of 33 percent. Obviously, the cable operators were not going to like it—and that was putting it mildly.

Because I ran ESPN's Denver office, a major part of my responsibility was to work with ESPN's senior executives to sell in the surcharge. Right off the bat, I knew it was going to take a Herculean effort, because many of the cable guys had tried valiantly to get the NFL deal for themselves, but had to give up on that plan when their consortium fell apart. It would be a natural reaction, I believed, for many of them to be angry with ESPN and hold it against us.

We began our sales effort by approaching the operators honestly and candidly. "Okay, you guys wanted punch-through programming," we said. "Well, we've finally got it, and if you want it as part of your ESPN service, it's going to have to be paid for." We also told them straight up that we paid $153 million for the three-year NFL package and that the goal of the surcharge was to break even. "We're going to be very democratic and transparent by showing you how your fee is calculated," we said.

In essence, the surcharge would be implemented on a "per-subscriber basis," we said. "The cost to ESPN is $51 million per year [$153 million divided by 3]. If we get all the current customers to sign up [45 million homes], it will be an individual increase of nine cents per month. That is our breakeven point." And then we assured them we would make available to their accountants all the numbers and calculations. The surcharge included our production costs, and as an added bonus to help them pay for it, we were going to give the affiliates four minutes per hour of local advertising per game, which was groundbreaking. Finally, we told them that if they signed up by midnight of a certain date, they would receive the best possible rate for the product. If they didn't want NFL *Sunday Night Football*, they didn't have to take it—or if they wanted to sign up *after* the deadline, they would have to pay a 20 percent penalty. "But your customers are going to want this product," we said to the cable operators.

Because this was still before the cable industry consolidated, we had to work with more than a thousand different cable operators. In the end, 99 percent of the industry signed up, but our fax machine was still running nonstop at midnight on the deadline date.

Of my entire personal client list, there was only one cable operator I could not persuade to take the deal. His name was Leonard Tow and he ran Century Communications back in Connecticut. When I was offered the promotion to manage the Denver office, I had asked for an account back east so that my wife and I could travel there once in a while to visit family. "Sure, George, we've got an account for you," they said with a wink and a grin. Leonard was both a legend in the business and an extremely tough guy to deal with, because he was a maverick. Still, he and I had managed to become friends, and because cable negotiations often extended beyond normal business hours, I called him at nine o'clock on the night of the deadline and spoke frankly. "Leonard, it's over," I said. "There's no more resistance to this. Everybody has signed up."

"No, George," he replied. "I won't do it."

"Leonard, your viewers are going to want the NFL. Don't cost yourself money, because we're not going to budge on the deadline. We can't. It's a matter of integrity with the rest of the industry. We've told everybody they had to sign up by midnight and, if you don't sign and you call us two days later, you're going to pay 20 percent more. I'm your account executive and I'm telling you it's over." But Leonard Tow was a tough guy and he still said no. *[Soon after, Leonard, realizing that* Sunday Night Football *was going to be a big success, signed up and paid the penalty.]*

On August 10, 1987, ESPN broadcast the first NFL game ever shown on cable television—a preseason contest between the Chicago Bears

Mike Patrick, Roy Firestone, and guest analyst Dick Butkus prepare to telecast ESPN's first *Sunday Night Football* game (and its first-ever NFL game), 1987.   *ESPN Images*

and the Miami Dolphins. That single game was watched by nearly every ESPN employee, because we all wanted to be part of history. And with a 9.9 rating and an audience of 3.8 million homes, it turned out to be the highest-rated, most watched program in ESPN history up to that point in time.

Beyond the games themselves, the NFL acquisition spawned several new, extremely significant shows for us. *NFL Primetime*, for instance, aired at 7 p.m. on Sundays and was able to use unlimited highlights due to our new NFL deal. So Chris Berman, who became ESPN's top NFL host, teamed with retired Denver Bronco standout Tom Jackson to recap the day's games. *NFL Primetime*, along with *NFL GameDay*, became two long-term staples of ESPN programming featuring a stellar crew over the years that included Joe Theismann, Steve Young,

Chris Berman and Tom Jackson hosting *NFL Primetime*, 2004. *ESPN Images*

Mike Ditka, Ron Jaworski, Andrea Kremer, Keyshawn Johnson, Chris Mortensen, Adam Schefter, Cris Carter, and Suzy Kolber.

On the advertising front, we were able to sell all of our commercial time for the NFL games (with a total of thirty-four national advertisers)—plus we picked up an additional five million subscribers. That meant we were being paid on 10 percent more volume at a higher per-customer rate. So now we had more cable subscribers, more viewers, more advertisers, and, of course, more revenue. You can do the math. Our acquisition of *Sunday Night Football* was not only punch-through programming for ESPN, it became a catalyst for the entire industry.

Overall, 1987 was a pivotal year in the history of ESPN—one of the most successful and dramatic ever experienced by a television network. In addition to televising the America's Cup and acquiring the

NFL, we advanced the ESPN programming ball with coverage of the Indianapolis 500 Time Trials, the NHL Stanley Cup play-offs, Davis Cup tennis—and our ratings increased by 33 percent.

A tremendous sense of pride began to spread throughout our company. Everybody knew we had turned the corner and were now in the big time of mainstream sports. After only eight years in existence, ESPN had finally grown to young adulthood. We had expanded our overseas distribution to more than forty countries and we were now seen in forty-five million American homes (the first cable network to surpass 50 percent of the U.S. market). ESPN was still the largest cable network in the United States.

While I was in the ESPN outposts of Dallas, Chicago, and Denver, headquarters in Bristol went through some ups and downs that occur when companies start to grow. Some new managers were hired, and the actions they took were counter to ESPN's values and culture. Generally, they wanted to do a lot of things that would make us more like the conventional broadcast networks. *SportsCenter* was cut back to fifteen minutes, for instance, to make it more like a local news show. That was enough to get people upset, but when they ordered Chris Berman to stop doing his nicknames (and tried to get the other on-air talent to be more staid), morale went downhill fast. *SportsCenter* started drifting and eventually came undone—to the point that the CNN sports show *Sports Tonight* was getting higher ratings.

As performance sagged, the new managers also started to fire people, causing a very bad environment. On a daily basis, particularly in and around *SportsCenter*, many employees didn't know when they came to work if it was going to be their last day. Bob Ley, for instance, worked for a year without a contract. He started looking for another job and almost quit. Others did quit, including solid on-air talent like

Sal Marchiano and Greg Gumbel. Even George Grande, who had tried to shield the *SportsCenter* guys from what was going on, couldn't take it anymore and went to work for the New York Yankees. ESPN in Bristol, at least, was becoming a difficult place to work.

The developing schism between New York and Bristol, which widened during this period, turned out to be both good and bad. Good in that New York trusted the original ESPN culture and allowed Bristol to operate on its own—but bad in that the problems were not quickly recognized and, therefore, continued to fester. It is somewhat ironic, but being located in Bristol turned out to be a great strength for ESPN.

Bristol was not a large Fortune 500 type of corporate headquarters. It had a strong blue-collar work ethic with a people-oriented culture that focused on treating others fairly. And during this tough time, ESPN people continued the bond they had forged early in our history. At first, they were so tight that they ignored the upper-level controversies, kept their heads down, and continued to produce great programming. With time, though, they started to revolt and squeeze out the people who did not buy into our values.

The ESPN culture carriers held things together, each doing what needed to be done in their own departments. Eventually, complaints from viewers about the changes with *SportsCenter* went through the roof, and the media hammered ESPN for cutting the show from an hour to fifteen minutes. In addition, during a prime-time interview, All-Star Kansas City Royals third baseman George Brett voiced concern that Chris Berman had been told to stop his nicknames. When fans heard that, they rebelled and called in or mailed tens of thousands of complaints.

The offending managers were finally fired, and *SportsCenter* got off the rocks and back to some semblance of normalcy. The show went back to an hour, and Chris Berman started doing his nicknames again. In the final analysis, sports fans (our viewers) made the difference.

And to me, that was paramount, because ESPN's unofficial mission had always been "to serve sports fans."

———

By 1988, I had celebrated my thirtieth birthday and the future was looking bright. Because of my work in Denver, I had gained the confidence of my bosses, who felt I'd done a good job in an important office for our company. Along the way, I had learned the basics of ESPN's business, and how to become a better leader in a corporate environment. I was also happily married with a wonderful family (my daughter, Kate, was one year old). Then, in February, I received a promotion to become director of affiliate sales for ESPN's Eastern Division, which required a transfer back to Bristol. We were going home.

———

I was in my first week as a midlevel sales manager at ESPN headquarters in Bristol when I ran into Chris Berman. "Hey, George, you're back!" said Chris.

"Hi, Boomer. Yeah, I'm back."

"Well, how'd it go?"

"Oh, pretty good."

As Chris and I were chatting and catching up, I suddenly heard a loud bell ringing.

"What is that?"

"Oh, that's John Walsh," came the reply. "He's calling a meeting."

"He rings a bell when he wants to have a meeting?"

"Yeah. It didn't go over very well at first. But now everybody's used to it."

John A. Walsh started as a consultant for ESPN in late 1987 and then was hired full-time by Steve Bornstein to become managing editor. What struck me about this move was that Walsh had never before worked in television. His background was in print journalism, where he had been an editor for such major publications as *Rolling Stone* magazine and the *Washington Post*'s *Inside Sports* magazine. Bornstein wanted to ramp up ESPN's reputation for quality journalism (for which, in my opinion, we never received enough credit), and we needed fresh thinking and innovative ideas to make it happen. So, by bringing in Walsh, Bornstein was putting an unconventional person in a conventional job.

I guess you could call John Walsh unconventional. He is an albino who wears a full beard and looks like Santa Claus. He is witty, outgoing, fun, and a whirlwind of action. He is one of the most unforgettable people I have ever met and, before long, he would shake up the status quo at ESPN—and be both lauded and lambasted for his efforts.

The first time Walsh came to Bristol, one of ESPN's mailroom drivers was assigned to go pick him up. "Hey, kid, go over to this Farmington hotel, pick up John Walsh, and bring him back here."

"Okay," responded young Mike McQuade, who was in his first day at ESPN. "How do I recognize him?"

"Don't worry, you can't miss him. He's an albino. He'll be waiting for you in the lobby. Now get going."

When Mike arrived at the hotel, he saw a big banner welcoming the National Association of Albinos, which was holding its annual convention there. And when he walked into the lobby, there were albinos everywhere.

Fortunately, Mike McQuade was a driver from the ESPN mailroom. He found Walsh, welcomed him to ESPN, drove him to Bristol, and completed his assignment.

Hail Mary

Much of a capacity crowd of sixty-two thousand fans were already seated in Candlestick Park when the earthquake hit. Batting practice was over. Larry Gatlin and the Gatlin Brothers had sung the national anthem. The ABC Sports team of Al Michaels, Tim McCarver, and Jim Palmer was on the air conveying the excitement of the evening. This was the "Battle of the Bay" World Series pitting glitzy San Francisco against disrespected Oakland. It was billed as beer versus wine, hamburger versus steak. The A's had already won the first two games at the Oakland Coliseum. Now it was the Giants' turn to play at home.

ESPN was on site to provide pregame and postgame coverage. Our trucks were positioned outside the stadium beyond center field, so our operations producer, Ron Semiao (who was part of a twenty-five-member crew), brought in a backup diesel generator in case of a problem.

Our team had completed its pregame show and had moved into place for the start of the game. Reporters Bob Ley, Chris Berman, Chris Myers, Joe Torre (between managerial stints), and producer John

Hamlin were assigned to an auxiliary press box about as high up as you could go in the stadium. Actually, it was more of a guard shack located behind home plate where technicians went to change stadium lightbulbs. A couple of television monitors had been installed in the box so the guys could see the local ABC station's broadcast. Their jobs were done for the moment. They were relaxed, chatting amiably, and looking forward to watching the game. It was a beautiful day. Unusually warm. No wind.

At 5:05 p.m., October 17, 1989, what sounded like a revved-up truck engine grew louder and louder until the floor of the shack felt like the guys were on a waterbed. Looking out across the stadium, they could see the railing of the upper deck undulating in waves. The foul poles were moving back and forth like needles on a metronome. And the stadium's expansion joints in center field split about six inches apart from the top all the way down to the ground. The ABC television picture went black and the last thing viewers heard was Al Michaels say, "You know what, we're having an earth..." Then all the power went out—the monitors, the scoreboard, the lights, everything. Bob Ley crossed himself. "Hail Mary, full of grace," he began. "The Lord is with thee. Blessed art thou amongst women and..." And then, before Bob could finish his Hail Mary, the shaking stopped.

There was a moment of silence while everybody processed what had just happened. Then many of the fans in the lower levels of Candlestick (where the intensity of the quake was less amplified) started cheering and chanting, "We will, we will, rock you!" Still caught up in the excitement of the World Series, they were unaware at that moment just how serious the earthquake had been. Nobody knew it had registered 6.9 on the Richter scale.

ESPN's reporting team hustled out of their positions in the upper deck behind home plate all the way to our truck beyond center field where Ron Semiao and the production team were waiting for them.

While power had been lost to communications outlets (including ABC's television broadcast), we were still up and running due to the generator Semiao had foreseen to bring in. We also had two working telephone lines, one of which we gave to the local police, because their radios were not working. *[Later, when the SFPD officers restored calm to the stadium, many lined up outside ESPN's trailer to use our phone to contact their families.]* Meanwhile, ESPN's technicians had us ready to go on the air.

Back in Bristol, John Walsh was watching ABC coverage of the game and rushed from his office down to the broadcast control room. Scott Ackerson, producing that night, was on the phone with Semiao. "What do you want us to do, John?" he asked.

"Just stay on the air, Scott," Walsh replied. "This is no longer a baseball story—it's a national news story." Walsh had made an immediate decision to trust the ESPN team on site to do the right thing. He knew they would cover the story the way it needed to be covered. And so they did.

Bob Ley prepared by gathering information from local police and from the control room in Bristol. Chris Berman, Joe Torre, and Chris Myers paired up with cameramen, like Jeff Israel, and rushed out to do spot interviews with fans and players. Minutes later, an ESPN SPECIAL REPORT graphic appeared on the network and we cut to Candlestick Park where Ley anchored our live coverage across the nation. Holding a reporter's notebook, working without a television monitor, and wearing an earpiece through which he was being fed information from ESPN's producers, Bob related the situation on the ground. "The quake, reported by KPIX-TV as the strongest to hit San Francisco since 1906, occurred at 5:05 Pacific Time," he said. Then we showed a live picture of the playing field from one of several ESPN camera operators who had ridden out the quake at the top of the stadium and were still at their posts. ABC would soon get back on the air but, for the moment, ESPN was providing the only national television coverage.

Bob Ley broadcasting live in the aftermath of the Loma Prieta earthquake, 1989.   *ESPN*

As police communications came back up, officers relayed additional information for us to broadcast and get the word out, including some first news reports that the Marina district was in flames, that several refineries were on fire in the East Bay, and that the upper level of the double-deck Cypress Street Viaduct (Interstate 880) had collapsed and killed a number of people. We also patched in a live helicopter video showing a collapsed fifty-foot section of the Oakland Bay Bridge (Interstate 80). That shot, in particular, drove home the seriousness of the natural disaster in San Francisco. A short time later, the grounds crew came out to pick up the bases and the camera started to shake. We were televising an aftershock live.

For the next hour and a half, ESPN's people spontaneously shifted from sportscasting to hard news reporting. No one needed to be told what to do—not the producers, not the on-air talent, not the technicians. They just swung into action—running on adrenaline and falling back on their professional instincts and skills. Once they had signed off, the enormity of the event began to hit home—the deaths, the fires, the damage, the raw emotions. They had been witnesses to an incredible, horrible tragedy. Some cried, some shook, some stood stoic, but they all had earned the right to hold their heads high.

I was a sales manager back in Bristol and I was very proud of them. People all over the company were talking about their performance, impressed that the entire team had risen to the occasion and acted so quickly and effectively in that moment of crisis. It inspired all of us, and I made sure to discuss the San Francisco events with all the people on my sales team.

As director of affiliate sales for the Eastern Division, I was now in charge of three regions—the Northeast, the Southeast, and the Midwest—which encompassed a total of thirty states. Early on, I spent most of my time traveling in order to get the lay of the land and build relationships with prospective and existing affiliates. As ESPN grew, I also found myself in constant need of new people to add to the team. However, I was very selective in whom I hired. One person I brought on board was Sean Bratches, a young go-getter working in television advertising sales in Dallas. Sean learned we had an opening and began calling me regularly to inquire about opportunities with ESPN. His persistence won me over, and I hired him as an entry-level account executive with responsibility for four states in the Northeast region. He hit the ground running and I knew early on he was going to be a winner.

In 1989, ESPN celebrated its tenth anniversary. By then, we were on firmer footing. Our new business model was established, we were becoming a stalwart of the growing cable television industry, and there was no question that ESPN was going to be at least a modest success.

A great example of our burgeoning reach was the signing of another landmark rights acquisition—our first contract with Major League Baseball. The $400 million, four-year deal called for us to broadcast 175 games a year (6 games a week). So, on April 9, 1990, ESPN began televising baseball games in multiple locations on various nights, and as was the case when we acquired the NFL, we received the right to use extensive MLB highlights to chronicle daily baseball action. That year we created a new show, *Baseball Tonight*, which became another ESPN staple hosted by anchors Dave Marash, John Saunders, Brian Kenny, and, later, Karl Ravech, with commentary by Peter Gammons, Tim Kurkjian, Buster Olney, Jayson Stark, and John Kruk.

Of course, ESPN received an immediate credibility boost with Major League Baseball due to our coverage of the World Series earthquake. I really believe the ESPN culture kicked in during that natural disaster. We saw total commitment, outstanding teamwork, and immediate action. Because empowerment is a key principle in how ESPN operates, our people in San Francisco were able to turn on a dime and do what they needed to do without waiting to ask for permission. On the contrary, Bristol supported them and gave them everything they needed to be successful.

The 1989 World Series revealed how big events can help transform companies. It demonstrated to everybody, both internally and externally, that ESPN was capable of serious news reporting. Externally, eyes were opened and the company's status was elevated. Part of our television coverage was shown on major news programs (such as *ABC World News Tonight with Peter Jennings*), which demonstrated to the nation that ESPN was capable of more than just reporting sports scores. Internally, it provided a big boost to morale and served as a big motivational force. It showed us that no story, no event, and no challenge was too large—and that our people come through when the chips are down.

Ultimately, both the San Francisco World Series earthquake and our acquisition of rights to Major League Baseball were additional turning points for ESPN. We were now on a new path that would lead to a higher level of professional sports reporting and sports journalism. I really believed there was no stopping us.

[The epicenter of the Loma Prieta earthquake was located in Santa Cruz, about sixty miles south-southeast of San Francisco. It was caused by a six-foot offset in the San Andreas Fault. Officially, 63 people were killed, 3,700 were injured, and 1.4 million lost power. It caused $10 billion in damage.]

Flood the Zone

When ESPN was created, high school student Robin Roberts set a goal for herself to one day work at the new sports network. But people told her it would not happen because she was a woman and, besides, ESPN wouldn't be around that long. An athlete in high school and college, Robin graduated from Southeastern Louisiana University in 1983 with a degree in communications. Her first job was as a sports reporter for a local television station in her native Mississippi. After only a few years on the job, Scotty Connal took notice and asked her to fly to Bristol to check us out. But Robin felt the network was a bit too disorganized and that she was too short on experience. So she moved on to Nashville, and then Atlanta, as a sports anchor and reporter for local television stations.

A Southern girl at heart, Robin was happy in Georgia and well thought of in her field. But, as she later recalled, "A sports reporter at a network affiliate was kind of like being the red-headed step-child of the newsroom." She often had to fight for two or three minutes of airtime to do an important story. And if there was bad weather or a national scandal, sometimes the sports segment would be cut altogether. Then, in 1990, ESPN came calling again—this time in the form of John Walsh.

During that visit to Bristol, Robin noticed a marked difference. Walsh talked to her about sports *journalism*, not just sports*casting*. He believed there was a great untapped area into which ESPN could step and forge a unique presence. Scores and highlights were the backbone of why fans tuned in to *SportsCenter* each night, but the variety of in-depth topics waiting to be explored was virtually unlimited. Also, Robin could make her personality part of the broadcast. But like everybody else, she'd have to start on the 2:30 a.m. *SportsCenter* broadcast and work her way forward.

Robin didn't hesitate. "Where do I sign?" she asked.

Robin Roberts was one of more than a dozen new sports reporters brought to ESPN by John Walsh, Steve Anderson, and Al Jaffe (who headed our talent acquisition office). As ESPN gained more sports rights and *SportsCenter* grew, we needed more on-air talent. They were simply spread too thin. So in addition to Roberts, some of their new hires included: Linda Cohn and Kenny Mayne (Seattle local television), Rich Eisen (Redding, California, local television), Craig Kilborn (Monterey, California, local television), Suzy Kolber (Miami local television), Andrea Kremer (NFL Films), Chris Myers (Miami local television), Dan Patrick (CNN) and Keith Olbermann (Los Angeles local television), Jimmy Roberts (ABC Sports), Mark Schwarz (Jacksonville, Florida, local television), Charley Steiner (New York Jets), Mike Tirico (Syracuse local television), and Jim Valvano (NC State). The one thing everybody had in common was that they were all passionate about sports—and it was a dream come true to be able to do more than just a two- or three-minute nightly segment.

Hiring a variety of new and talented sports journalists from across the country was part of John Walsh's plan to take ESPN to a new level—one on par with the print publications he had previously worked with. In a 1987 thirty-six-page report prepared for Roger Werner (now ESPN's president) and Steve Bornstein (executive VP of programming and production), Walsh had focused on *SportsCenter*, in particular. He noted that the licensing of sports rights would come and go, but *SportsCenter* was going to be there 365 days a year. As such, it should be *the* gathering place for sports fans every night where viewers could get the real story, in depth and with professional insight. "You have to invest in that franchise!" Walsh advised matter-of-factly. And to management's credit, Walsh was empowered to implement his vision.

Working with ESPN veteran Steve Anderson (*SportsCenter* managing editor), they formed three separate and distinct teams that included not only on-air talent but also a producer, director, production assistants (PAs), and associate producers (APs). The idea was to create a more effective working group and give viewers real consistency in whom they were going to watch every night. The 6 p.m. *SportsCenter* Monday through Friday featured Charley Steiner, Robin Roberts (who was quickly moved from the 2:30 a.m. slot), and Bob "General Robert E." Ley, as he was affectionately called by the team. (Bob Ley's *SportsCenter* desk was called the "General Store.") The 11 p.m. show teamed Dan Patrick with Keith Olbermann. The 2:30 a.m. "first team" was Chris Myers, Stuart Scott, and Rich Eisen.

In addition to forming teams, Walsh and Anderson insisted on changing the highlights rundown. Typically, sportscasters started with the biggest game of the night and, if that happened to be a baseball game, they would then show all the baseball highlights (no matter how unexciting the other games might be) before moving on to the next sport. Walsh's idea was to make it more like the front page of a newspaper, with the top big games or stories (regardless of sport) leading off the broadcast. He also advocated changing the chronological highlights of individual games to feature the most exciting and important moments. In baseball, they always presented plays chronologically by inning; in football and basketball, by quarter; in hockey, by period; and so on. But Walsh wanted to present the most exciting plays ranked from top to bottom, regardless of when they occurred in the games. New ideas were also popped into the highlight reels, including the "hero" highlight, the "goat" highlight, or the "last-second" highlight. And teases were put in so that viewers would stay tuned and watch the rest of the show.

The highlights rundown, the lead stories, and the order of game plays was decided by each *SportsCenter* team. The 6 p.m. group, for example, held a production meeting first thing in the morning that included all participants, including Steiner, Roberts, Ley, the director, the PAs, and the APs. It was run by producer Bruce Bernstein, but everybody at the table had an equal say. A second meeting was held at 2 p.m. to determine which stories they were going to lead with. And finally, a postmortem meeting was convened after the show was over to discuss what was done right or what was done wrong while it was still fresh in everybody's minds.

It turned out that forming separate teams worked amazingly well. Just like a well-functioning team in basketball, football, or hockey, members of the *SportsCenter* teams listened to and respected each other, especially during the sometimes heated discussions as to which stories or highlights to lead with. But when a final decision was reached, everybody took ownership and helped make sure the best possible show aired. There was nothing too big or too small for anyone to handle. What needed to get done got done.

That's not to say that there weren't bumps in the road, including the normal resistance when change is implemented in an organization. Walsh had to fight for everything—for the rundown, for the content, for the teams, for the culture of the newsroom, and for how many people could be hired. It was especially tough in the first year or two, because certain methods had been ingrained since ESPN's inception in 1979. Some individuals didn't want to change and claimed that when they did try new things, they were mocked by their peers in the industry. Reporters on the CNN sports show, for instance, laughed at *SportsCenter* for not doing all the highlights by sport. And some producers there thought John Walsh was nuts.

There were times when the pressure got to Walsh. Bob Ley, who would drive John home every night after the 11 p.m. show *[Walsh could not drive due to his poor vision]*, remembered him pounding the dashboard in frustration one night. "John, take it easy," Ley said. "People are afraid of outsiders and you're trying to change a lot of things. And by the way, you have a unique style, in case you haven't noticed—between the Santa Claus motif and ringing the bell for meetings. It'll be all right. Just give it some time."

It became obvious, though, that Walsh was a strong leader—and very determined in his mission. He butted heads with a lot of the anchors in the early going. Chris Berman, for example, could be a maverick and, at times, disrupt the team. So Walsh told him to knock it off and, to show that he was serious, didn't let Chris go to Foxborough, Massachusetts, to do a piece on the NFL's New England Patriots. Berman took it in stride and became more of a team player, because he really cared about the company. Of Walsh's discipline in that instance, Boomer even joked later that "Daddy took the T-Bird away."

Walsh also had a few flare-ups with Keith Olbermann who, when paired with Dan Patrick, created the kind of chemistry that made for great television. There is a skill to delivering sports highlights— telling a story, doing it in a way that is witty, putting in your own observations—and Keith and Dan were at the top of the game. Sports fans loved them and the signature catchphrases they used, like *biscuit in the basket* and *en fuego* (Spanish for "on fire"). People tuned in to watch them much as they had done to listen to Chris Berman and his nicknames—and soon, the Patrick-Olbermann *SportsCenter* combination was a ratings phenomenon.

But when Keith and Dan started constantly referring to their broadcast as "The Big Show," Walsh objected, stating that the name of the show was *SportsCenter* and the 11 p.m. show was no more special than any other *SportsCenter*. In response, Olbermann and Patrick started each show by saying "This is *SportsCenter*" (rather than "This is the Big Show")—and *that* became a new catchphrase.

While most of the on-air talent played ball, there were a few who simply could not handle either the discipline or the many changes Walsh brought to *SportsCenter*. In the early going, some just could not let go of the chronological highlights. Others could not accept that the industry was changing, that the world of sports was changing, and that ESPN had to change right along with it. Those who would not get with the program had to be helped out the door. And the truth is that Walsh and Anderson fired at least ten people that year. They had to. You cannot grow an organization if you have people in it who are not willing to change. It's true in all businesses.

Through all that resistance to change, John Walsh kept going, because he believed in a vision and because he was a good leader. He watched every *SportsCenter*. He was always at the office, setting the example. And he built solid personal relationships so that people finally came to realize that he cared about them. Walsh's confidence in them paid off, too, because as *SportsCenter* improved, more sports fans tuned in, and ratings grew.

In June 1991, I accepted a transfer from Bristol to ESPN's New York City office. Actually, I requested the move. Had I been in production and programming, I would have stayed in Bristol, but for my field of sales and marketing, the action was in New York. I was thinking more about my future plans and career, in part, because I now had a family of five to take care of (our son James had just been born, and George Jr. was about to turn two). After a full decade at ESPN, I was very happy with where I was and excited to be working in New York for the first time.

In my new job, as I was learning how to grow the revenue of the company, what the programming and production team was accomplishing in Bristol was of great interest to me. First, I was proud that the original vision of Chet Simmons for *SportsCenter* as ESPN's differentiator not only was shared by management, but was being realized. No other media company had anything that was even close. Second, *SportsCenter*'s increased ratings served to increase the value of ESPN, which helped tremendously in our sales and marketing efforts. It provided more wind in our "sales," so to speak, giving us more to talk about and also more to promote.

I also *watched* ESPN all the time. Just like in the early days when I was on the road and studying at night, I felt that to be successful in sales, it was critical to be as up to speed as possible on our product. And now that I was managing half of our affiliate sales department, I constantly encouraged my team to also be "students of the business" by watching our programming, reading everything they could, and knowing what was coming down the pike. ESPN was getting better and changing fast. If we fell asleep for a moment, those of us in sales and marketing would find ourselves playing catch-up, and I was not about to let that happen.

In addition to making changes to *SportsCenter*, ESPN also created two new cutting-edge programs that are now recognized as significant contributions to sports journalism. The first show, *The Sports Reporters,* was intended to be like a Sunday morning newspaper. Former *New York Post* sportswriter Joe Valerio (who went on to produce *The Sports Reporters* for twenty-five-plus years) reasoned that Sunday morning is relaxed. After church and a good breakfast, the average sports fan gets a cup of coffee, sits down with the morning paper, and looks at the day ahead in sports. So we set out to produce a show that explores the broad spectrum of sports issues with insightful commentary from newspaper columnists.

The Sports Reporters debuted in October 1988, originally hosted by

Gary Thorne, the legendary Dick Schaap, and later by John Saunders (for thirteen-plus years). The essence of the show was discussions featuring sports columnists from the nation's top newspapers, including William C. Rhoden (*New York Times*), Jemele Hill (*Orlando Sentinel*), Mike Lupica (*New York Daily News*), Bob Ryan, Jackie MacMullan (*Boston Globe*), Israel Gutierrez (*Miami Herald*), and Mitch Albom (*Detroit Free Press*), among others. Dick Schaap, who for thirteen years made the show a must-watch for serious fans, came from the era where sportswriters had newsprint on their fingers and, at the close of day, went to their favorite watering holes to talk sports. Schaap masterfully hosted *The Sports Reporters* just like he held court at many of those New York bars.

If *The Sports Reporters* was ESPN's equivalent of *Meet the Press*, then *Outside the Lines* (*OTL*) was our version of *60 Minutes*. OTL,

The Sports Reporters with Tony Kornheiser (*Washington Post*), Leonard Koppett (*Peninsula Times*), host Dick Schaap, and Mike Lupica (*New York Daily News*), 1991. *Cynthia Greer*

which was created by Walsh and Anderson, began episodically in 1990 as a one-hour show hosted by Bob Ley. The first two shows included a couple of great stories: "After the Cheering Stops," about athletes (both college and pro) trying to adjust to life after their careers are over, and "The Autograph Game," about the big market in baseball memorabilia. Soon we were doing four to seven shows a year and becoming progressively more ambitious. For example, in 1993, *OTL* unmasked swim coach Mitch Ivey for having inappropriate relationships with his female swimmers. And in 1996, Ley and the *OTL* team went to Russia to look at sports in the former Soviet Union. Part of that program focused on Pavel Bure (the "Russian Rocket" who, at the time, was playing for Vancouver in the NHL), and reports of his connections to the Russian mafia.

Both *Outside the Lines* and *The Sports Reporters* were successful for two very big reasons: (1) they were produced in a highly professional manner, and (2) they had earned credibility with sports fans. As Robin Roberts once commented, "Other networks have viewers; ESPN has *fans*—and there's a difference. You cannot fool a sports fan. If you look like you're faking it, or you seem like you don't know what you're talking about, you aren't going to be around very long."

John Walsh realized that part of gaining credibility with sports fans, and thereby earning their trust, was to present material to them through solid sports *journalism* along with standard sports*casting*. Sportscasters convey the atmosphere of the event and provide highlights. Sports journalists dig deeper. They tell stories that attract and hold the audience. ESPN was bringing that to the table and sports fans took notice.

Between 1989 and 1992, there were five big stories that changed *SportsCenter*, and therefore ESPN. Had they occurred a decade later, each would have been on the front page of the *New York Times*. It just so happened that these stories centered around sports—and back then, ESPN was the only media outlet (television, radio, or print) that was prepared to cover them like any other national news story would be covered.

In October 1989, the Loma Prieta earthquake at the World Series created a situation where our people on site had to act quickly and spontaneously. Earlier that year, however, our ESPN news team was proactively on the tip of the spear in reporting all the events that led to baseball great Pete Rose eventually being banned from the sport for life. We interviewed people who had knowledge of Rose's gambling, including sources close to the special prosecutor's office investigating the case. During coverage of this story, ESPN employed a completely new dynamic by sending reporters to different cities in an effort to obtain any and all pertinent information. Jimmy Roberts went to Cooperstown, Dan Patrick went to Cincinnati, Charley Steiner was on the streets of New York, Bob Ley was the centerpiece in Bristol, and Chris Myers was in Philadelphia where Pete Rose was. ESPN covered every element of the story and, finally, broke the news of baseball commissioner Bart Giamatti handing down a lifetime ban, which Rose accepted the next day. That broadcast broke new ground for *SportsCenter* by going forty-eight minutes straight without a commercial interruption.

This happened ten years before Howell Raines, editor at the *New York Times*, was reported to have coined the phrase *flood the zone* to denote a general strategy where a group of reporters is sent into the field to investigate, cover all angles, and get to the core with in-depth coverage *as the story unfolds*. For ESPN, it was not some pre-thought-out strategy that we were going to use when a big story broke. Rather, it was a method of operations that just came naturally to us. In those days, ESPN routinely threw our young, passionate people at breaking news stories. And often, what at first appeared to be a difficult problem turned into an opportunity to showcase what ESPN was capable of delivering.

The three other national stories we covered in a similar manner were the sudden and tragic death of Loyola Marymount University's Hank Gathers during a conference tournament basketball game in Los Angeles (1990), Earvin "Magic" Johnson of the Los Angeles Lakers revealing he was HIV-positive (1991), and boxer Mike Tyson's rape trial in Indianapolis (1992). After Tyson was convicted of raping eighteen-year-old Desiree Washington (Miss Black Rhode Island) in an Indianapolis hotel room, Walsh met with Robin Roberts and asked her to do an on-air commentary.

"What?" she responded. "We don't do commentaries!"

"Robin, now that he has been found guilty, it is nothing more than your thoughts as a journalist and as a black woman," replied Walsh. "It was a black woman who had the courage to bring the charges against him. How about it?"

In a piece separate from *SportsCenter*, Robin Roberts did a superb on-air commentary. It was a first for us and, in my opinion, a perfect example of the transformation of *SportsCenter* from merely sportscasting to top-of-the-line sports journalism. Circumstance played a part in that success, too, because John Walsh's original intent was simply to make *SportsCenter* a superb program and, in the middle of the transformation process, those five national stories fell into ESPN's lap.

Launching "The Deuce"

Steve Bornstein joined ESPN in 1980 as a program coordinator. In 1990, he was named president. By then, ESPN reached more than fifty million households. Only thirty-seven years old, Bornstein's energy and enthusiasm would result in a series of major changes in the early '90s that were not only *exactly* what the company needed at that point in our history, but would also set the stage for future growth. As competition from Fox and others mounted, his vision for ESPN foresaw an organization with a much larger reach, international in scope, and one that produced content across multiple media platforms.

Early on, at the urging of management consultant Tony Smith, Bornstein took a hands-on approach to creating ESPN's first formal mission statement. He formed a four-person team comprising himself, Smith, Ed Durso (general counsel), and Rick Barry (human resources director) to write the statement and then release it to the rest of the company. The statement articulated a number of principles upon which ESPN had been built. We were committed to enhancing our position "as the premier sports programmer in the world" in order to serve sports fans. ESPN people were our "most valuable resource" and deserved to be treated with "respect and dignity." The statement went on to note that "working together as a team" was the "heart of our success" and partly a result of "aggressive thinking and risk-taking." And finally, as a business ESPN was committed to a "healthy return on investment."

Personally, I really liked the idea of a written mission statement. As a growing organization, we now had an expression of what we stood for and where we wanted to go. And that turned out to be extraordinarily important as we set out on a massive effort to expand ESPN's brand both in the United States and around the world.

Discussions about brands can often be confusing, but they needn't be. A brand is nothing more than what people think of when a certain product or company comes to mind. Usually, brands are developed intentionally and with a lot of thought by a corporation's marketing department. But that's not the way it happened at ESPN. In the beginning, we didn't know what a twenty-four-hour sports network was supposed to be. There was little thought given to articulating a brand in the way we think of it in business today. Rather, we let our people experiment, innovate, and implement what seemed to work well—and we did so in an environment that was fun and fast-paced.

In that sense, ESPN's *culture* came first and, over the years, the brand grew out of simply performing the task at hand. Such things as Chris Berman's nicknames, our televising a wide variety of sports, *SportsCenter*'s highlights, Patrick and Olbermann's chemistry, Bob Ley and *Outside the Lines*—all contributed to forming the ESPN brand. Once established, our executives then began to build on it more proactively. Before Bill Grimes and Roger Werner left for greener pastures, for example, they established a merchandising department so that products with the ESPN logo could be sold more broadly rather than simply out of the backs of our vehicles at football games. Also under their leadership, we began to create a presence beyond U.S. borders by launching ESPN International and serving television outlets in over sixty countries around the world.

Bornstein's ambitious agenda for ESPN was to create more television networks and move into different media. ESPN Radio, for instance, was launched nationally on the first business day of 1992 in partnership with the ABC Radio Network. In the first major joint venture with our sister company since the 1984 acquisition, we began with only sixteen hours of programming per week on about fifty stations.

A few years later, ESPN became one of the first television networks to create a presence on the Internet. Doing so was a real gamble back then, because search engines like Google did not yet exist and email was not widespread. So to mitigate the risk, Dick Glover (head of ESPN Enterprises) led the company's effort to form a joint venture with software and website company Starwave, which was founded by Microsoft's Paul Allen. In addition to the technology we gained in the partnership, we immediately added significant Internet experience in house with new personnel who would go on to make a big impact at ESPN, among them John Zehr, Aaron LaBerge, Dan Benshoff, and Marie Donoghue. In April 1995, ESPN launched its first website, ESPNet .SportsZone.com. It quickly became one of the most popular sites on the Internet, serving 120,000 users per day with scores, statistics, features, polls, and chat. Of course, that early website set the stage for what would eventually become ESPN.com.

In early 1992, Steve Bornstein surprised everybody by bringing in John A. Lack as executive vice president of programming and marketing (essentially the number-two executive at the company). Lack had been instrumental in creating two groundbreaking cable channels—MTV and Nickelodeon. Soon added to ESPN's new marketing team were the top-notch advertising firm of Wieden+Kennedy (Nike's agency at the time) and Lack's colleague Harriet Seitler, a thirteen-year marketing veteran of MTV. The fact that Harriet did not have a background in sports may have contributed to her exceptional creativity at ESPN. Unencumbered by conventional thinking, she came up with ideas that, in my view, really shook up our traditional marketing efforts and resulted in some of the best promotional spots and advertising campaigns our company had ever produced.

In those days, ESPN's on-air promos were fairly pedestrian, consisting mostly of game footage and a voice-over with something like, "Tune in tonight at 8 p.m. to see St. John's battle Georgetown in a Big East clash." But the marketing triumvirate of Lack, Seitler, and Wieden+Kennedy started a whole new style of commercials designed to foster an emotional connection between ESPN and the sports fan. They brought in marching bands, celebrities, and even hired Spike Lee to direct one spot. ESPN had never seen anything like this before. It was a fresh, bold step in brand development for the company.

Around this time, my boss, Roger Williams, left the company and Steve Bornstein began looking outside for a replacement. A short while later, in November 1992, he offered me the job, which I gratefully accepted. Becoming vice president of affiliate marketing was a big move for my career, and a serious leadership role. The department was now a significant and growing contributor to ESPN's revenue, and if we couldn't distribute new products, the company's growth prospects would have been dim. Right off the bat, my new job thrust me onto the front lines of one of the most important events in our company's history: the launch of ESPN2—"The Deuce."

We had been thinking about launching a second channel for some time. Although we were no longer able to schedule everything we wanted to televise on ESPN, it was abundantly clear that there was plenty of product. The big thing we didn't know was whether or not we could sell a new network to our affiliates. So my department's first priority was to go out to the cable operators and see what kind of a demand we would have for a second ESPN sports channel. We began pitching that new idea in mid-1992.

To say that our first forays were met with skepticism would be an understatement. "You think you need *another* twenty-four-hour sports network?" we were asked. "Are you crazy, George? You'll be canni- balizing yourself. How is it going to be different?" And of course, we heard the underlying reason that is at the root of every such discus- sion: "Don't you think we already pay you enough?"

We weren't getting *anywhere* with the cable operators in our early efforts, and it was obvious that we needed a fresh approach in order to successfully distribute ESPN2. But what? That is where John Lack's marketing creativity vaulted to the forefront. He came up with the idea of a younger, hipper version of ESPN, one billed as an *alternative* sports network designed to reach a younger demographic. In addi- tion to the NHL, we would broadcast skateboarding, BMX (bicycle motocross), extreme sports, and other events that younger fans liked.

Lack conceived of "Jock'n Roll," a program that displayed box scores with rock-and-roll music playing in the background. The flag- ship show for ESPN2 would be *SportsNight*, a lighter, trendier version of *SportsCenter* hosted by Keith Olbermann, Suzy Kolber, and Mitch Albom. "This is not your father's ESPN!" became the mantra for ESPN2. We began pitching this new descriptive image for "The Deuce" in the spring of 1993, and it worked. We now had the attention of our affiliates as the new network vision gained some traction.

However, the U.S. Congress threw a wrench in the works that at first I thought would cause problems. For years, executives at tra- ditional broadcast networks were frustrated that cable systems just picked up their over-the-air signals and resold them as part of the fee for basic cable. So they lobbied Washington and got a provision added to the Cable Television Consumer Protection and Competition Act, which was passed in October 1992. The "Retransmission Consent" provision (or Retrans, as it was referred to in the industry) simply said that permission had to be first obtained from broadcasters before their signals could be used by cable operators, and that the broadcaster had the right to negotiate satisfactory fees. More simply put, cable systems now had to pay the broadcast networks for televising local channels.

This new law was hated by the cable operators, who said, "I'm never going to pay broadcasters, because after all, they send out their signals for free!" But the broadcasters retaliated by saying, "You guys are building a business off our backs, and we deserve to get paid." Pretty soon, these two very powerful factions of the television industry were circling each other like two boxers in the ring. Both were ready to fight and neither was about to back off.

It was during that period of difficulty that ESPN, sensing an opportunity, came up with a new idea, one that Fox Broadcasting was working on as well. Because we were part of CapCities, which also owned ABC, why not offer any cable operator signing up for ESPN2 the right to carry ABC programming, too? The cable guys could say they weren't really paying for ABC (which they were, because it was covered in the ESPN2 price), and CapCities, through the ESPN2 license fees, received value from the cable operators for the use of ABC's signal. It was a new model, but it just might avert a big problem in the industry.

That summer, while Retrans was being debated in the industry, I attended the national cable convention in San Francisco, and it was the only thing anybody was talking about—heatedly, I might add. "Retrans is coming and it's going to be a train wreck!" "We're not going to pay you guys!" "Yes you are! Yes you are!"

Hearing all of this, our team floated the first "what if?" "Hey, what if we could get you ABC Retransmission consent in exchange for launching ESPN2?" That idea gained traction right out of the gate and was quickly adopted by CapCities as a strategy.

The only problem now was that, by law, all the cable operators had to be signed up by October 1, 1993. That meant that the affiliate sales department had a period of about a hundred days to negotiate more than a thousand contracts. Personally, I never worked so hard in my life. We were so busy that summer that I had to hold staff meetings on Sunday nights by telephone, because everybody was on the road all week. When I asked my team if that would be okay with them, they all said, "No problem, George. What time?" Our group included Sean Bratches, who had steadily advanced in the company since I hired him.

That summer's sales effort was nonstop presenting, selling, and negotiating at all hours of the day and night. We even took most of ESPN's legal staff with us on the road to expedite the deal making. As part of our sell, I started making the audacious statement that ESPN was the nation's "most valuable" cable network. I didn't have any kind of official poll to cite as the source, but no one ever refuted me. So we just kept playing it up.

"Hey, if ESPN is the most valuable network, it stands to reason that ESPN2 will be very valuable, as well. So let's go! Sign up!"

As part of our sales effort, we created a slogan: "ESPN2—the wilder, crazier son of ESPN." We were doing okay with it until a female employee contacted me and said she didn't realize that ESPN was a male. Embarrassed that we had implied such an idea, we dropped the phrase. Plenty of women are sports fans, and clearly women had played an integral role in ESPN's success, both internally and externally. That was a lesson I would never forget.

Throughout the summer and early fall, we were able to sign up almost every cable operator in the United States. As it turned out, our idea to solve the Retransmission Consent problem became a primary driver of sales for ESPN2. Not only was it a big success, but we were praised for coming up with a win-win that kept everybody happy. With time, our model would be emulated by other broadcast and cable companies.

At 8 p.m. EST on October 1, 1993, ESPN2 successfully launched to a record ten million U.S. homes. On that first broadcast, Keith Olbermann sat next to Suzy Kolber at the *SportsNight* desk. Wearing a leather jacket, Keith spoke the first words on ESPN2 with a memorable, if irreverent, line. "Welcome to the end of our careers," he said with a wry grin. "The Deuce" was on the air.

That night, a raucous, over-the-top party took place in the parking lot on our main campus. ESPN people had worked so hard to launch the new network that they needed to blow off steam. Bornstein had also invited people from CapCities, ABC, NHL Commissioner Gary Bettman, and all the ad agencies to come up from New York to be a part of the celebration. The "adult beverages" flowed liberally, there was live music and dancing, and MC Hammer was there to perform. The ESPN2 launch party became legend in ESPN lore. People talked about it for years after.

But there was a problem. It only took six months for us to realize that the younger, hipper version of ESPN was not working with sports fans. Ratings were low, and our viewers voiced their displeasure. They wanted fewer gimmicks and more "stick and ball" sports. So we huddled together and quickly decided to evolve ESPN2 programming by dropping the rock-and-roll music and adding more mainstream sports, such as baseball, basketball, football, motor sports, and so on. Keith Olbermann returned to *SportsCenter* and reteamed with Dan Patrick. Suzy Kolber went on to become a versatile on-air talent focused primarily on the NFL. And Mitch Albom continued as a major contributor to *The Sports Reporters*.

Marketing "The Deuce" as the wilder, crazier version of ESPN worked for the launch, but the bottom line is that it did not work as a longer-term programming strategy. Yet despite the fact that we had a lot of time invested and were proud of the achievement, we did not let our egos get in the way when it became obvious that a change needed to be made. And that taught me that an executive cannot get too wedded to a single business model. When things aren't working, you have to move, and move fast. You have to deal with the cold hard facts, even if you worked hard to get to that point.

The launch of ESPN2 was the most successful launch of any cable network up to that point in time—and the leadership at CapCities was especially proud of our efforts. A few days afterward, Dan Burke sent out a memo to all department heads congratulating everyone and lauding ESPN's teamwork and professionalism. On my copy, he took the time to add a personal handwritten note across the bottom. "Dear George," it read. "My hope is that you are or soon will be someplace resting. You and your team did a *great* job with this opportunity! The rest of us are all proud and grateful." And he signed it again, "Dan Burke."

I have never forgotten Dan's gesture and how good it made me feel. And from that time forward, I resolved to send out as many of my own handwritten notes to co-workers as I possibly could.

On the evening of October 1, 1993, I was standing in my office looking down at the party going on in the parking lot. One major cable operator (the largest in the country), TCI out of Denver, had not signed up for ESPN2. Our negotiations had ended earlier in the day and, although time had basically run out, I was hoping against hope that they would still come on board.

At 8 p.m. on the dot, just as "The Deuce" came on the air and Olbermann's leather jacket appeared, my fax began beeping and clicking. Coming through was the signed contract from TCI. I ripped it out of the fax machine, put it in my pocket, and headed downstairs to the party. I first showed it to the members of my team and congratulated them. Next, I found Steve Bornstein and John Lack to give them the good news. The signed TCI contract put us over the ten-million-household mark. So Steve, John, and I hoisted some champagne and toasted our success. Then, at about nine o'clock, I headed home to my wife and family. I was exhausted.

Lockhorns, February 15, 2004. © LOCKHORNS © 2004 WM.HOEST ENTER-
PRISES, INC. Distributed by King Features Syndicate

"Not So Fast, My Friend"

Chris Fowler, Lee Corso, and Craig James were manning the *College GameDay* set just outside Memorial Stadium in Lincoln, Nebraska, on October 29, 1994. The big showdown between number two Colorado and number three Nebraska had just concluded with a dominant 24–7 Cornhuskers win and, while preparing for the postgame segment, they noticed on television that the students had torn down the goalposts in celebration and were hauling them off. Then, all of a sudden, a roar erupted in front of the set, the crowd parted, and students emerged wielding a large jagged piece of yellow metal goalpost and set it down right in front of the television cameras. Then the crowd went crazy, screaming and chanting: "We're number one! We're number one! We did it! Cornhuskers are the best! Yeah! Whoooo! Yeah!"

At that moment, Chris Fowler realized ESPN was on to something. "They brought that goalpost right to us," he remembered. "It was like a cat who had killed a mouse and was proudly showing it off—only in this case it looked more like a large giraffe." *College GameDay* was only in its first full season on the road, and the jury was still out as to whether the show was going to make it or not. But after this, Fowler's doubts dissipated. "When they brought that torn-down goalpost to us," he said, "I knew we were on the road to stay."

Lee Corso was part of the original team (along with Tim Brando and Beano Cook) when *GameDay* debuted in 1987 as ESPN's studio show for college football. Chris Fowler left *Scholastic Sports America* and became host in 1990, and Craig James joined the team in 1993. In those early years the show had a low profile, modest ratings, and every once in a while someone went on site to cover a bowl game. It was during those postseason bowls that the guys were able to experience firsthand the tailgaters, the buildup, and the community nature of college football games. Knowing it would be a lot more fun to actually go to the regular-season games, Fowler, Corso, and James consistently poked and prodded their bosses to let them take the show on the road. They bided their time for the right game, and when it came they pounced.

The opportunity they were waiting for occurred on November 13, 1993, when the number-one-ranked Florida State Seminoles visited the number two Fighting Irish of Notre Dame in South Bend, Indiana. It was as big a national game as anybody would ever see in the regular season. NBC was doing the broadcast and they billed it as the "Game of the Century." Two undefeated teams, two high-profile coaches in Bobby Bowden and Lou Holtz, a Heisman Trophy candidate in Seminole quarterback Charlie Ward, and an intraregional contest to boot—North versus South. Any way you looked at it, this game was going to be big. *College GameDay*'s time had come and we had to be there.

Steve Bornstein and his executive team gave the go-ahead to go on the road even though it was an expensive proposition. It was also risky production-wise, because we had little idea how to stage a show like this at the game site. There were a hundred questions we couldn't answer. How many cameras do we need? What kind of microphones should the on-air talent use? Should we interview guests live or should we tape all of our pieces? "All I knew was that we had maybe one chance to get it right," said Fowler. "If it had been a disaster, they weren't going to let us do it again.

The night before, *GameDay* set up on the Notre Dame campus right outside the basketball arena to cover the traditional pep rally. Being able to capture the energy and intensity of the cheerleaders, the band, the Leprechaun mascot, and all the students was pure magic. On the day of the game, the broadcast took place inside Heritage Hall, where all of Notre Dame's sports trophies were kept. It was a small production with a makeshift set and a couple of cameras for a one-hour pregame show from 11 a.m. to noon. About two dozen students showed up and stood politely behind a little rope except for some cheering when Lee Corso, caught up in the euphoria of the home crowd, took off his Florida State hat and put on a Notre Dame hat indicating a reversal of his pick to win the game.

After the Fighting Irish prevailed in an upset, 31–24, Coach Lou Holtz surprised everybody by triumphantly walking right up on the *GameDay* set during the live postgame show. Corso immediately gave Holtz his chair and microphone, and Fowler and James engaged the coach in a spontaneous and in-depth conversation about what had transpired during the game.

Although we knew there weren't a lot of people watching our broadcast that first time, it was pretty clear that similar fan passion for college football was going to be present at every future game we might show up at. So over the next several years, we gradually stepped up our on-the-road *GameDay* shows. We chose what we believed would be the best game of the week, despite who might be televising it. Game choices were announced a week ahead of time, which generated anticipation and excitement.

Soon, league commissioners and university officials began lobbying for *GameDay* to come to their home games. Then, on November 13,

1999, when we went to the Virginia Tech campus to cover the number two Hokies hosting the number nineteen Miami Hurricanes, the program was unexpectedly elevated to a level that none of us had ever imagined. That's when Head Coach Frank Beamer, who had an emerging football program led by quarterback Michael Vick, sensed an opportunity to use *GameDay* to show the world what Blacksburg, Virginia, was like. So he put the word out to the student body and, by the time our pregame show aired, there were an estimated *eleven thousand* fans behind the set screaming, waving, and carrying on.

In the years that followed, it was not abnormal for *GameDay* to have anywhere between ten and fifteen thousand fans show up for the broadcasts—and *that* was a whole new ball game. It resulted in a tremendous period of growth and creativity during which *GameDay*'s primary mission remained the same—setting the stage for the entire day in college football with the big game serving as the centerpiece. Incrementally, over the next twenty years, as the show grew in popularity, we increased its length from thirty minutes to three hours. Of course, some of the on-air players changed, but the passion and the teamwork remained the same. Over the years, Kirk Herbstreit, Desmond Howard, David Pollack, Erin Andrews, and Samantha Ponder were added to the crew. Chris Fowler and Lee Corso remained and provided important stability. Corso, for instance, always reminded new members of the team to check their egos at the door, and that they were "in the entertainment business with college football as the vehicle."

The "entertainment" on *College GameDay* started with the chemistry generated by the guys on camera. Their job was to have fun and to be more like fans at a bar talking football with the viewers eavesdropping.

In 2004, thirty-year-old Lee Fitting was named producer for *College GameDay*. It was a move that surprised a lot of people and raised some eyebrows, because he had skipped a couple of steps in the normal progression to reach that level. After graduating from James Madison University in 1996, Lee started as an entry-level temporary production assistant in ESPN's rigorous PA program. At the end of the seven-month trial period, Lee's boss pulled him aside. "They're voting on you right now," he said. "I don't know if you're going to make the cut." But after some anxious hours, ESPN decided to drop the "temporary" from Fitting's title and assigned him to produce special features for *SportsCenter*. His initial working hours were from 6 p.m. to 3 a.m., Wednesday through Sunday. In 2000, Lee began work as an associate producer for *College GameDay*, mostly producing features. But four years later, when the lead producer transferred out, he put together a written proposal and gave it to the executives in charge of the show and said: "Listen, I really want to produce *College GameDay*, and here are my ideas about how to make it better." A couple of weeks later, they got back to him. "Okay, Fitting," they said. "Let's go!"

When Lee began his new job, he was a micromanager. He had his hands in everything. It had to be done the way he wanted it. But because he was green, his bosses kept him on a short leash. So when he made mistakes, which he most certainly did, they were there to provide counsel and guidance. One of Lee's mentors was John Wildhack, who was progressing nicely in the company. Wildhack had started as an entry-level producer back in 1981, just as Fitting had in 1996. As such, he knew what Lee was going through and was the perfect coach for Lee until he was able to succeed on his own. And when that happened, Wildhack was able to confirm that *GameDay*'s management had decided to give the program a longer leash. "Okay, Lee, they're delegating responsibility to you. You're now empowered to act on your own. Go get 'em."

With time, Lee realized just how much that meant to him, personally. Being trusted by his bosses not only gave him more freedom to act on his own, it made him feel good—really good. And that, in turn, elevated his performance. So Lee decided to do the same for the people who reported to him. He no longer looked over their shoulders in the edit room. He no longer went into the on-site truck to make a final check of the graphics and videos. He stopped giving orders and started trusting people to do their jobs, just as ESPN management trusted him. In essence, Lee Fitting stopped micromanaging and started delegating. He stopped being just a manager and became a leader. And that resulted in a higher level of sustained performance, more creative thinking, and, ultimately, a better product. In my opinion, the transformation that Lee Fitting made—from manager to leader—is a good example of how ESPN's people-centric culture works. If you unleash the talent and energy of everyone in your organization, you're bound to be successful.

College GameDay has evolved into one of the biggest things on television. It is a brand in and of itself and, certainly, it has become a phenomenal success for ESPN. Companies now fight to become sponsors. The set is built by Home Depot, there is the DirecTV bus, and other prominent spots have been occupied by blue-chip companies, such as AT&T and Coke. So the initial risk taken by ESPN's executives turned out to be well worth it in the long run.

The show is also wildly popular among sports fans. At every college we visit, a festive tailgate atmosphere is created by the students, some of whom show up twelve hours before kickoff. And Lee Fitting likes to joke that *College GameDay* was the first television program to employ "social media," because on the third road show way back in 1994, one guy walked behind the set holding up a sign to express an opinion. By 1999, there were hundreds and hundreds of signs from the inconsiderate to the inexplicable. Some dissed the visiting team, others made fun of Fowler and Corso, and some espoused political views or individuality. There was even a proposal of marriage.

In 2010, when the program expanded to three hours, it included a live simulcast on ESPN Radio. The longer format suits the show perfectly, allowing for more in-depth interviews and features. Toward the end of each show, the on-air team also began discussing other games to be played later that day, with each member choosing a winner and bandying back and forth the merits of those picks among themselves. Lee Corso always went last and, if he disagreed with one of the other guys, he'd say, "Not so fast, my friend"—and that became his own popular catchphrase.

Every Saturday, *College GameDay* builds to Corso's pick for the big game, the one that will be played on site. And the ultimate moment in the show occurs when he puts on a mascot's head to indicate which team he has chosen to win. Corso used to just put on a cap with the team's logo, but all that changed on October 6, 1996, when number four Penn State visited number three Ohio State in Columbus. Before the show, Lee told Kirk Herbstreit (who had played quarterback for Ohio State) that he was going to pick the Buckeyes and asked if he could borrow a sign for him to show.

But Kirk had a better idea. He asked his future wife, Allison (former head of the cheerleading squad), if they could borrow the head of Ohio State's mascot. So at the end of the program, Corso made his pick by putting on the head of Brutus the Buckeye. Fans started cheering—and laughing, because Lee looked ridiculous wearing a suit and tie with Brutus on his head. So a tradition was born and, over the years, Corso has worn the USC Trojan helmet, Texas Tech's Raider Red, Kansas State's Willie the Wildcat, the Williams College Purple Cow, and countless tigers, elephants, dogs, bears—you name it. He even once rode a motorcycle with the Oregon Duck. Lee Corso's headgear at the end of every *GameDay* is TV gold. Viewers wonder who he is going to pick and what he is going to do. It is sixty seconds every week where everyone watching will smile—and *that*, as Lee likes to say, is entertainment. It's also pure fun for college football fans.

Chris Fowler, Lee Corso, and Kirk Herbstreit on the set of *College GameDay*, University of Nebraska, 2007.   *Scott Bruhn*

The desire and fervor in college football is as high as it gets in any sport. ESPN tapped into that passion from the very beginning when we picked up videotapes from the airport and broadcast the games on tape delay—and people still watched them, over and over again. The passion of college football fans for their teams is very similar to the passion that people at ESPN have for their company. And that results in passionate people serving other passionate people, which is a formula for success in any business. It has certainly made *College GameDay* not only work but become part of the fabric of college football.

On October 19, 2013, *GameDay* visited the campus of Clemson University for the prime-time matchup between the number three Clemson Tigers against the visiting number five Florida State Seminoles. At the end of the show, actor Bill Murray was invited to participate in the picks segment. But almost every time Murray made a pick, Lee Corso disagreed with him. "Not so fast, Caddyshack!" he quipped. "Not so fast, Ghostbusters!" In all, Corso disagreed with or said "Not so fast" to Murray six times.

After Lee left the set for a few minutes, Bill told Chris Fowler and Kirk Herbstreit that he was picking Clemson to win the big game, which sent thousands of Tigers fans into a cheering frenzy. Corso then returned to the set dressed as Florida State mascot Chief Osceola replete with headdress and spear, indicating, of course, that he was picking the Seminoles. Having none of it, Murray jumped from his chair and, as if in a pro wrestling match, grabbed Corso in the middle of his war dance and body-slammed him to the mat on top of a Clemson Tiger-paw rug. Then, after pounding Corso a couple of times with elbow drops and foot stomps, Murray victoriously grabbed Chief Osceola's spear and sent it sailing into the distance. All to the cheers of the Clemson faithful.

"Don't Ever Give Up"

Coach Jim Valvano had a habit of writing his dreams down on note cards and carrying them around in his coat pocket. An early one found by his wife, Pam, read: "Win the national championship." Jimmy V (as he was affectionately known) burst onto the national scene doing exactly that in the 1983 NCAA Basketball Tournament when his North Carolina State Wolfpack pulled off an electrifying last-second victory over the heavily favored Houston Cougars. Few who watched that game will ever forget the euphoric Valvano running out on the court at the end of the game, looking for someone to hug.

The underdog Wolfpack surprised sports fans everywhere by winning nine do-or-die games in a row on their way to becoming champions. At the end of the regular season, unranked nationally and laden with ten losses, they had to win the Atlantic Coast Conference Tournament just to get an invitation to the Big Dance. The Pack beat Wake Forest by one point, North Carolina (with Michael Jordan) in overtime, and then stunned the Ralph Sampson–led Virginia Cavaliers in the final. On the ESPN broadcasting team for that ACC championship game was Dick Vitale, who prophesized: "Cinderella! Upset City!"

As his team headed into the NCAA Tournament, Valvano's message to his players was, "Survive and advance—one game at a time." Back then, in college ball, there was no shot clock and no three-point line. Anything was possible. In the first round, State came from behind to beat Pepperdine in double overtime, and then came from twelve points down to edge UNLV. After the team made it to the Sweet Sixteen, the national press began referring to Valvano's guys as "The Cardiac Pack: Team of Destiny." In the Elite Eight matchup, NC State again beat Virginia (coming back from seven points down with seven minutes to go) to make it into the Final Four, where they bested Georgia in the national semifinal game.

That put the Wolfpack in the final against the number one seed in the tournament, and the number-one-ranked team in the nation, the Houston Cougars, who were nicknamed Phi Slamma Jamma. With players like Hakeem Olajuwon and Clyde "The Glide" Drexler, Houston was on a twenty-six-game winning streak and heavily favored to beat NC State. The media said that Valvano's kids "didn't have a chance," and that a Houston win was "a cinch." Looking back on it, Duke University Head Basketball Coach Mike Krzyzewski admitted, "I thought Houston would kill them. I didn't think there was any way NC State could win." Even Valvano joked that his own mother picked Houston to win by eight points.

In a pregame press conference, Jimmy V said he was going to slow down the game so that the Cougars couldn't run their fast-paced offense. Then he surprised everybody by having his team come out running, which caught Houston off guard and resulted in a seven-point halftime lead for the Pack. In the second half, Phi Slamma Jamma came roaring back to take the lead. But Valvano's team hung around by intentionally fouling to slow the clock and force the Cougars to shoot free throws, which they missed. On the final play of the game, with four seconds left and the score tied 52–52, senior Dereck Whittenburg (who had been electrifying on the Wolfpack's amazing postseason run) launched a desperate thirty-foot shot that came up short. But teammate Lorenzo Charles jumped over Hakeem Olajuwon and, in one fluid motion, caught the ball and dunked it into the basket as time ran out. NC State won the game 54–52. *Sports Illustrated* called it a miracle. ESPN labeled it college basketball's most memorable moment of the twentieth century. "The definition of unbelievable [was] NC State beating Houston," said Mike Krzyzewski. "*That* was unbelievable."

After the tournament, Jim's ebullient personality made him something of a national celebrity. He appeared frequently on television talk shows and gave countless well-received motivational speeches. In 1989, he retired from coaching and joined ESPN—quickly becoming one of our premier color analysts by entertaining fans with a combination of basketball expertise and humor. Once in a while, Jim was paired with Dick Vitale, and because of their similar passionate styles people started calling them the "Killer V's." Dickie V and Jimmy V grew to be very close friends during that time.

Embraced by ESPN people from the start, Jim became a true member of our team. One day, Robin Roberts was training to be a basketball play-by-play announcer, and Valvano happened to be in the building. John Walsh spotted him and said, "Hey, Jim, would you do a mock game with Robin?" "Yeah, c'mon, Robin," he said. "I'll help you cut your demo tape." The two of them went down to the recording studio, sat down together, and did play-by-play and color analysis of a taped game.

"Jim was a big star back then," remembered Robin. "He didn't have to do that." It was, however, emblematic of Jim Valvano. Just like when he was coaching basketball, nothing was too big or too small to help a member of his team. It was also the essence of ESPN's culture, I believe. We all wanted everybody else to succeed. Jimmy V fit right in.

In the summer of 1992, after experiencing some severe and ongoing pain in his lower back, Jim underwent extensive medical testing. He was finally diagnosed with a rare form of cancer that affected his glands and bones. The doctors told him that the cancer was fast moving and probably too far gone. He would have to undergo a strong regime of chemotherapy immediately and, if it worked, he might have a year to live. If not, only ten months.

Jim always wore his heart on his sleeve, so he shared with his ESPN family what he was up against before leaving to undergo treatment at Memorial Sloan Kettering in New York. A month or so after the initial chemo treatment, determined to go back to work, Jim shaved his head in anticipation of his hair falling out. But it grew right back in, and Jim went right back to Bristol to do two or three shows a week.

Those around him knew he was in a great deal of pain, but he never let the viewers see it. And to everybody, he was always his normal, upbeat, smiling self. Jimmy V believed he was going to beat cancer—and he made everybody around him believe it, too.

In mid-1992, ESPN President Steve Bornstein was contacted by Ray Volpe, who ran an independent production company called Kaleidoscope, and his associate, Edd Griles. The two, who had produced high-profile events such as the Miss Universe pageant, proposed to Bornstein the idea of creating a national sports awards show. Intrigued, Steve asked ESPN CFO Jim Allegro to meet with Griles and Volpe and, if he thought there was something to the proposal, to run with it. Allegro *did* meet with the two entrepreneurs and *did* like the idea, so he went straight to John Walsh to ask his opinion. "Funny thing," said John, "I suggested that very same idea back in 1987 in my thirty-six-page proposal to Bornstein. But it went nowhere, I think, because the time just wasn't right. Maybe now it is."

Steve Bornstein certainly thought so. He was still intent on developing the ESPN brand and, realizing there was a void in the entertainment business for a sports awards show, he became determined not to lose that space to anyone else. So when Allegro recommended going forward with the project, Bornstein readily agreed.

Walsh and Allegro led the effort to create what has come to be known as the ESPY Awards—and what a task it was. They had to decide what awards were going to be given out and how to pick the nominees and the winners. A trophy had to be designed. A thousand questions had to be answered. Where were we going to hold this event, and when, and should it be live or taped? Who would be the host? Who would be the presenters? We had to design, print, and sell tickets. We had to do everything you can imagine that needed to be done to televise a national awards show. After all, it was ours. We owned it.

In the process, the production team developed an idea to create an award for courage and name it after tennis great Arthur Ashe, who had recently announced he had contracted AIDS from a blood transfusion. I don't know if Walsh, Allegro, and Bornstein knew from the very beginning who was going to receive the Arthur Ashe Award for Courage at the first ESPYS, but it certainly was obvious that Jim Valvano was a strong candidate. What *was* clear, however, was that our executive leadership had decided to do something important to help Jim and the other members of the ESPN family touched by cancer.

On one of his trips to Bristol, Jim and his wife, Pam, had breakfast with Steve Bornstein and John Lack, who told them that ESPN wanted to do something to make a difference. "We would like to work with you to start the V Foundation for Cancer Research," said Steve. Both Jim and Pam were deeply moved, in part, I think, because corporations just did not often do things like that. But Bornstein, Lack, and the rest of our executive leadership were serious.

After Jim agreed to the proposal with his typical passion and enthusiasm, ESPN set up an office, allotted a budget, and assigned people to collaborate with him to get the new foundation off the ground. Despite being ill, Jim led the effort himself, drawing on his experience as a basketball coach. Finding a cure for cancer would be the V Foundation's mission. The first formal goal, he determined, would be to invest in young physicians and scientists to help establish their careers. Young people, Jim knew, had more energy and would not be bound by old ways of doing things. It was a young person, he believed, who would have the best chance to come up with a cutting-edge idea that might lead to a cure. A second goal would be to make certain that the vast majority of contributions received would go directly to researchers, rather than to a large staff. And just like he did when coaching at NC State, Valvano personally recruited a team of family and friends to champion the effort. The first chairman of the board was Bob Lloyd, Jim's former co-captain on the 1967 Rutgers basketball team. Other members of the initial board of directors included Dereck Whittenburg (from the 1983 NC State national championship team); Duke coach Mike Krzyzewski; Phil Knight, the CEO of Nike; Harry Rhoads, president of the Washington Speakers Bureau; and ESPN's John Saunders.

Jim and Mike had been opposing coaches in the Atlantic Coast Conference, where basketball rivalries were as tense and competitive as anyplace in sports. But in August 1993, when Jim switched from Sloan Kettering to the Duke University Medical Center to receive his chemo and other medical treatments, Mike went over to visit him nearly every day. Jim sent everybody else out of the room when Mike showed up—and the two talked for hours about basketball, about their families, and about life. Coach V and Coach K built a strong bond during that time. They became good friends.

The night before the first ESPY Awards, Dick Vitale (who was set to present the Arthur Ashe Award for Courage to Jim) attended rehearsal at the Felt Forum in Madison Square Garden. Dick knew that his buddy was not doing very well and that he was probably not going to attend the event. But when he saw the extraordinary video montage that had been put together for Jim, Dick put in a call to the Valvano household. Pam answered the phone. "I'm sorry, Dick, he's just not taking any calls," she said.

"Pam, I've got to talk to him. Please get him on the phone."

Jim took the call, but his voice was very weak. "Dick?" he whispered.

"Jimmy. You have to come to New York tomorrow, man," said Dick. "It's going to be great."

"Dick, I don't care about trophies and awards. I'm not going to see my little girl graduate from high school. I'm not going to walk my daughters down the aisle. Dick, I'm not going to New York."

Dick was now crying. "Jimmy, you've got to come, man. You've just got to."

Vitale's next call was to Mike Krzyzewski who, with his wife, Mickie, leapt into action and convinced Jim and Pam to attend the event. They would all fly to New York together the next morning. They already had the tickets and hotel reservations. Everything was arranged.

On the plane ride up the next day, Jim was weak and *very* sick. "He was throwing up the whole way," recalled Krzyzewski. "I just thought there was no way he could make a speech that night." When they got to the hotel, things seemed to get even worse. "In addition to the nausea and the back pain, Jim was now running a fever," remembered Pam. "So we had some medicine sent up to the room."

On March 4, 1993, the night of the first ESPY Awards, there was a bad storm in New York. Windows were blowing out of skyscrapers, traffic was extra bad, people had trouble arriving, and presenters were late. Dennis Miller was the host, and other celebrities there included Bill Murray, Raquel Welch, Mariel Hemingway, and Dustin Hoffman. About thirty awards were given out that night. Best Male Athlete (Michael Jordan), Best Female Athlete (Monica Seles), Best Coach/Manager (Jimmy Johnson), and College Basketball Play of the Year (Christian Laettner buzzer-beater) were a few of the serious awards. And in true ESPN style, the evening included some fun awards, such as: Outstanding Performance by a Sports Personality in an Attempt to Break into Show Business (Shaquille O'Neal raps with Fu-Schnickens on *The Arsenio Hall Show*) and Most Outrageous Play of the Year (rabbit scores a TD in a Michigan-Purdue game).

I was there with my wife, Ann, enjoying the evening and excited to see ESPN continue to grow with its own awards show celebrating sports. What I did not know at the time, however, was that what happened next would be just about the only thing anybody would ever remember about that night.

Dustin Hoffman was standing backstage about to introduce Dick Vitale when he noticed Dick was a little nervous. "I *was* nervous," recalled Vitale. "I saw Jimmy and Pam and Mike and Mickie sitting in the front row and I was so emotional, I wasn't sure if I could get through the introduction."

"Listen, Dick," said Hoffman. "It'll be okay. Just go out there and speak from your heart." And that's exactly what he did. After the video montage honoring Valvano ran, Dickie V paid no attention to his prewritten script and simply spoke about what Jim Valvano meant to him. Then he walked off the stage and down to the front row. "I wanted to just bring Jim a microphone and let him say thank you after the award was announced," said Dick. "But Jimmy said no."

"Just get me up there on that stage," Jim told Vitale. "I didn't come all the way to New York to just sit here and say thank you."

So Dick helped Jim up to the podium and then stood off to the side. "I thought he would take the trophy from me, say thank you and that he couldn't wait for the V Foundation to start, and then sit down," recalled Vitale. "I don't know where he got the energy to make a full speech."

As Jim began to speak (without any notes or preparation) the pain seemed to leave his body, and the national television audience would never know just how sick he really was. He began by thanking everybody and saying what an honor it was to "be mentioned in the same breath with Arthur Ashe." Then Jim acknowledged that he was, indeed, fighting cancer. "Time is very precious to me," he said. "I don't know how much I have left and I have some things that I would like to say.

"There are three things we all should do every day," Jim said. "Number one is laugh. You should laugh every day. Number two is think. You should spend some time in thought. Number three is, you should have your emotions moved to tears—could be happiness or joy. But think about it. If you laugh, you think, and you cry, that's a full day. That's a heck of a day."

Jim also talked about dreams. "How do you go from where you are to where you want to be? I think you have to have an enthusiasm for life. You have to have a dream, a goal. You have to be willing to work for it. Keep your dreams alive in spite of whatever problems you have."

He mentioned his parents, Rocco and Angelina Valvano, his wife, Pam, and their three daughters, Nicole, Jamie, and LeeAnn. "I urge all of you . . . to enjoy your life, [and] the precious moments you have," he said.

Jim Valvano at the 1993 ESPYS. *ESPN Images*

Then Jim said that he wanted to spend whatever time he had left to "give some hope to others." He announced the formation, "with ESPN's help," of the V Foundation for Cancer Research. "It may not save my life, [but] it may save my children's lives. It may save someone you love." He quoted cancer statistics and asked for help. "Try if you can to support...the foundation, so that someone else might survive, might prosper, and might actually be cured of this dreaded disease." The foundation's motto, he said, would be *"Don't give up, don't ever give up*. That's what I'm going to try to do every minute that I have left. If you see me, smile and give me a hug.

"I gotta go," said Jim, in closing. But he had "one last thing" to say: "Cancer can take away all my physical abilities. It cannot touch my mind, it cannot touch my heart, and it cannot touch my soul. And those three things are going to carry on forever."

As Dickie V and Coach K helped Jimmy V back to his seat, the crowd rose to its feet in a sustained standing ovation. There wasn't a dry eye in the house.

[Jim Valvano passed away less than two months later, on April 28, 1993. His wife, Pam, found one last note card in Jim's coat pocket. It read, simply, "Beat Cancer."]

The Olympics of Extreme Sports

In May 1995, I was named senior vice president of sales and marketing, which put me in charge of ESPN's two primary revenue streams. My responsibilities tripled overnight as I added the marketing and advertising sales departments to my existing responsibility for the affiliate sales department. On my first day in this new position, I learned that two of the three departments were fighting with each other—and they were the two departments in which I didn't have any experience. So my first priority was to find out what the problem was.

It all began when the marketing department created an advertising campaign called "Pig-Out." The idea was that men can't get enough of *Sunday Night Football* on ESPN—that they "pig out" on it. The campaign was very out-of-the-box—different, creative, and provocative. The marketing department had produced print advertising and commercials, and had purchased a thousand pink "Pig-Out!" piggy banks, which were to be sent to advertising customers. There was only one problem, and it was a big one. Our advertising sales staff, which presumably stood to benefit from the campaign, hated it. "It sends the wrong signal," they told me. "A slovenly piggish-like theme is not how we're portraying ESPN and its viewers. We're selling an upscale audience."

"Well, why didn't you make your feelings known before the campaign was rolled out?" I asked.

"Because nobody talked to us about it," came the reply.

Now I knew what the problem was. The "Pig-Out" campaign had been created in a vacuum, in a silo. People in the marketing department had produced a major ad campaign without consulting the people in advertising sales. For me, that was unacceptable. So I called a meeting and brought in one of the piggy banks I had altered with a circle and a slash around the words PIG-OUT! "Guys, I'm new in this job," I said. "But this isn't going to happen again. The next time we create a big marketing campaign, *all* departments will be involved while it is in development, certainly before it is finalized and rolled out."

Silos tend to be a result of corporate growth. People start looking inward instead of doing what is best for the organization as a whole. I was particularly concerned about this situation because communicating shouldn't have been too hard since both departments were located on the same floor in our New York office! I could understand how there might be a communication breakdown between Bristol and New York due to the 110-mile distance in geography, but the departments I now headed up didn't have that excuse. The fact that they were all on the same floor and not talking to each other made it even worse. But how was I going to break this tendency of human nature to huddle together in separate silos?

First, I appreciated that I was dealing with people—and that involves leadership. Each department was loaded with talented individuals who did not want to recognize that there were equally talented individuals in the other department right across the hall. I felt that if they just got to know each other, things would be a lot better. So rather than issuing an order for people to talk to each other, I needed a project that *required* them to work across department lines.

It turned out that the process to create what would eventually come to be known as the X Games would bring everybody together in a common endeavor—not only sales and marketing in New York, but also with production and programming in Bristol. Actually, virtually every department in the company would become involved in the project.

It all began innocently enough, with an idea from an ESPN employee who described himself at the time as "a front-line soldier." Ron Semiao joined ESPN in 1985 as an accountant. By 1989, he was the unit operations producer at the World Series who had brought in a diesel generator, which allowed ESPN to broadcast after the Loma Prieta earthquake hit. In 1993, Ron transferred to the programming department to help launch ESPN2, and he immediately began exploring what was referred to back then as "alternative" or "extreme" sports in order to appeal to younger, hipper sports fans.

To educate himself on the subject, Ron visited a local bookstore and was amazed to find individual magazines on just about every one of these sports. There were skateboard magazines, BMX magazines, snowboard magazines, surf magazines, and on and on and on. But there was no one magazine that covered all the sports together. So Semiao bought a huge stack of publications and spent an afternoon on his couch at home going through them.

At the end of the day, Ron had made three important conclusions. First, to contemporary youth, the pro athletes in extreme sports were revered and respected. To them, skateboarder Tony Hawk was just as awesome as Michael Jordan. Second, each sport was more than just an activity. They were *lifestyles* reflecting how young fans expressed themselves as individuals. And third, mainstream print advertisers were actively trying to associate their products with all the sports, because young people thought they were cool.

Ron likened the current state of extreme sports to the rock-and-roll movement of the 1950s and 1960s. Parents said it wasn't real music, but the kids sustained it to the point where it became an accepted part of the overall music culture. The same thing could happen with extreme sports, Ron realized. The kids were already sustaining them, and they just might become an accepted part of the larger sports culture. So why not have ESPN showcase all the sports in one major televised event? We could not only hold competitions, he thought, we could also feature the unique lifestyles of the athletes.

Ron Semiao had a new idea, but it was much broader than his job description of placing programs on ESPN2. He also knew that part of ESPN's culture was to listen to anybody who had a good idea. So Ron ran his concept by his longtime friend and colleague John Wildhack, who was then a manager in the remote production department. Wildhack's enthusiasm gave Ron the confidence to go to his own bosses, who also encouraged him to take it farther up the line. Semiao's next meeting was with David Zucker, senior vice president in charge of programming. In preparation, Ron reduced his pitch to one simple, easily understood sentence: "I want to create the Olympics of extreme sports," he told Zucker.

After some discussion, Zucker asked him to put his vision down on paper in the form of a memo, which he would send to Steve Bornstein. "Let's move on this before some other company thinks of it and beats us to the punch," said David. And the next thing Ron Semiao knew, his idea for a showcase of extreme sports was being seriously considered by ESPN's top executives in New York—and, as head of sales and marketing, that included me.

Should ESPN put on the Extreme Games (as it was called that first year)? If so, should we farm it out to a third party or stage and produce it ourselves? There turned out to be quite a bit of recalcitrance among the executive group, in part because we were looking at a $12 million price tag to stage the event ourselves. But when Bornstein went around the room, I voted yes. "Our salespeople are all over this," I said. "It's exciting and we can make it happen." Ultimately, Bornstein, who loved the concept, broke the logjam and declared that not only were we going to move forward, but ESPN was going to own, stage, and produce the Extreme Games ourselves.

That decision created both opportunity and risk. Clearly, we were looking at an opportunity to drive additional revenue streams by building a new proprietary asset—and that was *very exciting*. The risk, however, was that ESPN had never before tried anything of this magnitude. It not only required an entirely new business model, but a new department to stage the event, and additional expertise about the individual sports themselves.

Ron Semiao, who became the de facto leader of the project, put in a cold call to Jack Wienert, who had previously been involved in staging Olympic-style events. Jack was a former football player for the University of Missouri and jumped at the opportunity to work with ESPN. After flying Wienert in from St. Louis for a lengthy interview, we hired him to staff and head up our new Event Production Group. Wienert was now in charge of everything that had to do with staging the Extreme Games—building the bleachers, setting up the athletic courses, printing the tickets, you name it.

Because ESPN owned every aspect of the event, we were responsible for creating the sporting competitions, the rules for those competitions, and the manner in which they were going to be judged and scored. In our minds, we had to include the athletes in those decisions, because they knew more about their sports than we did. So we asked them to help us design the games. Although that notion sounded like common sense, it was anything but easy. Skateboarders, snowboarders, street lugers, and all the other athletes, by their very nature, walk to the beat of a different drum than the average professional athlete. As such, we had to persuade them to work with us. Some thought they were selling out to the establishment. But we finally were able to convince most that we were not asking them to sell out, we were asking them to buy in. Two of the better-known athletes who got involved in the early planning were pioneering skateboarder Tony Hawk ("The

Birdman") and professional BMX rider Mat Hoffman ("The Condor").
To their credit, as with all the athletes, they insisted that their sports
be covered professionally, with credibility, and not as circus acts.

Our role in sales and marketing was to present and sell this event
to consumers. Marketing had to position the Extreme Games properly
so that our sales guys could be successful selling advertising. At first,
though, we could not decide whether to treat the Extreme Games as
a competition or as a festival. The athletes, themselves, were more
on the festival side. They were not the jocks in high school, but they
all had a sport they passionately loved. And they were not really into
competition. If there were ten guys competing in a skateboarding
contest, the other nine were as happy for the winner as if they had
won themselves. The genuine jubilation to see their friends do well
was unique in sports and, I might add, very refreshing. So we went
with a "festival" for the first games.

We presented the participants as real athletes, not stuntmen or
daredevils, but artists with unique lifestyles. We educated the viewers
about the various sports, showed them that there was a lot of action,
and tried to entice people to tune in, because these sports were different. Clearly, ESPN was branching out beyond the core sports fan
and, to do that effectively, we had to use more than the traditional
medium of television. So in addition to running advertisements and
promotional spots on ESPN, we used ESPN Radio, ESPNet.SportsZone
.com, and print advertisements in individual extreme sports magazines.
ESPN also went off channel, purchasing time on other networks, such
as MTV, CNN, and various syndicated radio stations.

Our promotional advertisements not only had to be good, they had
to be agreeable to the sales department. After all, selling television
advertising time for extreme sports was nothing like selling it for, say,
an NFL or MLB game, where we could more easily sign up major
sponsors. Rather, we now had to attract companies that wanted to
put a skateboarder on their soda cans, or a logo on clothing or other

merchandise. We also had to sell sponsorships and signage beyond what aired on television. But no one in our sales department ever had to worry about where to hang a sponsor's sign at a skateboarding event. This time we had to approach potential sponsors by telling them, for instance, that they could place a certain-size sign at a certain location on the half-pipe so that the cameras would pick it up during the event. Details like that required an entirely new capability for the sales department, so they were forced to work closely with production, programming, and event planning. There was just no other way to accomplish our goals.

Preparation for the Extreme Games, therefore, became a catalyst for true teamwork at ESPN. Of course, our collaborative efforts were not always smooth sailing. But when disputes arose, Ron Semiao was always there to smooth things over and help build consensus. With time, people across various in-house disciplines began to develop more respect for each other—and that led to a stronger internal culture for all of ESPN.

In June and July 1995, the inaugural Extreme Games were held in Providence and Newport, Rhode Island. More than two hundred thousand fans attended the games, which included such sports as skateboarding, street luge racing, in-line skating, mountain biking, and sky surfing. ESPN and ESPN2 provided more than sixty hours of television coverage. To make the games more exciting, our producers placed miniature cameras on the helmets of athletes, on the walls of ramps, and along the racecourses. Wireless cameras were also put on skydivers, on street luges, and on helicopters that hovered over the events.

I attended the first Extreme Games and I was exhilarated by the enthusiasm and adrenaline-fueled atmosphere. Every participating athlete received a trophy. There was a big party on the beach and, true to form, the ESPN people who had worked so long and hard to put on the event had our own party and stayed out all night.

The next year (1996), we changed the name of the event to the "X Games," added more sports, more athletes, and started awarding prize money along with gold, silver, and bronze medals. In January and February 1997, we held the first Winter X Games in Big Bear Lake, California, which included such events as snowboarding, ice climbing, shovel racing, and snow mountain bike racing.

Over the ensuing years, the X Games continually improved as Ron Semiao and Jack Wienert and their team experimented with new venues, new angles, and new ideas. For instance, they added athlete lounges (with music and couches) so the participants could get away and relax. As ratings and popularity of the X Games increased, we were able to sell all of our advertising time each year. Some of our large sponsors included Mountain Dew, Taco Bell, Chevrolet, Nike, and Miller Lite.

But there were countless smaller companies that manufactured products for young people who could not afford airtime. Their products included energy drinks, video games, sports equipment, apparel, and such varied items as backpacks, gloves, and bindings. So Ron and Jack put all these companies in one large tent and allowed fans to walk around, much like the sponsor exhibitions you would see at any large convention. One year, as Ron was showing me around, we walked into the big exhibition tent, which was decorated in a Casablanca-like theme. "Ron, what's this?" I asked. "It looks like a hashish den! When do the hookahs come out?"

Semiao also tried to keep the young people happy by bringing in cutting-edge music bands, which I was not up to speed on. One year, he kiddingly sent me an email requesting suggestions. So I asked my teenage daughter, Kate, for her opinion. "Why don't you email Ron and suggest to him that he bring in Hoobastank?" she said.

"Who or what is Hoobastank?" I asked.

"C'mon, Dad. Hoobastank is great! They're only the best!"

So I photographed a Hoobastank poster and emailed it to Semiao. "Hey, Ron, what do you think about having Hoobastank perform at the next X Games?"

Ron's jaw dropped. "How do you know about Hoobastank?" he emailed back. "I thought you'd ask for the Eagles or the Rolling Stones!"

As the years passed, the X Games grew into an international brand—and everybody succeeded. Many of the sports (such as skateboarding and BMX) formed their own federations. Countless athletes became famous—such as Olympic snowboarding gold medalist Shaun White, who had grown up on ESPN, winning his first X Games medal in 2002. Even the International Olympic Committee (IOC) did a complete about-face in its perception of these sports. (Shortly after the first games debuted, one IOC member had referred to the Extreme Games as a "fad" that would not last.)

Soon, the IOC began a push to make the Olympics more relevant to a younger audience. In the 1994 Winter Olympic Games in Lillehammer, there were no "X Games" events held. By 1998, two snowboarding events were added as medal sports. By the time the 2014

Bucky Lasek skates in the skateboard vertical finals at Summer X Games 17 in 2011. *ESPN Images*

Winter Olympics in Sochi rolled around, there were twelve snowboarding and "X-Games-like" skiing events. As a matter of fact, the very first televised event on NBC that year was snowboarding slopestyle.

ESPN certainly profited from the tremendous success of the X Games. But our company also succeeded far beyond the financial rewards. ESPN's culture made it possible for a young man named Ron Semiao to bring his idea forward, have it quickly approved by upper management, and eventually become a worldwide success. That simple fact continued to inspire ESPN people every day to come up with their own new ideas, which kept our company on the leading edge of innovation. Moreover, in owning the event and putting it on ourselves, we enhanced and propelled the ESPN tradition of respectful collaboration and working together in teams. And from a business leadership perspective, *that* is the real message of the X Games.

In the middle of ESPN's preparation for the Extreme Games, I hired Judy Fearing to succeed Harriet Seitler as senior vice president of marketing. With twelve years at PepsiCo and an MBA from Dartmouth, she was a fantastic addition for us.

On Judy's first day, I asked her to come to my office, where I handed her a Rand McNally road map of New York and Connecticut.

"What's this?" she asked.

"It's a map," I replied. "Even though the marketing department is located here in New York, we have a lot of great production and programming people in Bristol. I want you to learn your way up there and show them the marketing department is their partner."

Merging with Mickey

s the new head of marketing, Judy Fearing quickly set up two meetings to bridge the gap between Bristol and New York. First, she drove up to Bristol and sat down with John Walsh, John Wildhack, and a host of other people. "Tell me what is wrong with marketing," she said to them. "Marketing does things in a silo," they responded. "You never ask for our input. We just see ads show up on the air, and most of them do not reflect what we are really all about." Judy made a list of all their comments and promised to take action. The second meeting she had was with our advertising agency, Wieden+Kennedy, to review all ESPN promotions (some of which Judy thought were pretty good) and discuss their interaction with production and programming in Bristol. She also asked them to present their view of the ESPN brand and how it influenced advertising campaigns.

The first important thing Judy heard from Wieden+Kennedy was that ESPN commercials "didn't generally require cooperation with production and programming, because they were not filmed in Bristol." Judy resolved to change that practice immediately. Shortly thereafter the agency presented a brilliant and creative document regarding its perception of our company's brand. "ESPN isn't a large network," it began. "It is, first and foremost, a *huge sports fan*—the type of fan who picks up the paper every morning and goes right to the sports section to read about the big game and study the standings. As a passionate sports fan, ESPN is knowledgeable, outspoken, and has strong opinions."

Judy Fearing loved the analogy of thinking of ourselves as a huge sports fan (rather than a big company) and immediately wanted to imbue it throughout the company. When she briefed me on the topic, I thought back to ESPN's first broadcast when George Grande articulated our mission to serve sports fans. To morph that into ESPN becoming a sports fan itself made perfect sense to me. So I encouraged Judy to run with it. Before long, the marketing department had come up with a few powerful statements so everybody could apply the idea to their everyday jobs, whether it was producing a show, programming the network, hiring talent, or selling ad space. One of those statements stated simply: "ESPN is a sports fan." Another read: "ESPN takes its sports seriously, but we don't take ourselves too seriously." Pretty soon, from their own perspectives as sports fans, our people were thinking about what *other* sports fans might want to see and hear.

It was at this point that Judy introduced the common marketing term *social currency* to ESPN. Like the weather, people talk about sports to facilitate social interaction. If they walk into a coffee shop in Chicago, for instance, and don't know anyone, they can always say, "Hey, did the Cubs win last night?" or "Hey, how are the Bears going to do this season?" Since nine out of ten Americans identify themselves as sports fans, there is an excellent chance of getting a reaction. Essentially, that's what social currency is—information shared that encourages further personal interaction. Sports is something that brings people together, because just about everybody likes to talk about it. Therefore, Judy Fearing reasoned that if we viewed ESPN as a sports fan, our *voice*—what we said on the air—could be used as social currency.

Although it was a term that most professional marketers were familiar with, I never heard anybody at ESPN use *social currency* before Judy arrived on the scene. And she introduced it in a most interesting, and very effective way. She simply started talking about it around the watercooler or in casual conversations over morning coffee. It was like planting a seed and allowing it to germinate. Pretty soon, it was commonplace in the company to be talking sports as social currency. Then they wanted to learn more from marketing about how to use it and make it work.

I recall Judy being invited to speak to the sales department about how to position ESPN to potential advertisers. "In the morning, our viewers tune in to see what has happened in the world of sports so they can be up to date when they meet with their friends, their clients, or their customers," she told them. "That is why you, Mr. Advertiser, want to promote your products on ESPN. Through our highlights, insights, and professional analyses, we attract these powerful, hard-to-reach sports fans. We provide them with the social currency they need to make connections and build relationships. That's why they tune in to ESPN. For them, it's a must."

Envisioning ourselves as a sports fan and using our voice as social currency were big steps in the development of ESPN's brand. In addition, out of those casual conversations about social currency flowed a new and powerful marketing statement: "ESPN should be part of the sports conversation wherever sports are watched, read, or discussed."

When our people read that simple sentence, the reaction was predictable. "Well, of course, we should!" everybody said. "That's a no-brainer." And where were those places that sports are watched, read, or discussed? Television, radio, print, the Internet—and any other new and innovative technologies that might pop up in the future. That new statement became a motivator and catalyst for us. Wherever the ESPN brand *could* travel, it *should* travel—and we were going to make that happen.

Out of all these discussions about branding, and out of the new interactions between New York and Bristol, came an idea that when executed, would elevate the ESPN brand to unprecedented heights. ESPN marketing and Wieden+Kennedy jointly agreed that more could and should be done to promote our flagship property, *SportsCenter*. So we decided to launch a new advertising campaign. But rather than begin the process in a silo, Judy sent a team up to Bristol to involve production and programming right from the start. The group, which included Judy's top lieutenant, Alan Broce, and our account staff from Wieden+Kennedy, spent a week obtaining a behind-the-scenes feel for *SportsCenter*. They went to production meetings, learned how stories were researched, watched the talent write their own scripts, select their wardrobes, put on their makeup—and then viewed the program live from the control room.

Brainstorming back in New York, the team played off a statement that Lee Leonard had made in the very first ESPN broadcast. "Hi. I'm Lee Leonard welcoming you to Bristol, Connecticut," Lee had said. "Why Bristol? Because here in Bristol is where all of the sports action is happening as of right now." The team then reasoned that if Bristol was the center of the sports world, wouldn't the world's greatest athletes be hanging out there, walking the halls and mixing it up with the talent? So why not do a series of humorous commercials with popular athletes right there in the Bristol facility? And then, picking up on the catchphrase used by Patrick and Olbermann, they decided to call it the "This is *SportsCenter*" campaign.

The first step in the production process was to drive back to headquarters and get the Bristol folks on board. So the marketing staff met with John Walsh and his *SportsCenter* team to explain the concept. We want to make celebrities out of the on-air talent. Is that okay? We want to have some of them poke fun at themselves and others be straight men. Is that okay? Do they want to get involved in helping shape the campaign? Do they have ideas on situations we could portray in the commercials? Despite some initial hesitation, the answer to all these questions was yes.

Our next step was to find top-tier athletes who would be willing to play ball with us in this new campaign. Initially, we didn't think that would be easy, because during their playing seasons, they didn't have a lot of time off and, besides, Bristol was a bit out of the way. But when we put out a major casting call to see who might be in the New York area and willing to participate, to our surprise we had a lot of takers. So we set dates when we could get a critical mass of people to Bristol to shoot the promos.

In one of the early commercials, we set up the ESPN entrance to look like a hotel lobby lounge with a bar and a piano player where people could come up and put tips in a glass on top of the piano. With Grant Hill dressed in his Detroit Pistons uniform and playing the piano, Dan Patrick walks in with his coat over his shoulder, looking kind of down. Grant stops him and says, "Hey, Dan, what's wrong?"

"Hi, Grant," replies Patrick. "Ah, bad show. Hair looked bad. Teleprompter went down. Made some mistakes on some highlights."

"I've got something to cheer you up," says Grant, who starts playing an upbeat tune. Patrick then smiles, shakes his head, and puts some money in the tip glass.

"Thanks. Thanks, Grant, I appreciate that."

"No problem, man," says Hill, who continues to play as Patrick pats on the piano to the rhythm of the music.

With time, commercials such as these became extraordinarily popular with our viewers. We had very little problem persuading athletes from virtually every sport to sign up. Just a few who participated have included: Peyton Manning and Ben Roethlisberger (football), Roger Clemens and David Ortiz (baseball), LeBron James and Candace Parker (basketball), Apolo Anton Ohno (speed skating), Shaun White (snowboarding), Alexander Ovechkin (hockey), Mary Lou Retton (gymnastics), Tiger Woods (golf), and Danica Patrick (racing).

External to ESPN, the "This is *SportsCenter*" advertising campaign became one of the most successful in television history. It was still on the air more than twenty years after it started. Internal to ESPN, the campaign also had a significant impact on how we conducted ourselves. For example, it further narrowed the schism between Bristol and New York by putting in place a new collaborative process. If an idea originated from marketing, we got buy-in and involvement from production and programming, and then we formed a diverse team to produce the product. The people in Bristol no longer thought ill of the marketing department in New York. "You guys don't work in silos anymore," they said. "You're okay." And everybody seemed to realize that working *together* made the results exponentially better. The whole process reminded me of a winning sports team where the final output is greater than the sum of its individual parts. That not only works in sports, it works in business, as well.

"This is *SportsCenter*" changed everything for ESPN. It helped us create an emotional bond with sports fans by showing that ESPN had a sense of humor all day long and that they were going to smile and

"This Is *SportsCenter*" commercial featuring ESPN's Charley Steiner, 1996. *ESPN Images*

laugh when they tuned in. The success of the advertising campaign also put considerable wind in the sails of the marketing department and inspired us to do even more with our brand. So we continued to tell our advertising customers how much social currency they had to run with in attracting sports fans and how powerful the ESPN brand really was. But then it occurred to me that it was about time we obtained some real data to back up those statements. That's when ESPN's head of research, Artie Bulgrin, conducted an extensive survey as to the strength of our brand.

The results surprised even the most optimistic ESPN people. "Our brand is not only the most powerful sports brand," said Artie, "it is the most powerful brand in television, period!"

On July 31, 1995, The Walt Disney Company announced it was acquiring CapCities/ABC for $19.5 billion (at the time, the second largest takeover in U.S. history). When that purchase was finalized in early 1996, Disney owned 80 percent of ESPN. *[The Hearst Corporation had purchased 20 percent of ESPN in 1990 for about $170 million.]* At first, people in our company were nervous about what this was going to mean for us. After all, Disney was a huge global corporation with more than 160,000 employees, compared with only 5,000 for ESPN. It also had multiple business segments, including, of course, the Disney World and Disneyland theme parks, a Hollywood film studio, consumer products, and the Disney Channel. Was Disney going to swallow us up? Were they going to roll us into ABC? Were we going to be relocated to Orlando? Was everybody going to be out of a job? Unfounded or not, all these questions swirled around the company. However, from an organizational standpoint, Disney CEO Michael Eisner announced in April 1996 that ESPN and ABC would remain as separate businesses, both reporting to Steve Bornstein.

From the very beginning, Eisner gave ESPN credit for what we had built. They kept us in Bristol, allowed us to maintain our unique culture, and set about building a solid relationship based on mutual respect and trust. Even though we experienced some bumps in the road during the transition, at the end of the day we all created a model template for how to make a major business acquisition work.

As head of sales and marketing, I could see clearly that Disney had done their due diligence when it came to ESPN. Michael Eisner, in his announcement of the acquisition, had compared us to Coca-Cola as "a magic name" in brands. He subsequently stated that we were also building it the right way. This was tremendous validation coming from The Walt Disney Company, one of the world's premier marketing organizations. We had all grown up watching *The Wonderful World of Disney*, and they were one of the most popular and best-known global brands. So most of us in marketing were pleased when, like a sage mentor, Disney began encouraging ESPN to nurture and enhance our brand. In a much more formal way than I ever recall it being discussed, they took the art and science of brand management to a new level.

Part of nurturing a brand, they said, is to expand it. So Disney executives (particularly Bob Iger) challenged us to make the ESPN brand even bigger, stronger, and more powerful. They admired the fact that we had been one of the first television networks to put our products on the Internet, first with ESPNet.SportsZone.com and then with our 1998 launch of ESPN.com. "Clearly, you're ahead of the competition," they said, "but you can do even more with your online presence." And that we did by ramping up our commitment with key personnel, including people like John Kosner, who was eventually made head of ESPN.com programming and development (in 1999) and then leader of all ESPN Digital Media (in 2003). *[Under Kosner's leadership, ESPN.com became a driver of ESPN's growth around the world, particularly as we transitioned from online to mobile. As of 2015, ESPN Digital Media owned a 35 percent share of the sports category in the United States (more than three times that of the nearest competitor).]*

Disney further encouraged us to take advantage of the strength of the ESPN brand and move into new businesses. "More products, more merchandise, and more distribution channels would allow ESPN to carry more weight," they said. So we, along with Disney's new ventures group, began searching for businesses in which to expand. We passed on a lot of opportunities, but did move forward with ESPN Stores to sell merchandise and ESPN Zone restaurants, which were high-end sports bars dedicated to giving fans a place to go to eat, drink, and enjoy games on large-screen televisions. Because ESPN had no previous experience in these markets, Disney's staff provided some of their vast resources to get us started and mitigate the risk. They supplied us with expertise, funds, and creative people to come up with the best possible products.

Overall, the acquisition of ESPN by The Walt Disney Company resulted in immediate benefits for our marketing and sales department. Disney executives gave us even more confidence in the power of our brand and where it could go. They emboldened us to push the boundaries. "Don't be satisfied with what you have today," they said. "As good as it is now, it can be even better tomorrow."

In 1996, we unexpectedly lost two valued and beloved members of our ESPN family. Tom Mees, one of our original *SportsCenter* anchors, died in a tragic drowning accident near his home. In the early days, Tom teamed with Chris Berman five or six nights a week for the late *SportsCenter*. He was a pioneer in the new world of sports television, delivering highlights and commentary with a combination of professional insight and sheer joy. As a longtime hockey fan, I really enjoyed listening to Tom do play-by-play. He shaped ESPN's coverage of the NHL and college hockey in those early days. Tom was only forty-six years old. He left behind his wife, Michele, and two daughters, Lauren and Gabrielle.

We also lost Scotty Connal, who passed away suddenly from a heart attack while attending the Summer Olympics in Atlanta, Georgia. Along with Chet Simmons, Scotty was the early heart and soul of ESPN. He hired many of the talent who set our company on the path to success. He gave unproven young people like me an opportunity to show what we could do. He set the tone for how ESPN would operate as a company, creating a culture of optimism, integrity, passion, and family. I think Scotty's son Bruce said it best when he simply stated: "Dad was a people person, and it didn't matter if you were a security guard or a high-level executive." Scotty Connal left behind his wife, Til, eight children, and eleven grandchildren. He was sixty-eight years old.

"Tell Me How You Did That, Again"

Right after the Disney acquisition, our competitive juices were flowing and we were driving hard on brand extensions. So when a sudden burst of competition appeared, we acted quickly. Fox Sports, which had formed in 1994 after acquiring broadcast rights for the NFL, had launched a new show called *Fox National Sports Report* airing twice nightly (at 6 and 10 p.m.). It was their answer to *SportsCenter*. Then, in February 1996, Time Warner announced that CNN and *Sports Illustrated* were joining forces to create CNNSI, a new cable channel that would offer sports news twenty-four hours a day. It was to debut in mid-December of that same year.

It didn't take long for ESPN's management team to get together to discuss this latest development. "We're not going to sit around while somebody else launches something like that," we collectively said. "If the viewers want twenty-four-hour sports news, we need to provide it." Everybody in the room agreed with that statement, so we determined to create our own sports news channel and have it up and running *before* CNNSI even went on the air. Part of the need for speed was a direct result of Disney's influence. Michael Eisner was constantly pushing ESPN to expand our brand, and Bob Iger, soon to be president of Disney, constantly encouraged us to "pack light and travel fast."

We made a public announcement right away that ESPN would be launching a new all-sports-news network. Then we got to work on creating one. Rather than air everything live, we decided to have a half-hour news wheel that repeated until we produced a new show. Our focus would be to air sports news, highlights, press conferences, and, if necessary, overflow events from our other two networks. After six months of Herculean efforts by every department in the company (just as we had done with ESPN2 and the X Games), ESPNews launched on November 1, 1996, with Mike Tirico as its first anchor.

CNNSI launched six weeks later on December 12, 1996. Almost immediately, rumors circulated through the industry that CNN and *Sports Illustrated*, two large divisions of a big corporation, had gotten off to a rocky start. But while CNNSI struggled, ESPNews got off to a roaring start, benefiting from both solid teamwork and our established business relationships with cable operators and recently created satellite companies. *[In 2002, Fox discontinued its* National Sports Report *and CNNSI shut its doors. Word in the business also had it that CNNSI threw in the towel, in part, because people from the two companies couldn't work together. However, ESPNews stayed on the air and thrived.]*

In 1997, also due, in part, to the urging of Disney, ESPN decided to expand our brand into the area of print journalism. Four years earlier, Disney had started a joint venture with Hearst to produce its own magazine called *Total Sports*, but it had not fared well. The idea to start over with an ESPN magazine was the brainchild of John Skipper, senior vice president of Disney Publishing. Skipper turned out to be the perfect fit to bridge Disney's world with ESPN's culture. Previously an executive for *US* magazine and *Rolling Stone*, John was not only an exceptionally creative individual, but a passionate sports fan to boot. Not surprisingly, he struck up a partnership with John

Walsh (who had also worked at *Rolling Stone*) to develop a vision for the new magazine.

ESPN let Skipper and Walsh operate in a relatively independent manner from everybody by providing the magazine staff with separate office space in New York. They quickly formed a new team, which included Gary Hoenig, Dick Glover, and John Papanek (who had been managing editor at *Sports Illustrated*). Looking to do something different, the group decided to go for a younger demographic than *Sports Illustrated* by featuring emerging athletes, humorous stories, lots of photos, sports culture, and fashion. In addition, *ESPN The Magazine* would be larger physically—and published every other week.

ESPN The Magazine debuted in March 1998 with a cover featuring the headline NEXT and stunning photographs of Kobe Bryant, Eric

The debut issue of *ESPN The Magazine* establishing the NEXT franchise, March 1998.   ESPN The Magazine

Lindros, Kordell Stewart, and Alex Rodriguez. That first issue shouted to readers right off the bat that this was not going to be your father's sports magazine. It was going to be different, and would be looking ahead, not back. It would feature up-and-coming athletes under the title "NEXT." Over the years, ESPN's new publication became famous for its lighthearted covers and the "BODY" issue, an ode to athletic bodies. *ESPN The Magazine* was successful from its inception. Eventually, it moved offices to Bristol and earned its spot as a thriving member of the company's content machine.

Back in 1987 while I was in Denver, ESPN had won the rights to first broadcast *Sunday Night Football*. At the time, we came up with the innovative idea of implementing a surcharge to cover our costs. That deal with the NFL took ESPN to another level, and we were fortunate to have renewed it several times through 1997.

After the Disney acquisition in 1996, I began looking ahead to upcoming negotiations with the NFL, which would occur in early 1998. On the table at that time would not only be ESPN's contract for *Sunday Night Football*, but also ABC's deal for *Monday Night Football*. The financial power of The Walt Disney Company, I believed, might provide ESPN with added strength to outbid Turner Broadcasting for the entire season package *and* retain *Monday Night Football* for ABC, as well. *[In 1994, Turner had joined the NFL party by acquiring the other half of* Sunday Night Football.*]*

In other words, a great opportunity was going to present itself in a couple of years, and I knew we were going to have to come up with something new and creative to take advantage of it. So as I always did when sizing up a big opportunity, I assembled the affiliate sales team to talk about it.

Our first conversation centered on one question: How can we leverage this situation so that if we can get a full season of *Sunday Night*

Football, it would catapult ESPN to a new level? Almost immediately, we began talking about creating a new era of affiliate agreements. Somebody suggested that we eliminate the surcharge of the 1987-era contracts and replace it with an option to increase our rate *if* we were able to obtain a full season. In essence, we would be betting on the come.

Then the question became: Well, how much should the option to increase be? Because there was no precedent for us to use, we decided to be aggressive. "Let's say we have the right to raise our rate up to 20 percent per year," we said. "That would be nice."

We started negotiating these new affiliate contracts in 1996 and 1997. The business environment was pretty good during those years. Cable television was still growing fast and operators were signing up new homes every month. Sports and movies were driving their sales, and the fact is that most people didn't want to have cable without ESPN. So we never stopped talking about the network's value. Our major pitch to get the operators to sign up involved a combination of eliminating the NFL surcharge and painting a vision of improving our product with a full season of *Sunday Night Football*. Additionally, the potential increase was an option *if* and *only if* ESPN was able to obtain the full season. Depending on our needs for revenue to pay for NFL rights, we would have the right to adjust our fee by up to 20 percent each year for the length of the contract.

Nobody really knew what was going to happen. But a lot of the cable operators didn't think we had a prayer of getting Turner Broadcasting's half of *Sunday Night Football*. Ted Turner was a major power player and an insider in the cable industry. It was also well known that over the previous decade, he had outbid ESPN for broadcast rights to such things as the NBA and major college football. "They'll never get Turner out of the NFL," was the prevailing sentiment. "ESPN's not going to get a full season, so what's the harm in signing this contract?"

But one of our strengths was that we had established solid personal relationships with most of the cable operators, some going back to 1979. They liked our team, believed in us, and had respect for us, in part because we always did what we said we were going to do—that is, produce a product coveted by their subscribers.

Based upon those long-term relationships, we ultimately were able to sign everybody up before negotiations with the NFL even began. And those contracts turned out to be a source of tremendous strength in the discussions.

During those talks, several key factors impacted the eventual outcome. First, ABC was concerned about the financial performance of *Monday Night Football*. But the network still wanted their flagship show and, as it turned out, so did Disney CEO Michael Eisner. Second, NFL Commissioner Paul Tagliabue (who had succeeded Pete Rozelle in 1989) was driving a hard bargain for the league's Monday and Sunday night packages. In the end, if ABC wanted to keep *Monday Night Football* and get a full season of *Sunday Night Football*, it was going to cost The Walt Disney Company a whopping $8.8 billion.

Because there was no consensus among the company's top executives, Eisner called me. "George, what do you think?" he asked.

"Well, renewing *Monday Night Football* is important to ABC, and getting a full season of *Sunday Night Football* for ESPN would be a game changer," I replied. "What ESPN gets from the cable operators on this deal will be significant enough for Disney overall."

"Are you sure?" he asked. "I mean, how much are you talking about?"

"We can increase rates a maximum of 20 percent every year for the next seven years."

"Impossible!" said Eisner. "Nobody will pay that."

"Michael, it's already in the contracts," I said.

After a long pause, Eisner said, "Okay, George. Thanks." And then he hung up.

The next thing I heard was that Disney had secured the deal.

ABC would continue its twenty-eight-year run with *Monday Night Football*, and ESPN received an eight-year (1998–2005) contract to televise a full season of *Sunday Night Football*. Most cable operators were surprised by the news and they certainly expected us to raise our rates the full 20 percent that first year, which we did. Each year, we looked at our product, our business environment, and what the market would bear. After a few years of adjusting our rate the full amount, the cable operators started to protest: "We don't like the price," they said. "Your increases are too high."

In response, we took time to manage the situation very carefully. Each year, before the increase, a detailed letter was sent to our affiliates laying out what we had done the previous year to improve ESPN. We stressed our value, the product we were providing, and how great business was in the cable industry. But before the letters went out, I made personal telephone calls to the top twenty cable and satellite CEOs to inform them of the upcoming increase. I stressed that ESPN provided a terrific product and that we were worth the new price. "Now, I know this is not something you want to hear, but it's going up for everybody," I'd say. "This is the price of poker."

I really didn't relish making those phone calls and, certainly, our affiliates didn't like the 20 percent increases. But they appreciated the fact that I took the time to call them rather than just let the word reach them in a cold and formal letter. More than once, a CEO responded to me with something like, "George, we hate the price, but we like you."

Part of business leadership is maintaining the personal relationships you've built with your customers, and that's really what I was doing. If you make it a habit to deliver the tough news as well as the good news, and if you do so honestly, straightforwardly, and with respect, more often than not you'll maintain your relationships and keep your customers.

For each of the next six years of ESPN's new NFL contract, we raised our rates the maximum 20 percent. During that time, the fee to cable and satellite operators to carry ESPN went from about eighty cents to roughly $3. That overall increase separated ESPN from the rest of the cable industry. It added billions of dollars of asset value to The Walt Disney Company. The revenue realized during those years changed the course of Disney, ESPN, and, really, the entire cable industry—and that is not an overstatement.

For years afterward, whenever Michael Eisner and I got together, he would ask, "Tell me how you did that, again, George?" And five years after he left Disney, Michael sent me a memorable email recalling the 1998 NFL deal. "George, it happened because of one phone call. You told me you could build ESPN off this deal with what you could get from the cable operators. I went forward only because of that conversation. That is why the deal was made. We built (you built) billions of dollars in value for Disney. Those are the facts. Keep this email to read to your great grandchildren."

In the fall of 1998, a copy of an internal memo mysteriously showed up on my desk. It was from Steve Bornstein to Michael Eisner and contained only two sentences: "I want to make George Bodenheimer president of the company. I'll talk to you later."

Our offices were right next to each other, so I walked next door and handed Bornstein the memo. "Steve, I think this was sent to me inadvertently," I said.

After glancing at it, he replied, "Yes. That's what I'm working on. Sit tight."

A few weeks later, I learned that Bornstein was leaving for California to run Disney's new Internet portal Go.com. It was at the height of the Internet craze, AOL was busting out, and Michael Eisner wanted to turn in that direction. He had just purchased Infoseek, a popular search engine, had it reengineered, and changed the name. The plan was for Go.com to host content from Disney, ABC, and ESPN. But Eisner needed somebody to run it, so he tapped Bornstein, who couldn't say no, because his star was on the rise.

Steve then chose me as his successor, Eisner and Iger okayed it, and on November 19, 1998, I was named president of ESPN. Personally, I felt blessed. And I couldn't have been more proud. From the mailroom to the latest NFL deal, I had worked as hard as I could for ESPN over the previous seventeen years. I had grown up here, married, had children, and made tons of friends. I felt as though I knew just about everybody at ESPN, and I could tell they supported the move.

The night of the formal announcement, I celebrated with my family. Ann, the kids, my mom and dad, and my sister, Sue, and her family were all there—and it meant the world to me to be able to share the moment with them. My father seemed particularly proud. "Too bad we can't go down to The Clam Box for another beer," he said. *[The venerable Greenwich, Connecticut, restaurant had closed its doors in 1985 after forty-six years.]*

"Yeah, Dad," I replied. "Remember that advice you gave me about making a career decision rather than a money decision? Seems like it's working out!"

"It sure is," he said with a smile. "So tell me, what are you going to do for ESPN now that you're president?"

"The Works"

It's a formidable thing to wake up one day and realize you are in charge—that the buck stops with you and that you are responsible for the whole operation. Usually, there is a transitional period when you assume the top spot, but that didn't happen in my case. On my first full day as president of ESPN, Steve Bornstein had only a few minutes to chat, because he had to catch a plane for California. "Congratulations, George," he said. "I hate to do this to you, but we're in court with Major League Baseball and you're about to lose the Senior PGA Tour. Don't worry, I know you can handle it. Good luck!"

Our problem with Major League Baseball occurred earlier that year when ESPN acquired the rights to a full season of *Sunday Night Football*. Doing so put us in a pickle, because we also aired *Sunday Night Baseball*, and the two seasons overlap in September. As soon as we announced that our intention was to televise the NFL on ESPN on Sunday nights, Major League Baseball executives objected. "Hey, wait a minute," they said. "We have a contract for Sunday nights on ESPN."

"Well, we'd like to move your games to ESPN2," we countered.

"But you don't have the right to do that."

"Well, we're committed to football on ESPN on Sunday nights."

So our dispute with Major League Baseball ended up in court.

I had never met Commissioner Bud Selig, but I knew I needed to see him in person quickly if we had any chance of resolving this situation successfully. So my very first call as president of ESPN was to the New York City office of Major League Baseball to set up a meeting as soon as possible.

"Bud, I'd like to get off to a fresh start," I said when we sat down together. "We have a very successful partnership between ESPN and MLB, and my goal is to continue that. Can we resolve the lawsuit?"

Selig smiled, but rejected my suggestion outright. "Not unless you relent," he told me. I knew there wasn't much of a chance of changing Bud's mind right off the bat, but at least we were now speaking and had the beginnings of a relationship.

I also contacted PGA Commissioner Tim Finchem that first week. Back in the 1990s, we often televised the Senior PGA Tour live in the late afternoon and early evening on weekends, and that contract was coming up for renewal. However, because *SportsCenter* was growing in importance, we had made the business decision to televise our flagship property live on weekends at 6 p.m., which created a scheduling conflict with the Senior PGA Tour. During that conversation, I was as honest as I could be in laying out the situation to the commissioner.

"Well, we certainly want to televise our tournaments live," replied Finchem.

"I know," I said, "but we just can't guarantee it, because we need more consistency for *SportsCenter.*"

"Okay, George. I understand. Thanks for telling it straight."

"Thanks for your time, Tim. We've had a good partnership and I hope you'll stay with ESPN."

There was really nothing contentious in our conversation, but neither one of us was prepared to change our position regarding the air schedule. Because our contract was up, I knew Finchem had other options. But we agreed to keep talking.

Several weeks later, I was sitting in a New York federal courtroom with ESPN's chief counsel, Ed Durso, and two of Major League Baseball's top executives, Paul Beeston and Bob DuPuy. We were in front of a tough-as-nails judge who was used to dealing with serious criminal cases. Our dispute was really only about contract terms and money. It was not a capital crime and no lives were going to be lost. After explaining our respective positions to the judge, who had already reviewed the depositions and relevant materials, she said to us, "I think you guys are a bunch of jerks! I'm willing to offer you one of my conference rooms and I suggest the four of you go into one of them, resolve this ridiculous dispute, and not bring it back here. I assure you that if you do, you'll all regret it!"

Knowing we had a good partnership, both sides wanted to continue and, not wanting to incur this judge's wrath, we went into one of her conference rooms and started to negotiate a deal for ESPN to continue to carry Major League Baseball games.

Previous to these negotiations, ESPN had simply purchased "television" rights, in general. It was a simple business when all you needed from a negotiation was the right to air the event or game on a single network. But times had changed. We now had multiple television networks, the Internet had started, and we needed broader rights for our growing businesses. The future of our industry was becoming clear... ESPN's future was becoming clear, too.

After the four of us agreed on a six-year, $2.4 billion deal, the two Major League Baseball executives were all smiles, because they thought the negotiations were essentially done. Then, to their surprise, I handed them a piece of paper and said, "Here's what we want for that price." Internally, we called it "The Works," as when you order all the condiments on a hot dog, and it included everything we could think of at the time, such as all kinds of multimedia rights and rights for different networks both in the United States and internationally. Our proposal went well beyond just the basic contract to televise baseball games on a single network. "The Works" was a detailed two pages in length—a far cry from a few lines scrawled on the bar napkins of negotiations in years past.

It took us another three or four days of round-the-clock negotiations to work out just what it was ESPN was buying for our $400 million a year. But any way you look at it, back in 1998, this was a groundbreaking deal for sports rights broadcasting. "The Works" is now more artfully referred to as a multimedia deal, which includes mobile rights, online rights, multiple television networks, and so on. While it is commonplace now, I'm proud to say that ESPN pioneered this new-era deal—one that would influence all future contracts in our industry.

Of course, Major League Baseball and ESPN did continue our relationship and we've been great partners ever since. However, we weren't successful with the Senior PGA Tour: Tim Finchem signed a new contract with CNBC. In my opinion, one can make the case that the Senior PGA Tour would have been better served by staying with ESPN. However, I understand what Tim was trying to accomplish. Overall, we won one and we lost one, so I was batting .500. But I had a higher percentage in forging relationships, because Tim Finchem and Bud Selig would both become friends of mine.

After Ed Durso and I (along with a team of lawyers and accountants) worked through several nights to complete the negotiations with Major League Baseball, we went out and had breakfast. After ordering, I placed a call to Chris Berman. "Hey, Boomer, this is George," I said. "I want to let you know the good news. We just closed the deal with MLB. We've got them locked in for the next six years. I knew you'd like to know, given how much you love baseball."

"George! That's great, man. Way to go. Thanks for calling."

"You bet, Boom. Talk to you later."

Baseball Tonight is a staple of ESPN's MLB coverage. Shown here (L to R) are Karl Ravech, John Kruk, and Barry Larkin at Dodger Stadium, 2011. *Allen Kee / ESPN Images*

Chris Berman and I shared a bond, as did all of us who were there in the early days of ESPN. After nineteen years in Bristol, Chris had become famous. His spontaneous nicknames for baseball players and booming voice had helped put *SportsCenter* on the map and jump-started the growth of the ESPN brand. Virtually every sports fan in America knew his name. And even though Chris had opportunities to go somewhere else, he stayed with ESPN, because ESPN was *his* company. "I loved what I was doing," he later told me. "Besides, we never stopped growing and that made it exciting to be here."

About the time I assumed the top spot, ESPN reached eighty million cable households in America and another one hundred million around the world. We had not only become a very profitable company for Disney, we were now one of the best-performing media assets in the world. ESPN, "the Worldwide Leader in Sports," as we liked to call ourselves, was number one in sports entertainment (as noted by virtually every poll or measurement you could think of).

The trick now, of course, was to keep us number one.

Many people bluntly told me that ESPN was not going to be able to keep up our record of continuous growth. But I had never seen ESPN rest on its laurels—and now that I was president, I was determined to continue that tradition. We had become successful by continually improving our content, by utilizing new technology, and by creating new networks and new products. I was very confident we could stay ahead of the competition by continuing to do things better and faster. Nonstop innovation was going to remain the order of the day. We would never be complacent. Of course, just saying so wasn't going to make it happen. And now that ESPN had demonstrated how to be successful in the twenty-four-hour sports business, we were facing significant competition from all the broadcast networks and scores of regional cable channels, Internet companies, and radio programmers.

As our ratings increased, people started jumping to the competition as other networks offered opportunities. Keith Olbermann, for instance, left for MSNBC in 1997. Often a negative disruption among the *SportsCenter* staff, and frequently at odds with management, Keith had finally been suspended by John Walsh and Howard Katz (executive vice president of production) for two weeks after he made a couple of unauthorized appearances on other networks. On one of those broadcasts, he referred to Bristol as "a godforsaken place," which upset a lot of people at ESPN, including me. Once Olbermann left, things began to calm down behind the scenes at *SportsCenter.*

From a leadership perspective, I felt that it was good for everybody that Keith had moved on. Unfortunately, he had burned a lot of bridges before leaving and, for a couple of years afterward, there was something of a public battle of words flowing back and forth between him and some ESPN people, which wasn't good for anybody.

Then, in 1999, Fox Sports hired Olbermann away from MSNBC as part of a major challenge to ESPN's leadership in the marketplace. The company put all their regional sports channels under one banner and openly declared war on us. In particular, they said they were going after *SportsCenter* and its huge national audience. As part of their assault on ESPN, Fox took out several full-page ads in the *Hartford Courant* replete with pictures of palm trees and invitations to ESPN employees to leave Bristol for a "nicer place," such as Los Angeles, where Fox was based.

As president of the company, I thought it was very important for me to be supportive of Bristol. After all, it was a nice place to work, a nice place to raise a family, and we had good schools throughout the area. In short, I was not about to apologize for where ESPN was located. As a matter of fact, I felt that Bristol had contributed mightily to our culture over the years. With its good old New England work ethic, Bristol had truly been one of the secrets to ESPN's success. "Be proud of Bristol and the surrounding area," I told our employees. "We don't lock anyone in. There are a lot of people who would like to work at ESPN. If you don't want to be here, please leave...*this afternoon*. And by the way, no hard feelings."

When I arrived early to the office on my second day as president of ESPN, there was a message on my voice mail from the night before. An excited but familiar voice came over the phone:

"George! George! I'm sitting in the Atlantic City airport and I just heard that you're the new president of ESPN!" said an ecstatic Dick Vitale. "Yeah, yeah! 'Am I ever going to have a career here? All I do is drive you around!' Remember saying that to me back in '81? George, I'm proud of you! Congratulations! You're not a diaper dandy anymore. You're Awesome, baby—with a capital *A*. By the way, I don't want to retire and get a wristwatch. How about a new contract?"

It's All About People

That's all fine, George, but why don't we have more light in the parking lot?"

"Yeah, and don't you know that Styrofoam is bad for the environment? Why are we still using Styrofoam coffee cups?"

"George, can we expand the hours of the fitness center?"

I had just completed my first company-wide videoconference as president of ESPN and had opened it up for discussion. I expected people to ask specific questions about our strategy or about my remarks. After all, in preparation, I had studied long and hard to learn every aspect of ESPN and could basically recite our issues and projected growth for any of our businesses in the United States and around the world.

Later, people told me that all the statistical stuff was great and that they felt very comfortable with ESPN's future. But they also made it crystal clear to me that they were just as interested (if not more so) in the issues that concerned them directly on a day-to-day basis. So I learned an important lesson in the top of the first inning of my presidency. While corporate leaders certainly have to know every aspect of their business, they also better pay extra-close attention to things that are important to employees.

With that in mind, I made a big push to see that the first new building on our Bristol campus would be a cafeteria (something we'd never had). In ESPN's early years, while the *SportsCenter* staff haunted the White Birch between shows, I was buying hamburgers two at a time from a vending machine and devouring them. Back then, it was everybody for themselves as far as food was concerned. By the time the early 1990s rolled around, one of the departments occasionally ordered in food for a meeting and word quickly spread through the building that there was "food on 3," so every platter would be picked clean in a matter of minutes. In those years, we ate more baked ziti (a local catering specialty) than the southern half of Italy.

My proposal to build a cafeteria was initially rejected by Disney for budgetary reasons. That, in turn, led to a lot of back-and-forth discussion that took months. In the meantime, I acted on my own authority and just said, "Build it."

A couple days after we opened, my roommate from the early days (and ESPN veteran) Don Colantonio and I were in my office looking out the window as people walked in for lunch. "Hey, your first big accomplishment as president, George," said Don, pointing in that direction. "Congratulations!"

"Yeah, we've finally got hot food," I replied. "How about that!"

"Did you get any flack for it?" asked Don.

"Well, the purchasing department at Disney called me yesterday, and said, 'Hey, we have to talk about approving this cafeteria expenditure.'

" 'Well, you'd better hurry up,' I said, 'because today's special is meat loaf and it's being served in there right now!' "

I was very proud of the fact that we now had a central place on campus where everybody could get something to eat. We served good food, too, which kept the place busy. I must admit, however, I had not anticipated that ESPN's first cafeteria would play such a large role in enhancing our culture.

Suddenly at lunch, everybody was bumping into other employees they would not normally see in the course of a day—and sometimes they hadn't seen in years, because the campus had grown so much over two decades. People from different departments started mixing. On-air talent ate with technicians. Managers chatted with the mail-room guys. It seemed like everyone was swapping stories, sharing information, and talking about new developments where they worked.

"Wow, Bob. That was a terrific story last night on *Outside the Lines*. How did you guys come up with that?"

"Well, sit down and let me tell you about it."

The next thing you knew, people were holding on-the-spot informal meetings that led to new ideas. Without ever planning for it to happen, our new cafeteria immediately began facilitating communication and collaboration among all departments. People were making new friends, building relationships, learning about other aspects of their company—and all over a good meal. I couldn't have been more pleased.

Earlier, we had purchased a nearby Gold's Gym and converted it into a fitness facility for ESPN employees. Of course, people did meet and mix there, but in smaller numbers. When I observed the phenomenon taking place in the cafeteria, I began thinking about having even more places on campus that would not only serve people's needs, but also provide opportunities for us to get together outside our daily jobs. Eventually, we would build a new state-of-the-art fitness center not far from the cafeteria, and we would provide the number one most requested employee item: an on-site child-care center. These investments paid for themselves many times over with improved morale, higher energy, and innovative thinking.

As part of my new responsibilities, I worked hard to split my time between our New York City offices and the Bristol campus. And whenever I was in Bristol, I made it a point to eat in the cafeteria, to work out in the fitness center, and to park where everybody else parked. Being visible and available is important for a leader. So I tried to make it easy for people to talk to me, and I met with anybody who ever asked to see me. I also made it a point to get to know people's names, whether they were security guards, cashiers in the cafeteria, or department heads. Pretty soon, employees began noticing that I was calling a lot of people by their first names. "George, how is it that you can remember so many names?" they'd ask.

"My memory's no better than anybody else's," I'd reply. "I just make an effort, because the job is all about people."

Actually, it drove me nuts if I *could not* remember a person's name. And from a purely business standpoint, when employees see a senior leader saying hello to everybody by name, they understand that they work in a place where friendliness, respect, and cordiality are part of the culture.

By 1998, ESPN's culture was deeply embedded in the DNA of those of us who had been there since the early days. But we were immersed in our work, growing fast, and adding people every day. So it was natural to expect some dilution in our standards, which I began to sense when getting to know some of the company's younger employees. At this point I realized that if ESPN was to remain number one in our industry, we were going to have to recapture some of that hungry magic we had in the early days. So I made it my personal mission to focus on and amplify ESPN's culture across our entire organization. It had been our strategic advantage back then, and I was determined to make it the main driver of ESPN's future efforts.

The importance of culture to a company cannot be overstated—and it becomes even more valuable as the organization prospers and grows. In my view, there are three main reasons why culture is important in business. First, it is the only thing leaders can truly control. Most variables in business are beyond the direct influence of any single individual. You can't control sales and, in ESPN's business, we can't always produce good ratings. Every now and then, we experience a blowout or a bad game, and people change channels. That's just how it is. Also, how many times do we see a business plan that looks great on paper? There are always dozens of tables and charts to demonstrate that it should work, but it often doesn't, because people in the company cannot make it work. That's where culture comes in. Culture is all about people and the environment where they work. And because people take their cues from their top executives, setting the culture is "job one" for business leaders.

Second, culture supports everything a business is trying to do. It drives quality, profit, and employee passion. Leaders cannot be in every meeting, in every conversation, or at every cocktail party. But a dynamic culture empowers people to act *on their own* in the company's best interests. If your people develop their own initiatives through their own creativity, you know your culture is working.

Third, a great corporate culture attracts an industry's best people— and that results in more action, superior products, and better efficiency. In the early days at ESPN, we had a workplace where creativity and innovation were rewarded, where everybody was respected, and where we knew we were part of something bigger than ourselves. That environment engendered loyalty, gave people a reason to stick around, and directly contributed to nonstop annual growth.

The first thing I did to amplify ESPN's culture was to start talking about it both casually and in more formal settings. I emphasized maintaining an entrepreneurial spirit and an underdog mentality. "Let's not sit around and read our own headlines," I said. "Let's operate like the entrepreneurial start-up we used to be. It'll result in faster action, keeping egos in check, and outworking our competitors." Some people started calling this my underdog speech, but I also talked about work-life balance by encouraging everyone to make their own families their top priority. "It's okay for ESPN to be a close second," I told everybody, "but never confuse the order. Your family comes first!"

Indeed, in the 1980s, ESPN operated like one big family. We cared about each other and, as all families should do, we helped each other along the way. So I let everybody know that if they wanted the company's help, we were going to provide it. "Tell your supervisors what your goals are, what your dreams are, where you want to go, and what you want to do," I advised. "We'll provide opportunities to help you get there." And finally, I encouraged everybody to enjoy themselves while they were at ESPN. "Remember, we take our sports seriously, but we don't take ourselves too seriously. So have some fun along the way."

The most important thing I did to amplify our culture was to promote ESPN's "culture carriers" into positions of authority and build around them. These were the people who embodied the values of hard work, honesty, integrity, and respect for others. Culture carriers are among our most passionate employees and are always positive influences on everybody around them. Personally, I knew who they were and, within a year or two of becoming president, I made a number of them my direct reports. For example, I promoted Chuck Pagano to vice president in charge of engineering. Chuck had been the technical director on the very first ESPN broadcast in 1979, had progressed nicely in his career, and was widely regarded as one of the leading creative thinkers on the engineering side of the business.

When Judy Fearing was promoted to head up marketing for Disney Consumer Products, I tapped her top lieutenant, Lee Ann Daly, to take over our marketing efforts. I kept in place Chief Financial Officer Christine Driessen (who had joined ESPN in 1985 as controller) and Rosa Gatti as senior vice president in charge of communications. Rosa was one of ESPN's early trailblazers and had been hired in 1980 by Chet Simmons, himself, to form the department. Her top reports were ESPN "trailer" veterans Chris LaPlaca and Mike Soltys. Sean Bratches was the head of affiliate sales, and Ed Durso (who had ten years of service with the company) rounded out the executive team as chief counsel and head of administration.

Russell Wolff, who served as head of our Asia-Pacific group in

Hong Kong and then head of programming at ESPN STAR Sports in Singapore, moved back to the United States to head up all of our international operations. To lead advertising sales, I hired Ed Erhardt, who had never before worked in television much less sold a unit of cable advertising. Ed had been vice president and group publisher for *Advertising Age* magazine, and I was sure he would bring new thinking to ESPN just as we were about to enter the frontier of multimedia sales. Because Ed came from outside the company, I experienced some negative reactions for hiring him. But that kind of blowback never really bothered me. It's imperative for leaders to have confidence in their decision making.

Part of ESPN's culture is to work in teams. It has always been that way and, I hope, always will be. While it's a proven fact that people working together get more done and achieve better results than the same number of people working separately, effective teamwork can be a tricky business. Just like on a sports team, you can have the best players in the world, but if they don't play well together, you've got nothing. In business, it's a delicate balance to treat everyone as individuals and also insist that they work well together.

At ESPN, the senior executive in charge of each department reported directly to the president, which is similar to the concept behind a flattened organization. However, having no go-betweens requires leaders who are willing to collaborate with each other. Otherwise, it's too easy for silos to form. Ever since I experienced the "Pig-Out" campaign back in the mid-1990s, I had placed a major emphasis on people in different departments always talking to each other. So from day one as ESPN's new president, I focused on teamwork and demanded collaboration among departments. Now I had just one more leadership tenet left to drive home.

Leadership is about people. People. People. People.

Everything a leader does has to be centered around treating people with respect. Not playing favorites. Not playing politics. Treating everybody fairly. Letting them do their jobs. *Helping* them do their jobs. Encouraging them to try new things. Letting them make mistakes (as long as they are honest mistakes). Not punishing them when they fail, but praising them when they succeed, and always making sure to give credit where credit is due. And most important, truly caring about them.

Additionally, empowering people is one of the most important aspects of leadership. So is *involving* people—not only in the day-to-day aspects of the business, but also in the public's perception of the company. And that starts in the local community. When I got the top job, I wanted to involve everyone—and I do mean everyone. So one of the first things I did was to centralize and expand our corporate outreach program. At the suggestion of Rosa Gatti, we renamed it TEAM ESPN and gave it the slogan "Fans Helping Fans." Our first charity was the Special Olympics, followed by a variety of worthy endeavors from Habitat for Humanity to the Bristol Family Center for Girls and Boys.

TEAM ESPN working in the local community, 2006. *Lisa Kovlakas*

TEAM ESPN was formed because most people really do care about their community and want to give back. But volunteerism is not easy for everybody. So when a corporation organizes and facilitates outreach programs, it is truly appreciated by many employees. I can also say from firsthand experience that TEAM ESPN generated a great deal of internal passion and pride. People genuinely were proud of the fact that their company cared about something other than just the business of making money. ESPN was already great in so many ways, but our corporate outreach programs added an entirely new dimension to how we viewed ourselves. Employees felt good when they volunteered in the community. And when people feel good about themselves, they tend to be happier and more productive in their jobs. I can say with 100 percent certainty that TEAM ESPN added significantly to our company's overall performance. There's no doubt in my mind.

I've always been proud to be a part of ESPN. And when I became president, it was important to me to be the same person I was when I was a driver in the mailroom. I was still just a member of the team. The friends I had back then, I still had. But I worked hard to maintain those friendships. And as president, I began to realize that the higher a leader rises in an organization, the more important it is to build and maintain interpersonal relationships—both inside and outside the company.

ESPN was growing very fast, we were adding people all the time, and every time I turned around, I saw someone new. I remember walking outside with Bob Ley one day and seeing John Walsh talking to somebody. As they approached us, I turned to Bob and asked, "Who is that walking with Johnny, Bob? What's her name? What's her name?"

"Sorry, George, I just don't know," replied Bob.

"I should know. I should know what her name is. I've seen her before." Fortunately, Walsh bailed me out by mentioning her name as we stopped to chat.

Over the years, I've made it a point to study great sports coaches. And it has not escaped me that much of their sage advice involves observations about teamwork. Vince Lombardi once said, "The achievements of an organization are the results of the combined efforts of each individual." And Casey Stengel, when congratulated on winning another World Series, replied by saying, "I couldn't have done it without my players."

Those two legendary sports figures knew what they were talking about. And their wisdom applies not only to sports, but to business, as well. If you put people first, profits will follow.

Make It a Priority

In the first quarter of 2001, ESPN's television ratings dropped 19 percent over the previous year. It was the low point of a gradual decline we had experienced from our peak ratings in 1996. We were now at a record low and, because ratings are the lifeblood of a television network, we were clearly in the midst of a major crisis.

Most industry experts believed our decline was inevitable and due to "fragmentation," the impact of viewers having many more choices. The old twelve-channel cable systems had become "digital" and were rapidly evolving toward a "five-hundred-channel universe." Common thinking at the time was that more viewer choice would lead to fewer viewers for any one channel, that media was a zero-sum game. Adding to the equation was the growing popularity of direct-broadcast satellite (DBS) providers, such as Dish Network and DirecTV. ESPN's past years of exponential growth were due, in part, to the regular addition of new subscribers and expanded product coverage (to the point that we increased profits even if our ratings were flat or slightly down). But in 2001, I was presented a proposed 2002 budget with revenue based on an annual ratings decline and, to me, that was totally unacceptable.

I was not going to approve a budget projecting that we were going to do worse next year than we did this year.

I immediately convened an off-site meeting of our top executives in Greenwich and laid out the facts. "We've got a problem here," I said. "Our ratings are tanking and we don't have a specific plan for turning them around. What are we going to do?" Within a matter of minutes, someone in the room said, "Why don't we make raising ratings a priority?" Everybody thought that was a such a good idea that we decided to set that as our number one company priority and, while we were at it, added three more. By the end of our multiday meeting, we had collectively come up with: (1) increase our ratings; (2) provide ongoing support for our affiliate sales and marketing efforts; (3) support the growth of ESPN.com; and (4) further develop our technology.

Before we developed a detailed action plan, we decided to first take a more in-depth look at the root cause of our ratings decline. To do that, we handed the ball to ESPN's research department, which was headed up by Artie Bulgrin. Artie had come to ESPN in 1996 from ABC-TV, where he had directed national sales research for its nationwide system of television stations. I was so confident in our research department that I knew they would get to the bottom of what had caused the problem. A few weeks later, Artie presented his department's findings to the "Priority One" team. "For this study, we have created a new form of enhanced research," said Artie. "We call our detailed reports 'Audience X-Rays.' We've never done anything this scientific before, but I believe the results are really telling."

It turned out that fragmentation was, indeed, part of the cause for our ratings drop, because the number of people tuning in to ESPN over the course of any quarter was beginning to show systematic decline. But there were other dynamics involved. The emergence of the Internet was a factor, as were digital video recorders (DVRs), such as TiVo, which had just appeared on the scene. However, according to the research department, most of ESPN's downturn in ratings was attributed to our own programming. "Viewers are telling us that they are ESPN fans," reported Artie, "but they are switching channels because many of our programs are uninteresting to them. Research also shows that our promotional efforts could be more focused. By the way, *SportsCenter* remains very strong. They still love our flagship show."

Artie Bulgrin's research department had determined that despite the changing landscape, we certainly did, in fact, have influence over our ratings decline. We could not blame our misfortune solely on outside influences that were beyond our control. It was our own fault. ESPN's leadership, I felt, had to accept responsibility and take action to correct the problem.

As part of our "Priority One" team action plan, we decided to completely reevaluate ESPN's programming lineup. We would look at each and every program to determine which shows were working and which weren't worthy of ESPN's airtime. Artie's department called their strategy "Regression to the Mean"—a combination of scientific ratings determination and statistical analysis. They created a distribution chart across all ESPN networks with the highest-rated programs, such as *Sunday Night Football* and *Sunday Night Baseball*, at the top. At the lower end of the distribution were poorly rated programs, such as exercise and outdoor shows, cheerleading, and re-airs of the X Games. Artie's reasoning was that if we could move the bottom of the distribution higher, then our overall rating would go up (in other words, regression to the mean, or the middle).

So over time, we revamped our programming by eliminating low-rated shows and expanding the live hours of news and information shows like *SportsCenter*. We also implemented a long-range strategy to develop more programming in the tradition of great ESPN storytelling (along the lines of *The Sports Reporters* and *Outside the Lines*, both of which were still performing consistently). A good example is *E:60*, a one-hour investigative newsmagazine (overseen by ESPN veteran Vince Doria) covering American and international sports, and featuring Jeremy Schaap (Dick's son), Chris Connelly, Lisa Salters, and Tom Rinaldi.

There were also a variety of efforts undertaken throughout the company's different departments to increase ESPN's ratings. For instance, a new statistical model was developed to prioritize our on-air commercial promotions, which were often handled on an ad-hoc basis by individual program producers. From that model, we learned that to effectively advertise a professional golf tournament, for example, we had to promote it twenty times over four days prior to the event. So to become more consistent and effective, we decided to revamp our entire on-air strategy and coordinate it at a higher management level. There was some pushback at first among producers, but once they saw how the new methods actually increased ratings, the resistance quickly evaporated.

Looking back, our 2001 television ratings plunge could have been disastrous for ESPN had we not taken immediate and effective action. At the time, I didn't realize how profound a simple suggestion like "why don't we make it a priority" would impact ESPN long-term. Although it seemed like common sense, our new process eventually became something of a five-point template for how we would handle future crises: (1) get everybody together to discuss the problem; (2) make fixing it a priority; (3) determine the specific cause of the problem; (4) create a detailed plan of action; and (5) communicate it to the entire organization and encourage *everybody* to help. It worked, too, because by 2002 (only one year later) our ratings had rebounded, increasing by 14 percent. Even better, we went on a nine-year run, which culminated in 2010 with our highest-rated year ever. Not coincidentally, over that time ESPN experienced continued revenue growth, averaging double digits annually.

The 2001 ratings crisis was a turning point for ESPN. The fact that we had reversed the situation so quickly (despite conventional wisdom that there was really nothing we could do about it) was not lost on our executive leadership team. Actually, we turned that crisis into an opportunity by applying the lessons learned to our future operations. The power of setting a single goal that everyone bought into, for instance, resulted in the new ESPN business staple of setting annual company priorities.

The process was fairly simple. We first solicited ideas from across the company. The hundreds of submissions we received were analyzed and grouped into themes. They ran the gamut from business development, programming, revenue, international, and people-oriented— depending on our current needs and our vision for the upcoming year. Then we gathered sixty to seventy of ESPN's top leaders for an off-site meeting.

Because a common complaint you hear in business is that many meetings are just a waste of time, I was determined to make certain these priority meetings worked. To kick off the meetings, I presented an overview of the company and then turned it over to a moderator already selected from within our group. Then I sat in the audience, listened, and weighed in from time to time. I also made sure that we had a free and open environment where everybody was encouraged to participate in the discussions. Opposing views were welcome and I made sure that nobody got their head chopped off for speaking their mind. Some people started referring to the way we ran meetings as a "culture of candor." But I was very serious. I did not want to hear what people *thought* I wanted to hear. I wanted their true opinions. After all, they were in the trenches, doing the hard work, a lot closer to the day-to-day operations of the company than I was, so they would naturally have very pertinent insights. Besides, looking at *all* options in any given situation inevitably results in a better decision.

During these meetings, we reviewed and debated a laundry list of suggestions submitted from the rest of the company. Eventually, we whittled the number down to ten, and then to three or four formal priorities—making sure that each was worded simply and clearly.

Actually, we used a democratic voting process during the entire meeting. In the early years, it was just a show of hands and, eventually, we moved to electronic voting. Almost always, at the conclusion of the last vote, the room burst into thunderous applause. Not only had we worked very hard to get to that point, but there was no set time for adjournment. The meeting ended when the priorities were set. Period. No exceptions. So everybody not only felt we had done something great for ESPN, but we could also finally go home.

Once back in Bristol, "champions" for each priority were chosen to form a team, develop a game plan, and to report back to the company on a regular basis. Then we communicated that year's priorities to everybody in the company. Initially, we thought that rolling out the list via email would work, but it didn't. So to make certain everybody got the message, we sent out team members to discuss and explain why each particular item had been made a priority. Additionally, we printed the priorities on cards and distributed them to all employees.

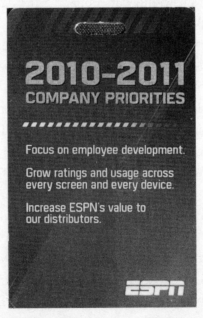

Company Priorities Card, 2010–2011. *ESPN*

Many people began punching holes in the cards and wearing them on their belts, along with their ID/security cards. We never asked anybody to do that, nor was it a requirement and, eventually, we started manufacturing the cards with pre-punched holes. The priorities had become a point of pride. Everyone was now involved and, by unleashing an army of ESPN employees, every priority had a whirlwind of activity behind it.

With experience, ESPN learned that there are four major benefits to setting annual priorities. The first is <u>Focus</u>. During our pursuit of that very first priority, everybody began pulling in one direction. We were going to increase our ratings, come hell or high water. There was just no doubt about it. That intense corporate-wide focus was an amazing thing to witness—and I was deeply impressed by it. To drive the point home, I hung a photograph on a wall near the entrance to my office that illustrated the point. Incredibly, it showed a 1964 high school football game being played while a three-alarm fire raged in a school building right behind the stands. The students, coaches, parents, officials, and spectators were intent on playing that game. *Nothing* was going to deter them.

The Northfield Mount Hermon High School (Massachusetts) football game versus Deerfield Academy went on despite a three-alarm fire consuming the school's science building behind the stands, November 20, 1965. *Photo by Robert S. Van Fleet, courtesy of Northfield Mount Hermon Archives*

The second major benefit to setting annual priorities is <u>Motivation</u>. In many companies, while senior executives are privy to all of the important goings-on in the company, most of the rest of the employees are shut off and are thirsty for information. It is empowering for employees to be informed about their company's priorities—and once armed with information, it actually motivates them to take action. People in the department responsible for a priority get their phone calls returned faster, and those in other departments use the priorities to help in decision making. "Hey, George, I was in a meeting last week," someone once told me. "We had a problem and we didn't know which way to turn. Then someone pulled out their card and we decided that we had to go in the direction that best supported our top priority."

For me, as a leader, it doesn't get any better than that. Nobody was sitting around in a meeting saying, "Well, we'd better call the senior vice president to see what we should do." Nonsense. They know what to do. They are experts in their fields—whether in accounting, production, communications, engineering, etc. They know what the priorities are. They can take action themselves and keep our company moving quickly to serve sports fans. As I always tell people, "If you're waiting for a memo from the corner office to tell you what to do, it's going to be an awfully long wait. You have to figure it out yourselves."

The third benefit is <u>Pride</u>. In 2013, at our Bristol headquarters, I ran into the executive who heads up ESPN in Buenos Aires, Argentina. "Hi, Guillermo, nice to see you," I said. "What's going on?"

"We're up here presenting our plan, George," he replied. *"You know we're a priority this year!"* Guillermo was proud of that fact—and pride is a strong motivator.

The fourth benefit of setting annual priorities is that it helps <u>Develop the Culture</u>. Once something is named a priority at ESPN, it becomes embedded in our daily activities and interactions with each other. Even if it is not named a priority the following year, everyone knows that the initiative is still important, especially if it happens to be one that deals with people issues.

After several years, word about ESPN's annual priorities spread around the industry. At a national conference, one CEO came up to me and mentioned it. "Hey, George, I hear you guys set company priorities," he said. "And I hear that you print them on a card. And I hear that you give one to each of your employees. Can you tell me about it?"

"Well, sure," I replied. "Each year, we set company priorities. We print them on a card. And we give one to each of our employees."

After the CEO stopped laughing, I said, "That's really all there is to it. But guess what? It works! We've got seven thousand people who know precisely what the company priorities are for that year. And it's part of their jobs to figure out how to relate to those priorities in whatever area of the company they happen to be in. *Everybody* is encouraged to participate."

Secretariat Over Mantle?

In mid-1999, about six months after I was named president, various Disney divisions began ratcheting up activity to expand ESPN's brand projects, including ESPN Zone restaurants, ESPN Stores, and a variety of other initiatives. Their expertise in the field of brand management was unquestioned, but the sheer volume of what was being proposed began to affect us, and people started to complain. "Do we really have to do all this stuff, George?" they asked. "If we do, then something else has to go, because we only have so many resources." My time was also being heavily impacted and, frankly, I was not enamored with some of the proposed ideas. So I called Michael Eisner.

"Michael, you have to tell me how I'm supposed to act here," I said. "We've got all these new friends from Disney. Are they telling us what to do... or asking us? I need some guidance."

"George, your job is to manage the ESPN brand," he responded. "If you don't want to do something, you don't have to do it."

"Thank you very much, Michael," I said.

It was good, clear direction, and Eisner had been emphatic. He and Bob Iger had put me in this job and they were going to let me run ESPN with little interference. The job was mine to define, and

I had the creative freedom to make the most of it. "Decentralized management" had been part of the culture at ESPN ever since Tom Murphy and Dan Burke of CapCities entered our world in 1985. And when Michael Eisner gave me that particular bit of advice, it was just one more reason for me to believe that our acquisition by Disney was going to be a great thing for ESPN.

I had been lucky to have reported directly to Steve Bornstein before becoming president of ESPN, because he also gave me a lot of freedom to succeed or fail on my own merits. Bornstein, for example, had taken my advice back in 1997 on a project that would help me years later when faced with the ratings plunge crisis of 2001. That advice was to move forward with a project called *SportsCentury.* The original idea was to have ESPN produce one hundred hours of programming taking a look back at the twentieth century in sports and defining who the great players were, why they were great, what the major events were, why they made a difference—and then putting everything in context with a broader view of American history. Bornstein was on the fence about moving forward, in part because a few executives viewed the project's proposed budget of $20 to $25 million as something we simply could not afford. But I joined forces with Steve's top adviser, Bill Creasy, in pushing hard to get *SportsCentury* off the ground. "Steve, we can't afford *not* to do this," I said. "I don't want to be sitting around in the year 2000 and see that one of our competitors thought ahead to do a project like this—and we didn't. How many times are we going to get a chance to look back on an entire century of sports? ESPN has to do this. Who else could do a better job?"

Bornstein not only gave the okay to move forward, he approved Creasy's and my recommendation to name twenty-six-year-old Mark Shapiro as *SportCentury*'s coordinating producer. Naturally, people questioned the selection. "What are they thinking?" ran some of the criticism. "ESPN's going to have a kid define the past hundred years of sports." But Creasy and I didn't back down. We had been watching

Shapiro since 1993 when he joined the company as a production assistant. A graduate of the University of Iowa, Mark had left a good job with NBC Sports, had accepted a lower salary to work for us, and had done extraordinarily well at everything he touched. "Shapiro is the right person to head this project," we said. "He has the energy and the smarts we need and, besides, it's part of ESPN's culture to place promising young people in positions of authority. He's also a history buff. He'll get it done."

In order to give the project as much independence and focus as possible, *SportsCentury* was given separate offices in Westport, Connecticut (about sixty miles from Bristol). Shapiro immediately set to work bringing in his own team of about sixty people. He personally interviewed and hired every editor, researcher, producer, and secretary. Some transferred from ESPN in Bristol and others were tapped from the larger pool of creative talent in nearby New York City. But Mark's first two hires were his most important, as he was able to convince widely respected veterans Bud Morgan and Pat Smith to come in on the ground floor and lay the strategic groundwork for the project. Morgan was a legendary production manager who knew virtually everybody in the business, and Smith was a seasoned writer who knew all the angles. By choosing two sports broadcasting pioneers, Mark gave himself some instant credibility with any critics who thought he was too young to handle the job. Additionally, ESPN's Dick Schaap provided sage counsel to Mark, while John Walsh supervised the entire project.

It was important to have these seasoned veterans on the team, but what made the biggest difference in Mark Shapiro's leadership was the fact that he worked side by side in the trenches with people every day—always on the job, always willing to do whatever was necessary. He also constantly reminded everybody that *SportsCentury* was more important than any one person. "ESPN is entrusting us with the brand," he'd say. "We have a huge responsibility with this project."

All of 1998 was spent preparing and producing *SportsCentury*. The team worked long hours at a frenetic pace seven days a week. They combed the twentieth century's television, radio, magazine, and newspaper archives for any and all sports information. Not only did they perform a tremendous amount of research, writing, and filming, their early decision to use only original interviews with living subjects resulted in more than five thousand new interviews. Everything hinged around the determination to get every detail right, to verify all the facts, and to produce the highest-quality programming possible.

SportsCentury's centerpiece was a weekly series of half-hour profiles on the top fifty athletes of the past hundred years. Selections were made by a special panel of about fifty sports journalists, production executives, and other noted observers, most of whom were interviewed for participation in the project. While no professional athletes were on the panel, it did include many well-known sports figures, such as Roone Arledge, Shirley Povich, Mitch Albom, David Halberstam, Bob Costas, Curt Gowdy, Sally Jenkins, Bryant Gumbel, Robin Roberts, and Chris Berman. The voting was wide open. Nobody knew who anybody else was voting for, and no list of nominees to choose from was provided. Moreover, just like all the viewers, every panel member had to watch ESPN to find out who had made the list and in what order, because we kept the final results secret and made no advance announcements.

SportsCentury: Top 50 Athletes of the 20th Century began airing in January 1999 with a new biography every week. We started with number fifty, tennis champion Chris Evert, and did a countdown until we arrived at Christmas Day when we aired bios of the final two athletes, Babe Ruth (number two) and Michael Jordan (number one). Reviews were good and ratings spiked during the final few weeks, because everybody wanted to see who made the top ten. After Jordan and Ruth, the list included Muhammad Ali (three), Jim Brown (four), Wayne Gretzky (five), Jesse Owens (six), Jim Thorpe (seven), Willie Mays (eight), Jack Nicklaus (nine), and Babe Didrikson Zaharias (ten).

Perhaps the most controversial moment came when Secretariat came in at number thirty-five, two spots ahead of Mickey Mantle (number thirty-seven). Even a couple of members of the selection panel were shocked. "What is a horse doing on the list?" they demanded to know. Much of the public found the choice amusing and, actually, the controversy only served to increase publicity and ratings. Sports fans loved the debate.

Sprinkled in between the weekly athlete countdowns were more than twelve hundred one-minute *SportsCentury* "moments," airing throughout the day on ESPN. "On this day in 1951, Bobby Thomson hit 'the shot heard 'round the world' off Ralph Branca as the New York Giants defeated the Brooklyn Dodgers to win the pennant." "This week in 1963, CBS debuted instant replay at the annual Army-Navy game in Philadelphia." "This week in 1972, Franco Harris of the Pittsburgh Steelers made the 'Immaculate Reception' to beat the Oakland Raiders in the last thirty seconds of the AFC divisional play-off game." On top of it all, ESPN's *SportsCentury* team also produced five two-hour specials that looked back on the most influential sports people of the century, the greatest games, the most controversial figures and decisions, the greatest dynasties, and the greatest coaches. When it was all said and done, the project was unprecedented in terms of its scope and quality. Everybody was watching ESPN. Our company was very proud of what we had produced. And most important, *SportsCentury* not only set a new standard for excellence, it was also a fitting tribute to the history of sports in the twentieth century.

As ESPN rolled into the new millennium, the *SportsCentury* project ended, the team disbanded, and everybody went on to new things. Some stayed with the company, others went back to what they were doing in New York, and some retired with the feeling that they had capped their careers with something very special. But I was still the president of ESPN and, like the coach of any championship sports team, I was always looking for good athletes. I knew I had one in Mark Shapiro, so I decided to increase his salary and create a new executive position for him.

Back in 1997, we had purchased Classic Sports Network and renamed it ESPN Classic. Given that much of the *SportsCentury* programming was now going to be re-aired on Classic, it seemed like the perfect vehicle for Mark, so I decided to try something different by making him head of Classic. It was new, because Shapiro would be the first single individual placed in charge of one of our networks. Here's how the conversation went when I told him about his promotion:

"Mark, we want you to move to Bristol and become vice president and executive producer of ESPN Classic," I said.

"What does that mean?" asked Mark.

"It means you're in charge of the network."

"Well, what does that mean, exactly?"

"I don't know what it means, exactly," I replied. "What I know is that Classic is in about thirty million homes, it broadcasts the history of sports every day, and for us to get into another thirty million homes and be profitable, we need a leader—and you're the guy!"

"I like the sound of that, George, but I'm still not sure what I'm getting into. For instance, will the affiliate sales and advertising guys working on Classic report to me?"

"No."

"Well, they're trying to sell ESPN, ESPN2, and ESPNews. Where will Classic be in the pecking order?"

"I don't know. You'll have to figure that out with them."

At that point, Shapiro got quiet and looked at me kind of quizzically. "Listen, Mark," I said, "you've already shown with *SportsCentury* that you can work across the aisle, bridge gaps, and win people over. If you could do it there, you can do it on a bigger platform. Even though these people don't report to you, I'm telling you that you need to work with them. So go build relationships. Make it happen."

"Okay," said Mark, finally. "I got it."

I knew I wasn't providing Shapiro with much specific direction, but that was by design. My focus as a leader is to encourage everybody to work as a team and that wasn't going to change just because Mark was now involved at a higher level. I wanted Mark to run ESPN Classic and, at the same time, support the flattened organization I had set up among the executive team. Essentially, I put him in a spot where there were few rules—and I wasn't going to hold his hand. My simple message was: "Get in the game, get along, and make it work."

For the majority of its programming, ESPN Classic had been running mostly archival footage. As soon as Mark got involved, the staff began incorporating interviews that had already been shot for *SportsCentury*. So, at the same time viewers were watching a classic game, such as the controversial 1972 Soviet gold medal basketball victory over the Americans at the 1972 Munich Olympics, they could hear commentary from Doug Collins, who played on the U.S. team. Essentially, Classic began weaving more storytelling into game watching—and it worked. Ratings immediately went up.

Encouraged by positive feedback about these early programming moves, Shapiro's team not only re-aired *SportsCentury: Top 50 Athletes of the 20th Century*, but decided to add to it by creating a new series titled *The 50 Greatest Athletes and Beyond*. Now, if sports fans were disappointed that one of their favorite stars hadn't made the first list, they might have an opportunity to see a profile of that particular athlete. Not only did we end up expanding the list to the top hundred athletes of the twentieth century, we doubled the length of each episode to a full hour. Additionally, Classic eventually began producing new one- and two-hour documentaries based on the books of iconic sportswriters. The first was based on Dick Schaap's *Flashing Before My Eyes*, which was soon followed by David Halberstam's *Summer of '49*.

As ESPN Classic's programming improved, the network received more publicity and higher ratings; cable operators started requesting it for their cable systems. Gradually, the people of ESPN realized that Shapiro and his team were making Classic a real winner. So Sean Bratches, the head of affiliate sales and marketing, went to Mark and asked him for an unusual kind of direct support. "We need to get into more homes in Chicago," he said. "Is that something Classic can help us with?"

From that one request, Mark's team produced a whirlwind of activity. First Classic aired an entire week of *SportsCentury* shows about famous Chicago athletes (Walter Payton, Ernie Banks, Dick Butkus, Michael Jordan, and so on). Then we ran a week of great Chicago games, including those of the Bulls, the Cubs, the White Sox, the Blackhawks, and the Bears. All this programming (aimed directly at Chicago sports fans) was coordinated with ESPN's marketing and communications groups, which promoted it locally and on ESPN and ESPN2. We also set up a studio in Chicago and broadcast live for an entire weekend.

In between broadcasts, famous Chicago athletes visited the studio for interviews. Bratches even arranged for the president of a local cable operator to appear on the show and talk about the pulse of the Chicago sports business. Consequently, the visibility of ESPN Classic exploded and the demand for it among cable subscribers increased dramatically. The next thing I knew, Mark Shapiro and Sean Bratches were setting up similar programming and "road shows" in Dallas, Miami, Los Angeles, Atlanta, and Buffalo.

From a leadership perspective, I was ecstatic. Everybody was working together. There were no silos. And for the first time, the affiliate sales team could rely directly on the programming team to help expand distribution. Overall, ESPN had more subscribers, more advertisers, and, of course, more revenue.

Just as Mark Shapiro was making great strides with ESPN Classic, our 2001 ratings crisis came to a head. After the meeting to set company-wide priorities, we established a long-range strategy to develop new and better programming. With that in mind, in mid-2001 I sat down with our marketing and programming people to talk about ways to broaden ESPN's audience. Our goal was to attract more female viewers and more casual sports fans, and bolster the slower summer months. So we decided to form a new division dedicated solely to creating nontraditional programming, such as made-for-television movies, talk shows, game shows, reality TV, and so on. We called our new division ESPN Original Entertainment (EOE for short). And right away, I asked Mark Shapiro to help out where he could, because I wanted to expose him to the company more broadly.

EOE was just one of the initiatives I personally pushed for to help solve our ratings crisis. One of my biggest moves in that vein really shook up the status quo at ESPN. I decided to put Mark in charge of all ESPN programming. In contemplating that action, I thought back to the early days of ESPN when we were short on staff and operating like a start-up. To solve problems, we often threw young, passionate people into jobs—and suddenly the problems became opportunities!

In this case, the problem was our ratings decline—and I believed I had the young, passionate employee in Mark Shapiro to turn it into an opportunity. His success at *SportsCentury* and ESPN Classic had demonstrated an ability to get things done and, at the same time, work well with people. I knew, however, that this move was going to be somewhat controversial. First of all, Mark was only thirty-two years old, and nearly everybody else at ESPN's senior level was older. Second, the programming department contained hundreds of employees, and its work reflected the ESPN brand more than just about any other single thing we did.

When I was ready to set things in motion, I called Mark to my New York office and took him for a walk in Central Park. I wanted to chat without any outside interruptions.

"Mark, I'm going to put you in charge of programming for all of ESPN," I said calmly.

"What?" he replied.

"Look, you've been doing a great job and I like your leadership and energy. My gut's telling me you'll do well in this position. What do you say?"

"Well, George, this is bound to cause some problems."

"I'm glad you brought that up," I said. "There are going to be people who will not like it. Some will not want to take orders from a thirty-two-year-old."

"I understand that, George. But what do you want me to do?"

"I want you to win them over. That's what I want you to do. They are members of our family and I want you to take care of them. Understand?"

"Yes, I understand."

During that walk in Central Park, I didn't mention to Mark that his most important objective was to increase ratings. He already knew that. It was ESPN's number one priority. The message I was really trying to impart was that we had to respect and care about the people in our company while we went about achieving our business goals. I was hopeful Mark could do both. Time would tell.

[In 1999, SportsCentury *won ESPN's first Peabody Award and the 1999, 2000, 2001, and 2005 National Sports Emmy Awards for Edited Sports Series. ESPN Classic had thirty million subscribers in 2000. Seven years later, that number had grown to sixty-five million.]*

Thirty-One F-Bombs

Mark Shapiro's first move as ESPN's new senior vice president in charge of programming was to hold a lengthy town hall with all eighty people in the programming department. At that meeting, he introduced himself and reaffirmed that the department's number one priority was to raise ESPN's ratings. After opening up the floor for discussion, Mark was asked about his reputation for being a workaholic. "You can't push accountability if you aren't the model for it," he said. "So I'm not going to ask anybody to worker harder than I would myself. But I don't think that's going to be a problem, because hard work is what ESPN is all about." Then I think Mark surprised people by vowing to meet with every single person in the room one-on-one to discuss the future of the department and their ideas for making things better. "I'm going on a listening tour for the next thirty or forty days," he said. "Based on what you all say, we'll come up with a new strategy and a new plan to raise ratings."

Sure enough, forty days later Mark rolled out his comprehensive plan. "This is going to work," he told me. "I know we can make it happen." Personally, I loved Mark's optimism and the fact that he had involved virtually everybody in the programming department to craft his plan. As such, I approved it, offered support, and gave him the freedom to implement it.

The initial phase of the team's strategy was to lengthen *SportsCenter*, because it had always been consistent in garnering solid ratings. Having already successfully expanded the Sunday 11 p.m. *SportsCenter* to ninety minutes, we now did the same for all the Monday through Saturday 11 p.m. *SportsCenter*s. The strategy worked as we continued to receive solid ratings.

The next move for Shapiro's team was to attack weekday afternoons by creating new programs that would lead into *SportsCenter*. Our thinking at the time revolved around the belief that sports fans love to debate every aspect of their sport. So on October 22, 2001, under the direction of Jim Cohen (ESPN's vice president of news), and in conjunction with independent producer Erik Rydholm, we launched a new program called *Pardon the Interruption* (*PTI*), hosted by Tony Kornheiser and Michael Wilbon (both sportswriters for the *Washington Post*). The half-hour show aired at 5:30 p.m., just before *SportsCenter*, and featured discussion and debate of the top sports stories of the day.

PTI became popular, in part, because Tony and Mike were passionate, humorous, and displayed tremendous on-air chemistry together as they ticked off topics on a "rundown" graphic appearing on the right-hand side of the television screen. Almost immediately, *Pardon the Interruption* was a game-changer. Ratings were high, as were those for *SportsCenter* due to the *PTI* lead-in. Then Norby Williamson (ESPN's executive vice president of production) pointed out that live games airing after the *PTI-SportsCenter* combination also increased. That meant that *PTI* lifted everything higher as viewers simply stayed tuned to ESPN throughout the early evening and into prime time. It was a big success. We knew we were on to something, and we wanted more of it.

We then launched *Around the Horn,* a sister show to *PTI*, at 5 p.m. in November 2002 with host Max Kellerman (followed in 2004 by Tony Reali). It was a combination sports talk show and sports information competition where the host put four newspaper columnists through "rounds" consisting of daily sports headlines and stories. *Around the Horn* was fun and entertaining—and viewers responded accordingly. As a matter of fact, both *PTI* and *SportsCenter* enjoyed even higher ratings.

After that, the floodgates opened as our programming department created a series of new shows one after the other. *1st and 10* explored the ten biggest sports questions of the day. *Dream Job* was a reality show in which participants interviewed for a job to become a *SportsCenter* announcer. The winner was Mike Hall who did, in fact, join the ESPN staff. *Cold Pizza* was our version of a morning show. And *Stump the Schwab* featured contestants trying to get the better of longtime ESPN staffer and in-house sports trivia expert Howie Schwab. All these new shows did well and allowed us to start promoting the entire afternoon as one huge block of engaging programming.

Concurrent with these very successful new programs, EOE began producing made-for-television films in a major effort to create buzz and attract new viewers. Our first production was *A Season on the Brink*, based on John Feinstein's bestselling book about the 1985–86 Indiana University men's basketball team coached by Bobby Knight. It was a full-length movie that cost about $2.5 million to make. EOE commissioned the script and produced the entire project, including directing, filming, editing, and casting (veteran actor Brian Dennehy played Coach Knight). When the first cut was completed, Mark Shapiro brought it in and we watched it together. After the film ended, I turned to Mark and said, "You know, I didn't realize the script called for this kind of language."

"It's pretty realistic, I think," replied Mark.

"Well, yes, I understand that strong language is prevalent in the world of sports. But ESPN has a lot of young viewers and we're considered a family-friendly network."

"What do you want to do, George? The shooting is completed."

"I don't know yet. But we're going to have to figure something out."

Mark and I then assembled fifteen ESPN people to screen the film together and to try to come up with a solution to what I perceived to be a serious problem. We very carefully chose a diverse group to make sure we didn't miss any elements of either the viewing audience or our own internal opinions. Sitting around the executive conference table that day was a real diversity of age, gender, race, political persuasion, professional expertise, and position levels in the company. After watching the movie, nearly everybody said they liked it. But before I could mention the problem, somebody else said, "What are we going to do with those F-bombs?"

"Yeah," said somebody else. "I counted thirty-one of them."

Then people started voicing their opinions. "I think they have to go." "Well, I think they should stay." "Yeah, they're realistic. That's the way athletes and coaches talk." "But they're offensive to some people." "I find them offensive." "I don't." "Leave them in." "Bleep them out."

"Okay, what are our options?" I asked.

"Well, we can certainly bleep them out," Mark responded. "Or we can leave them in. Or we can shelve the film completely."

"We can't just wash $2.5 million down the drain!"

"Why don't we just use the power of our own networks and various platforms?" someone else said.

"That's a good idea."

"Yeah, we could air the movie on ESPN and ESPN2 at the same time. One version would be unedited, and the other would bleep out all the F-bombs."

"We could market the movie that way in advance. 'For those of you who are uncomfortable with strong adult language, you can watch the edited version.'"

"That would do it for me," said one of the people who was initially upset about all the profanity.

In the end, that's exactly what we did. On March 10, 2002, *A Season on the Brink* aired simultaneously on ESPN (unedited) and ESPN2 (edited). The next day, *USA Today* ran a story with the headline: ESPN DOMINATES PROGRAMMING FOR THE WEEKEND: VIEWERS LIKE 'BRINK' UNBLEEPED. The unedited version on ESPN garnered an incredible 3.4 rating. ESPN2 had a 0.6 rating. So by running it on both networks, we did a combined 4.0!

Previous to this, the only program that registered as high as 3.0 on any of our networks was *Sunday Night Football*. So the "problem" turned into a great success. We received far more publicity by airing the movie on both networks, and we did not receive much pushback from parents, the FCC, or anybody else in Washington. Personally, I believe it was a direct result of assembling a group of diverse people around the table and encouraging them to speak freely and come up with a reasonable and workable solution.

From 2002 to 2005, EOE produced six made-for-TV movies, including: *The Junction Boys*, *3: The Dale Earnhardt Story*, *Hustle*, *Four Minutes*, and *Code Breakers*. We put a great deal of marketing effort into each movie and all of them turned a profit and were solid ratings successes. Overall, however, we did not feel we were getting enough bang for our buck, nor were we happy with the controversy some of the films generated. And if I thought that F-bombs were a problem, I had only to wait for our first TV series, *Playmakers*. Airing weekly from August 26 to November 11, 2003, the drama depicted various aspects of the personal lives of fictional professional football players. But the NFL Players Association, team owners, and NFL officials all voiced their concerns that some of the content portrayed the league negatively. So I made the decision to cancel the series after eleven episodes despite the fact that ratings were very high. Personally, I just did not think it was good business to continue a program that was so upsetting to one of ESPN's major partners.

At the end of the day, we decided not to pursue made-for-television movies or TV drama series as part of our long-term strategy in generating new programming. In the big picture, however, I viewed the entire effort as a success, because we did add a lot of new viewers, we did increase ratings, and we did provide an avenue for ESPN people to expand their horizons. Most important, the experience in getting our company's creative juices flowing set the stage for a fabulously successful new documentary series we would begin producing in 2009 to mark our thirtieth anniversary.

Another big part of our major effort to increase ratings centered on my challenge to our team to acquire additional rights to major sporting events. After all, "stick and ball" sports, as we liked to call them, were ESPN's bread and butter, so why not work at expanding our brand and stay ahead of the competition in that very valuable arena? As such, Mark and I set our sights on reacquiring the National Basketball Association after a twenty-year absence from ESPN. We last had a contract with the NBA way back in 1982—a two-year agreement for forty regular-season games and ten play-off games. NBC and Turner had provided television coverage for the past dozen years, but their contracts were up for renewal at the end of 2001, so the time was right to act.

When we first approached NBA Commissioner David Stern, he did not want to change horses, because he had enjoyed great success with both NBC and Turner through all the Michael Jordan years. In those days, coverage of professional sports was usually split between a broadcast network and a cable network. So the conventional thinking now was that ESPN would have to oust Turner to get the NBA. But Shapiro, an unconventional thinker, came up with an excellent strategy. First, he proposed a plan for us to both coexist with Turner and go after NBC's package, reasoning that, as a traditional broadcast network, NBC would be more vulnerable. Second, Mark employed ESPN's strength with varied media platforms to help persuade the NBA that we were best positioned to lead the league's future growth.

Our first meeting with the NBA took place in New York around Thanksgiving, 2001. It was the first time we used our new "360 Model," which was a creative tool for demonstrating to a sports rights holder why they should go with ESPN over other networks. Basically, on one sheet of paper, we drew a wheel with spokes radiating from the hub (in this case, the NBA) leading to different ESPN media assets, including: ESPN, ESPN2, ESPNews, ESPN Classic, ESPN Radio, ESPN.com, ABC, and Disney (each of which could be used to launch, broadcast, or promote the sport). The truth is that, by then, ESPN had built a better mousetrap, and no other network had anything like it, certainly not NBC. Commissioner Stern immediately saw our advantage and agreed to come to the table for serious negotiations. That's when things began to get both interesting... and tense.

We had numerous discussions in the ensuing weeks, but the last and most arduous was a round-the-clock meeting in the executive conference room at the NBA's headquarters on Fifth Avenue in New York City. There were only five people present: David Stern; two of the NBA's top executives, Adam Silver and Ed Desser; Mark Shapiro; and me. One of the last significant items we had to work out was how many WNBA (Women's National Basketball Association) games ESPN was going to carry. Stern was the mastermind behind the formation of the WNBA back in 1997, and he wanted us to carry twelve games. Shapiro countered with ten. It was two in the morning and everybody was tired, so Desser tried to close up the deal by suggesting we compromise at eleven. But without pausing, Mark rejected the offer. He didn't notice my reaction, but I winced. And Stern begrudgingly said okay to ten and that pretty much ended the negotiation, except for dotting a few *i*'s and crossing some *t*'s.

On January 22, 2002, in a major accomplishment for ESPN, the National Basketball Association announced that we had secured the rights to broadcast more than one hundred regular- and postseason games, including the NBA finals. It was a six-year deal for which we paid $2.4 billion ($400 million a year) that provided for coverage on multiple platforms (ABC, ESPN, ESPN2, ESPN Classic, ESPNews, ESPN Radio, and ESPN.com), as well as the emerging technologies, such as video on demand, interactive TV broadband, and video game development. And now, for the first time in the history of cable sports television, one network had the rights to televise all four of the major professional sports leagues—the NFL, the NHL, Major League Baseball, and the NBA.

It was definitely a proud moment for all of us and, purely from a business perspective, having all four major sports took the public's

"Dr. Naismith meet Lord Stanley."

"Lord Stanley, this is Mr. Doubleday."

"Mr. Halas, Lord Stanley."

"Dr. Naismith, this is Mr. Halas."

"Mr. Doubleday meet Dr. Naismith."

"Mr. Halas, we'd like to introduce Mr. Doubleday."

The NFL, NHL, MLB and NBA together at last, only on ESPN and ESPN 2.

ESPN print advertisement noting that ESPN was the first network to acquire rights to the NFL, MLB, NHL, and NBA simultaneously, 2002. *ESPN Images* perception of ESPN to a new level. But we didn't stop there. Shapiro's programming team also closed a five-year $300 million deal to broadcast Wimbledon, the crown jewel of tennis majors, beginning in 2003. Additional programming we were able to add or renew, included the French Open, indoor lacrosse, and expanded coverage of Indy 500 racing, the PGA, and Major League Baseball.

While each of these new additions helped increase our ratings, one nontraditional event came along and surprised everybody. In 2002–03, we acquired long-term rights to broadcast the World Series of Poker (WSOP) from Las Vegas. ESPN had broadcast the WSOP from 1988 to 1995 with modest success. But times had changed and the game had become enormously popular, especially with the advent of online poker. Everything we did with poker seemed to work. We expanded coverage to include most of the tournament rather than just coverage of the final table. We added mini cameras so that viewers could see the players' hole cards, which led to commentary about the strategy of poker. We re-aired taped events at off hours and still received good ratings. Eventually, the WSOP became a real ratings hit on ESPN and, for a time, poker was a national craze.

Overall, Mark Shapiro and his team successfully helped turn around ESPN's ratings crisis of 2001. More than that, however, I was impressed how Mark, himself, raised the visibility of the company's ratings performance. One of the things that led to the crisis, I believe, was that when our ratings were declining, many of our executives were not sufficiently tuned in to the problem. But Shapiro regularly posted ratings in company-wide memos and emails, talked about them to anybody who would listen, and generally amplified the issue so that every person in the company was following our progress on a regular basis.

⸺

After coming to an agreement with David Stern, Adam Silver, and Ed Desser to cover ten WNBA games as part of our overall NBA package, we decided to take a break and reconvene at 10 a.m. when we would finalize the agreement. It was about two thirty in the morning as Mark Shapiro and I walked along the streets of New York to find an all-night restaurant so we could get something to eat. Mark was all pumped up, talking excitedly about the negotiations, and just thrilled about securing the deal.

Finally, we stopped and I put my arm around his shoulder. "Mark, I love your energy, your passion, and how you're trying to win for our company," I said. "But I just want you to know that you should have taken the compromise that Desser offered you. The difference in one or two games is completely insignificant. Eleven instead of ten would have been okay. Even if you're right and even if you don't want to, sometimes compromising is the right thing to do, especially when you take into account long-term relationships. You might have done some damage with the commissioner tonight."

I didn't want to burst Mark's bubble, and I didn't speak to him in a chastising manner. But he needed to know how I felt at that moment. And Mark took it in stride. He later told me that he modified his future actions because of that conversation. Instead of always having his foot on the gas pedal, he periodically paused to ask himself, "Is this a place where we should compromise?"

[During the years 2002–05, ESPN experienced fourteen straight quarters of ratings growth—quarter over quarter, year over year.]

Saludos

In Bangalore, India, the car Russell Wolff, Christine Driessen, and I were riding in pulled up a couple of blocks short of the cable operator we were headed to see. Our host asked us to step into an ornate horse-drawn carriage and, the next thing I knew, we were in the middle of a parade replete with local dignitaries, people dressed in regional costumes, and a band. When we arrived at the cable operator's office, there was a big banner on the outside of the building that read WELCOME, MR. GEORGE BODENHEIMER, ESPN. The staff greeted us personally as we stepped out of the carriage, and once inside they welcomed us with gifts and specially prepared food. "Wow," I remember thinking to myself at one point, "this sure is a long way from sitting on a box in the back room with mom-and-pop cable operators in Biloxi, Little Rock, and Waco." But that was more than twenty years earlier and, since then the expansion of ESPN around the world had been meteoric.

This particular trip was one of the many excursions Russell Wolff and I had made together since he'd assumed the position of senior vice president of ESPN International in 2002. Russell first came to ESPN in 1997 from MTV Networks, where he had primarily worked on domestic issues. His first three years with us were in Hong Kong as vice president of our Asia-Pacific region. Then he transferred to Singapore as head of programming for ESPN STAR Sports, our joint venture with Rupert Murdoch's News Corporation, which served twenty-six countries in Asia.

Even in the early days of ESPN, we were looking at the possibilities for overseas markets. Our original efforts were handled by general counsel Andrew Brilliant, and consisted of selling American sports content to foreign broadcasters. As ESPN's top lawyer, Andy was best suited to understanding the laws and regulations of other nations. In 1989, we formally created ESPN International to take advantage of the growing satellite markets in Latin America, Asia, and Europe. In addition to selling content, we established new networks, often by leveraging resources through joint ventures. ESPN Latin America was launched in 1989, followed by ESPN Asia in 1992. By 1993, we had gained a foothold in Europe by joining Eurosport in partnership with French broadcasting giant TF1 and Canal Plus (a French premium pay network). In 1994, two-year-old ESPN Asia was incorporated into ESPN STAR Sports based in Singapore.

By the turn of the century, Russell Wolff and Christine Driessen had revised ESPN's international strategy and embarked on one that was multi-local in nature, focusing on local products with local staffs. Basically, we wanted to serve sports fans the world over in as many places as it made sense to do business. It was a big step for us, because we chose to respect individual cultures and customs by partnering with and hiring local employees rather than sending in expatriates to do everything. We also emphasized decentralized management so that each organization would have as much authority and responsibility as possible without having to contact Bristol to obtain permission for everything they wanted to do.

As the leader of ESPN International, Russell urged me to go on trips with him several times a year. "Our mission," he told me, "is to grow the ESPN brand around the world profitably, within budget, and as fast as we can. To make that happen, I need the president of the company on the ground in as many countries as possible."

"All right, Russell," I replied. "You set them up and I'll go with you."

So we began taking several international trips a year. Each was meticulously planned in advance and usually lasted from four to seven days. Wherever we were, as soon as we touched down, we were on the move. Most days, we started at seven in the morning and ended at ten at night. We visited with our affiliated cable and satellite operators, rights holders, advertisers, and potential partners. Usually, we timed our trip to coincide with a local major sporting event where we could join clients, potential customers, and dignitaries. On every trip, our main focus was to sell ESPN, to grow our business, and to visit and inspire the local ESPN people. There were a lot of "meet and greets" on these trips. And I learned to make a toast in many different languages—"Cheers," "Prost," "Yung sing," "A votre santé," "Saludos," "Cin cin," and so many others.

In 2002, we went to Europe, starting in London (ESPN's European headquarters) and then traveling to France, Spain, Italy, and Germany. In 2004, we toured Asia, beginning in Hong Kong where we joined Michael Eisner and others from Disney to see the progress of Hong Kong Disneyland, which was then under construction. From there we traveled to China and spent time with NBA officials and players as they played basketball on a goodwill mission. In Beijing, we formally kicked off China's version of *ESPN The Magazine*. ESPN had small offices in both Hong Kong and China, but we finished the trip in Singapore, where we had a staff of five hundred people working for ESPN STAR Sports.

Russell, Christine, and I went to India in 2006, where that cable operator welcomed us with that parade in Bangalore. We also had the pleasure of touring many remote areas of India where we were sometimes greeted with garlands, candles, and even fireworks. We timed that trip to coincide with a big cricket match between India and

Pakistan—and it felt like everybody in India, in every little town or big city, was following that match. Just like in the United States, we encountered passionate sports fans wherever in the world we happened to be. Sports as social currency are truly international.

These trips to Europe, to Asia, to India, and to other parts of the world had a profound impact on me, both as the president of ESPN and as a human being. From a business perspective, it was critically important for our executive team to visit our international offices. The local employees were honored that we would devote the time to fly across an ocean to meet with them personally, to shake their hands, and to build personal relationships with them. It was a big deal for me, too, because I had the opportunity to talk about what was happening with ESPN and how each of them played an important role in our success. I also made sure they knew that we were all part of the same ESPN family and that it was part of our company's culture to help them with whatever they needed. Those many interactions brought home the point, once again, that in many respects people the world over are the same. We all care about our jobs, our families, and each other.

After gaining an appreciation for what our company was doing outside the United States, I began talking about ESPN as a global sports media company. Just calling ourselves an American company with an international division really did not give our overseas people their proper due. They worked just as hard, were just as devoted, and were as much a part of ESPN as anybody in America. And my telling them so made a difference in the way they felt and how they interacted with each other and, importantly, with our Bristol-based employees. Our company started operating as a single team globally. The international press soon picked up the new phrasing and started consistently referring to ESPN as global in nature.

In my view, if a company doesn't have a workforce that reflects its customer base, it is missing opportunities to produce the best possible product. It is also putting itself at risk for making errors and not being sensitive to all people when producing that product. Therefore, a company with a global presence must have as diverse a workforce as possible. That's why, at ESPN's 2003 annual priorities meeting, we considered adding "Embrace Diversity" as a formal priority. But when we first began discussing the idea of putting this "people" item up for consideration, there was some resistance. "Wait a minute, our priorities are supposed to be about business," someone said. "Yeah, if you make people a priority, how do you ever take it off the list?" another said. "How can we possibly measure a people-related priority, anyway?" Others, however, were really passionate about diversity and wanted to embrace it wholeheartedly.

We appeared to be deadlocked on the issue when I stepped in. "You know what, I don't know what the number of priorities is going to be this year, but one of them *is going to be* diversity," I said. "So let's decide what all the others are going to be." At first, there was silence in the room, because I almost never interjected myself in such a forceful manner. But the topic was so important to me and to ESPN that I felt compelled to say something. However, I cautioned everyone that this was not something we were going to be able to check off next year and say, "Okay, now we're diverse!" We were going to have to take a long-term view of things, and it was likely going to take several years to make a significant difference in our company.

The importance of diversity in business cannot be understated. Diversity of expertise is needed, as well as diversity of thought, diversity of life experiences, and, certainly in a global corporation, diversity of geography and ethnicity. If a U.S.-based media company is going to create a Hispanic television network, the process should not start with only non-Hispanics on the team. Rather, people with expertise in Spanish-speaking countries need to be seated around the table. When we set up ESPN Latin America in 1989, for instance, we hired full-time people from the countries in which we did business.

When ESPN's ratings hit the low point in 2001, our advertising revenue naturally went down. In turn, that put pressure on the company's financials, which resulted in a detailed look at spending in every area of the company. After a review of the international department, we sent out a company-wide memo announcing that Latin America was losing money and that if we did not turn the situation around, we were going to have to take drastic action. Similar to how we handled the ratings crisis, we assembled all of our Latin America leaders, presented the facts, and asserted that we were going to have to fix this problem together. Once we explained the situation, I'm proud to say that attitudes changed quickly, everybody rallied to the cause, and over the next few years, ESPN's Latin American operations were on the road to better financial footing, ultimate profitability, and solid long-term growth.

Russell Wolff had a major hand in that turnaround. For example, he took a close look at our international *SportsCenter*s, which were not working well (especially in Latin America). Years before, when we first started *SportsCenter* outside the United States, we created a "one size fits all" version that would be broadcast throughout Latin America, Europe, and Asia. As such, it included a huge range of sports, such as soccer, cricket, NFL football, rugby, polo, and NBA basketball, to name a few. And because it was going to be used in multiple territories and in multiple languages, it was a highlight show only with no on-air talent (just voice-over). Unfortunately, the concept didn't work. People in India weren't versed in the NFL, and Latin Americans weren't particularly interested in cricket. So, by trying to make one *SportsCenter* work in *all* of the territories, it ended up not working in *any* of the territories.

In order to make *SportsCenter* work outside the United States, we went back to the roots of ESPN by making the show locally relevant, with familiar on-air talent, and, in short, more fun. One of the first non-U.S. *SportsCenter*s we produced in this way was in Buenos Aires,

Argentina (chosen, in part, to beef up the financial footing in Latin America). Heading up the Argentine office at the time was Guillermo Tabanera, who led a staff of all Latin Americans, mostly natives of Argentina. Needing to stay within budget, Guillermo rented a big house attached to a warehouse in downtown Buenos Aires and turned it into a fantastic *SportsCenter* studio.

To show our support and appreciation for everybody's hard work, Russell and I flew down for the initial broadcast, and I was particularly gratified by how proud and motivated our local employees were. They knew that *SportsCenter* was the flagship franchise at ESPN and they were deeply honored to be expanding it to their country. They were *bursting* with pride. There we were, over five thousand miles from Bristol seeing the familiar *SportsCenter* graphics and hearing the familiar *SportsCenter* theme music—only the broadcast was in Spanish. Personally, I was quite moved by all I saw that night.

Camilo Perez and Vanessa Palacio anchoring ESPN *SportsCenter* in Argentina, 2012.   *Joe Faraoni / ESPN Images*

Spreading *SportsCenter* around the world was not only good for brand growth, but it also contributed to our overall strategy of having in place the same ESPN culture wherever we might be located. We wanted fans in Argentina, for example, to feel the same way that fans in America felt about ESPN. And we wanted our employees to feel connected to Bristol while, at the same time, feeling empowered to make ESPN an expression of their own local market. However, creating a consistent culture in a globally diverse company wasn't as easy as it sounded, and it would take time to achieve.

Our strategy was fourfold. First, we brought employees to Bristol to experience the culture for themselves. Second, we sent ESPN culture carriers to our international locations to assist in any way possible. Chuck Pagano, for instance, was instrumental in the technical setup of many of ESPN's new international offices. Third, we continued to hire people in local areas whom we felt were a good fit for ESPN (those who were passionate sports fans who possessed values consistent with our own). And fourth, just as we did in Bristol, we promoted the local ESPN culture carriers. The final test on whether or not we had succeeded was when any ESPN employee from anywhere in the world visited another ESPN location anywhere in the world and could honestly say: "This feels like ESPN."

On one of our trips to Latin America, Russell Wolff and I visited ESPN's office in Mexico City. At one thirty in the afternoon, we met about forty employees for lunch at a very nice restaurant. In front of each place setting were three glasses filled with different-colored beverages. I found out later that it was a version of the popular Mexican Flag Shooter (the three colors representing the colors of Mexico's flag). It reminded me of the shooters we used to drink at the White Birch after a hard day's work in ESPN's early days, only these were larger three-ounce shot glasses. One had red tomato juice in it, the middle glass was filled with white tequila, and the third looked like green crème de menthe.

After greeting everyone, we all sat down and I spoke for a few minutes. The entire ESPN Mexico City staff was there—on-air talent, sales and marketing people, technicians, everybody. I told them how important they were to ESPN, how proud we were of their efforts, and I complimented them on the outstanding job they were doing in their homeland of Mexico. Then I picked up the middle glass of white tequila, held it up high in a toast, and said: "Here's to you and ESPN. Saludos!" And I drank it down in one gulp, like a shot.

For a moment, there was a kind of stunned silence around the room. Then everybody picked up their glasses of tequila, raised them, said "Saludos!" "Saludos!" "Saludos!" and drank them down in one shot. Then I sat down to some murmured laughter and applause.

No one had told me that, by tradition, our Mexican colleagues *sip* this tequila. So, being polite, everyone had followed my lead.

The restaurant's waiters were confused and didn't know what to do. So they quickly went around and refilled everybody's empty glass with more white tequila, which we sipped for the rest of the lunch. As you might imagine, that turned out to be one of the most lively and spirited luncheons on record.

Less Expensive than a Cup of Coffee

I was on a conference call with Michael Eisner and several other Disney executives who were asking me questions about ESPN's annual budget when I proudly announced, "Next year, our affiliate fee is going over $1 per subscriber per month for the first time." A dollar would certainly be a milestone in the cable industry.

"What's the big deal?" asked one of Eisner's lieutenants. "We get three dollars for a soft drink at the theme parks."

At first, I was taken aback, because they didn't seem to understand the significance of what I had just told them. "Well, it's unprecedented," I said. "Nobody else gets a fee like that."

I stewed about that comment for several days after the phone call ended. Finally, it dawned on me. If you put the price of ESPN in context with other consumer products, it's a fantastic bargain. At that time (1999), a simple cup of coffee at Starbucks was more expensive than an entire month's worth of ESPN programming. A turkey sandwich at a deli was more expensive. They even charged more for a slice of pizza at a shopping mall food court. So when you looked at it in that way, ESPN was a great value. Where else could you watch sports for that price? Heck, if you took a family of four out to dinner and a movie, you were going to spend a lot more money.

After I had this eureka moment, my first thought was to pass the analogy on to the affiliate sales force, where I had spent so many years of my career. They were the people on the front lines who were always getting beaten up by cable operators about our rates. So I walked into an affiliate sales meeting with a cup of Starbucks and put it up on the lectern. "Guess how much this cost me?" I said with a big grin. "Almost twice the price of having ESPN in your home for a month! Now, that puts things in perspective, doesn't it? So don't get defensive about our rates—*ever!* Be confident in the value of our product." And for years thereafter, when traveling, I would send them emails. "Hey, I'm in Cincinnati. Just bought a cup of coffee. Guess how much it cost? $2.67!" They knew what I meant. Over the years, though, my cost of coffee comparison wore out, so I switched to other items. "I was in the Fort Lauderdale airport yesterday. I bought a bottle of water, a turkey sandwich, and a cup of fruit—$18!"

ESPN's rate officially went over $1 in 1998 as a result of the first increase after we acquired a full season of *Sunday Night Football*. From 1998 to 2003, our fee went from $1.07 to $2.67 and, during that time, I tried to smooth over the 20 percent increases by personally calling the top twenty cable company CEOs. But after five straight annual increases, Jim Robbins of Cox Communications got mad. "ESPN's price increases are too much," he said. "We're not paying it. This has to stop."

Our dispute began privately with Cox threatening to pull ESPN off its cable systems, and us insisting on another 20 percent increase. But things escalated to a new level when Cox went public by stating in national interviews that ESPN was driving up the cost of basic cable. We countered with advertising spots on ESPN Radio stating that Cox wanted to take away the listener's sports. Then the dispute really escalated. Both sides took out full-page ads in major newspapers across the country and launched competing websites advocating our respective positions.

Jim Robbins and I then held dueling press conferences in New York and Washington, DC. He stated that ESPN was already the most expensive sports channel and that our prices were "way out of whack."

"You can't talk about price if you don't talk about value," I countered. "ESPN is much more valuable than any other network Cox carries on its cable systems." I backed up my statement with year after year of industry surveys confirming ESPN's value. We also had the Disney lobbying staff going into full gear. Finally, everything came to a head when the U.S. Senate held hearings on cable industry rate increases.

Overall, this was the most visible dispute we'd ever had with a major operator (Cox was then the fourth largest in the United States, with 6.2 million subscribers). The actual mechanics of the back-and-forth weren't really much different than they had been in previous years. What was different was that emotions were elevated, because we were on a public stage that involved the media, Congress, and the FCC. The stakes were high.

Eventually, and out of the glare of the media lights, Jim Robbins and I met privately for serious talks. Personally, I always had a sense that things would work out, because Jim and I had maintained a solid personal friendship for many years. Those talks echoed the way I generally tried to negotiate, in that I simply treated everybody with respect and did not play games. I also tried to be straightforward and truthful. If ESPN couldn't do something the other side wanted, I said so. If they asked for something that was possible, I said we'd consider it (and we did). I listened, attempted to be a voice of reason, and avoided being adversarial. I believed being respectful of other people helps in negotiating good business deals. It's not always only about the money.

The dispute ended up like any negotiation that ends up well—both sides gave a little and realized that we had more in common working together than apart. While still defending our position and the value of ESPN, we took what I considered to be the high road. We modified our pricing in 2004 by dropping down to a 10 percent increase. The crisis was resolved, Cox's executives felt they had won, and we let them declare victory. Our 10 percent increase was on top of $2.67, so we were getting twenty-six cents while most of the other networks received far less. Overall, ESPN had just come through an extended period of unprecedented pricing in the business and, in the long run, we had significantly raised the bar, set the stage for ESPN's next fifteen to twenty years of growth, and distanced ourselves from our competitors. Looking at it that way, our compromise turned out to be a big win.

One of the lessons I took from the Cox dispute was similar to what I had told our affiliate sales force when reminding them that ESPN cost less than a cup of coffee. Business leaders must have confidence in the value of their products and make those products the best in the business. This is particularly important if they're going to charge a premium price. That's really how I felt when we were battling Cox on a national stage, when I was testifying in front of Congress, and when I was sitting across the bargaining table. I believed in the value of our products, and nobody was going to tell me that ESPN was not worth the price we were charging.

As president of ESPN, I delivered that message wherever I went. Even when I was in Washington lobbying members of Congress, I let them know that ESPN was on the top of the heap as far as cable networks were concerned. During the Cox dispute, I met several times with Senator John McCain of Arizona who, as chairman of the Senate Commerce, Science, and Transportation Committee, actually called the hearings. Even though Senator McCain was one of the toughest critics of our pricing, he watched ESPN all the time. McCain loves sports. He's a boxing fan. The pricing issues were not easy, but first chatting about boxing and Arizona sports helped ease the tension between us. Walking the halls of Congress, I always referred to ESPN.com on my phone so, when I met with another senator or congressman, I was knowledgeable about the upcoming games in their state. "Hey, Senator, your Michigan team is 6–3 and they've got a big game this weekend," I'd say. "Oh, yeah!" the senator would reply. "Big game Saturday! They should win." By starting each conversation with sports, I was able to ease right into the serious business issues.

Sports is social currency. And every state in America is a sports state.

Through the years, I frequently attended annual owners meetings of the major professional sports leagues. The NFL usually went to a resort for several days, brought all the families, and invited ESPN and their other television network partners to attend. The NBA, Major League Baseball, and the NHL held similar meetings, most of the time for only a day or two. When invited to their meetings, I often made a presentation to provide an update on ESPN or address any pending issues.

The owners of the National Hockey League, for example, were always knocking ESPN for not showing as many highlights of their sport on *SportsCenter* as we did for football, basketball, or baseball. And often, they were quite vocal about it.

In June 2002, NHL Commissioner Gary Bettman invited me to make a presentation at the NHL Board of Governors meeting. At that time, ESPN had a four-year contract to broadcast NHL games so, of course, I accepted his invitation and asked *SportsCenter* managing director Steve Anderson to attend with me. We planned to address the "highlight issue" head-on in our presentation.

The meeting took place at a hotel in Toronto. Two representatives from every team were seated around a large U-shaped table with a microphone in front of each individual. Accompanying staff were in the background, so there were about a hundred people in the room when Steve and I began our presentation.

Using PowerPoint graphics, well-researched statistics, and video highlights, we discussed ESPN's history with the NHL and made a solid case to show that we did, indeed, provide a great deal of hockey coverage and an appropriate amount of highlights. Our presentation lasted about forty-five minutes and, after we were done, I stood up at the front of the U-shaped table, thanked everybody for their time, and asked for comments or questions.

There was an unusually long pause as people just looked around. Finally, Brian Burke, then the general manager of the Vancouver Canucks, leaned forward and turned on his microphone. "You guys don't do anything for the NHL," he said. "I think ESPN is shit!" Then he flipped off the microphone.

Sitting right next to Brian was Bill Wirtz, the longtime owner of the Chicago Blackhawks. Bill smiled and leaned forward, clicked on his microphone, and said: "I think ESPN is fantastic! And I love what you guys are doing for the NHL."

Then there was another extraordinarily long pause as everybody waited to see what my response would be. In that moment, my choices were limited. I knew that sports owners are very opinionated and they don't like BS, so I didn't think it would be appropriate to simply thank Bill for his compliment. Nor did I want to take the bait from Brian's body slam and react emotionally.

So I finally said, "Well, there you have it, gentlemen. We're somewhere between shit and fantastic. You all will have to decide for yourselves where we fall in that span."

That got a big laugh and ended the presentation.

Wow

Construction on ESPN's vast new digital production center was more than half complete in late 2001 when Chuck Pagano (head of technology and engineering) dropped by my office to give me an update. At 120,000 square feet in size, the facility was going to be one of the largest of its kind in the television industry. Our plans also called for it to be equipped with the latest, most exciting state-of-the-art technology. As a matter of fact, we had already put out requests for price quotes on the hardware.

"George, we've got a problem," Chuck said.

"Oh?" I replied.

"Yeah. High-definition television [HDTV or high def] is coming soon and our plans currently call for standard definition."

"Okay," I said. "Well, we approved this plan just a year or two ago and had to jump through all sorts of hoops to make it happen."

"I know, I know," replied Chuck. "But if we build it that way, it will be out of date in a couple of years. I'm telling you that this technology is moving faster than anybody ever dreamed it would. And high def *will* catch on."

I really knew only the basics when it came to the technical aspects of our business. That's partly why one of my first moves as president of ESPN was to put Chuck Pagano in charge of technology for the company. I trusted him implicitly. If he said we needed to go in a new technical direction in order to be the best, that was good enough for me, even if it was something as significant as what he was now suggesting. Chuck was always up on all the latest technological advancements, and his creative mind was able to look down the road and envision what it would mean for ESPN. As Pagano liked to say, he was always looking to apply the "Wow" in technology. If it wowed Chuck, I knew it would wow sports fans. So whenever he spoke, I listened.

"Okay, Chuck," I said. "Let's get the team together and solve the problem."

We didn't take very long to make a decision once everybody was assembled and the facts were presented. First, it was obvious that the crystal-clear picture associated with high-definition television was going to be a game changer. And it was more than reasonable to believe that once sports fans were exposed to it, they were going to demand it. Second, Chuck informed us that development of HD in the industry was being hampered because there was no consensus about how to move forward. "All the broadcast networks are looking at it," he said. "But there are two formats and the engineers can't agree on which one to make standard." Third, Pagano made the key point that another reason for the delay was that flat-panel HD television sets, which were needed to display the new picture, were not yet widely available in the marketplace. "But everybody knows we're moving to flat-panel high def sets," he said. "It's just a matter of time."

Then our executive team began probing the risks involved in a midstream construction change like we were contemplating. "Isn't it a little late to make a major change like this to the digital center plan?"

"No," Chuck replied. "I want us to get out in front of the curve and lead everybody else."

"But aren't all of our mobile production trucks outfitted with standard-definition equipment?"

"Yes. They'll all have to be re-equipped to accommodate high def, along with everything else now planned for in the digital center."

"Well, how much more is that going to cost?"

"I don't have the exact numbers yet, but it will be a significant amount."

"Where is that money going to come from? It's not in the current budget."

"Listen, I'll handle the technical specifications," said Chuck. "You guys work with Disney on the budgeting."

"Hey, what happens if we choose one format and the rest of the industry chooses the other? Are we going to be stuck with a Betamax system while everybody else goes to VHS? You know, like Sony back in the '80s with cassette recorders?"

"No, no, that's not going to happen," said Chuck, reassuringly. "We'll make the right choice and ESPN will set the standard for the rest of the industry."

After a couple of hours, we reached a consensus. Because we were steadfast in our mission to provide the best possible product to sports fans, and because we intended to continue as leaders in our field, we had to move to high def. There was no question it was the right thing to do. It was right for ESPN and it was right for the future. So ESPN's executive team chose to make that decision *now* and figure out the rest *later.* "All right," I said, concluding the meeting. "Let's do it."

While the team and I worked with Disney on revising, resubmitting, and getting approval on a new budget, Chuck Pagano went to work. He realized that there was real potential with this project to both reinvent ESPN's business and, at the same time, significantly impact our industry. Because high def was brand-new, he also had the benefit of starting with an open book. And Chuck was such a free thinker that he was not encumbered by the past ways of doing things.

Through detailed research and discussion with peers in the industry, Pagano's team explored all the ins and outs of HDTV's two competing technical formats. The "interlace" format, they concluded, was based too much on the old analog technique and produced poorer resolution than the "progressive" format. CBS and NBC had already started down the path to high def with interlace, but progressive produced superior motion clarity. As Chuck explained it to me, "If you're watching NASCAR with interlace, the wheels on a race car are blurred, because you only get half the resolution. With progressive, you can see the slots in the wheels turning clearly. Oh and by the way, George, the new flat-panel televisions are all going to display images using the progressive format."

ESPN's differentiator, then, was to use the progressive format for HD television. Once that decision was made, Pagano started working within the industry's engineering community, which was far more of a support structure for each other than a competitive crowd. While ABC engineers were already planning to use the progressive format, Chuck also spoke to his counterparts at Fox and told them why ESPN was going to use it. "Join us," he said. "It'll be far better for everybody in the long run." Eventually, word got around that "Pagano was going to use progressive" and, pretty soon, everybody was calling ESPN to learn more.

Sharing that kind of information with the rest of the industry could have been viewed by some executives as poor judgment or "giving away secrets." But I didn't see it that way. Chuck was an established leader in the industry. He was making sure that others didn't choose the wrong format, which might hinder the overall progress of high def in the business. And besides, Pagano's team was so far ahead on the detailed research, and ESPN was so fast in taking action, that I knew we were going to be way ahead of our slower-moving competition.

A couple days before ESPN's new HD digital center opened for business on June 7, 2004, Chuck gave me a personal tour of the facility and, man, was I impressed. The place was gleaming. There were three high-def studios and more than $100 million in new technology that existed nowhere else in the world. So imagine my surprise at Chuck's answer when I asked him what he was most proud of. He walked over and opened up a coat closet. "What are we looking at here, Chuck?" I asked. "This is a closet."

"I know, George," he said. "You asked me what I'm most proud of and this is it. When we were building this place, I asked our team what they needed most, and they told me, 'A place to hang our coats.'"

I'll never forget that. And the honest truth is that I was more impressed with Chuck's answer to my simple question than all the fancy equipment in the new digital center. You can invest in all the technology you want, but it's your people who make it work. Chuck Pagano listened to and really loved the people on his team, which was one reason he's a great leader.

Appropriately, ESPN's first high-def broadcast from the new digital center was the 6 p.m. *SportsCenter*. I was standing outside the studio with thirty or forty executives and members of the press who had gathered for the occasion. The atmosphere was festive and upbeat. But about thirty minutes into the show, I heard somebody say over the PA speaker, "Okay, we're going to videotape."

"Videotape?" I thought. "What's going on? We're all digital now." It turned out that all the computer servers had failed. Fortunately, they went down one by one, so there was time for action before we went off the air completely. Without missing a beat, Norby Williamson, *SportsCenter*'s top executive, and Bill Lamb, Pagano's top lieutenant, gave the orders to start running videotape. The transition was seamless and the viewing audience had no idea that anything had gone wrong. That gave ESPN's technical team a chance to take action without interrupting anything. Bill later told me that when the system went down, "My whole life flashed before my eyes. But we got everything back up and running—and then we all went downstairs and broke open a couple of bottles of champagne to celebrate. Heck, Chuck didn't even mention the server failure."

"First mover advantage" is important in business, and being the first sports media company to go high def turned out to be a tremendous success for ESPN. Sports fans loved the better pictures and, as a result, our ratings and ad revenue increased, and our affiliates were ecstatic. Additionally, because sports fans wanted to see games in high definition, there was more demand for HD flat-panel television sets. After a few years, the head of the Consumer Electronics Association not only said that ESPN helped sell more TV sets than anybody, he gave us credit for "changing the track of HD on this planet." Pushing into new technologies had always been a part of the ESPN culture—and always would be as long as I was heading up the company.

By being the first major network to launch HDTV, we not only gave ourselves about a five-year head start over everybody else, we demonstrated how the technology could work successfully. And that opened the floodgates. Pretty soon, everybody was converting to high def. And to think it all started when Chuck Pagano came into my office and simply told me we had a problem.

On November 15, 2004, I arrived home from a busy day at the office, had dinner with my family, and settled in front of the television with my wife to watch *Monday Night Football* (*MNF*). That evening's game pitted the Philadelphia Eagles against the Dallas Cowboys in Dallas. About a year earlier, I had been named president of ABC Sports along with ESPN, and we were managing them as two separate entities with separate business models and separate personnel. If I wasn't actually at an *MNF* game (which I often was), I always watched the broadcast.

Monday Night Football, the crown jewel of ABC Sports, had an iconic opening with Hank Williams Jr. singing a song that asked: "Are you ready for some football?" Each week, the show's producer, Fred

Gaudelli, created an entertaining video, referred to as an "open," to precede it, one that was both topical and designed to capture the audience. *[Fred had also started his career in the ESPN mailroom and had grown into one of the top sports television producers in the business.]* A month earlier, ABC's new drama, *Desperate Housewives*, had aired for the first time. Ranked number two in prime time, it was a huge hit for the network. Looking to capitalize on that success, this week's football open was going to parody the show.

Although these opens were a point of pride for our network, I did not make it a habit, nor did I feel the need to review them beforehand. Actually, no one outside the staff involved in producing *Monday Night Football* ever saw them before they were aired. So as the clock ticked down to 9 p.m., I was looking forward to seeing what the team had come up with this week.

I had no idea what was coming.

The scene was an empty locker room with Eagles star wide receiver Terrell Owens about to go out on the field when he is confronted by Nicollette Sheridan (in character as divorcee Edie Britt from *Desperate Housewives*). Wearing only a white towel and saying she had just taken a "long, hot shower," Edie asks Owens to skip the game for her. After he refuses and starts to walk away, she further entices him by dropping her towel to the floor. (Sheridan was shown only from the back.) Finally relenting, Owens grins and says, "Aw, hell, the team's going to have to win without me." Then Sheridan jumps into his arms and they twirl around in glee. Cue the Hank Williams song, "Are You Ready for Some Football?"

After a moment of silence, I looked over at my wife and said, "Wow!" And before I knew it, my phone rang. It was Chris LaPlaca in our communications department. "George, this is blowing up on us!" he said excitedly. "The press wants comments! We need to get in front of this quickly." I spent the rest of the night on the phone, either fielding calls or making them myself. Although one NFL owner

Monday Night Football opening video with Terrell Owens and Nicollette Sheridan, 2004. *ABC*

told me he loved the open, virtually everybody else was concerned or upset about it—and the firestorm that ensued over the next several days was something to behold.

Dan Rooney, owner of the Pittsburgh Steelers, called the skit "an out-and-out disgrace." Chicago Bears Coach Lovie Smith said it was "pretty close to pornographic," and in a congressional hearing Senator John McCain labeled it a "disgraceful performance." Other comments reported in the media included the words *trashy, smutty, degenerate*, and *disgusting*. Calls and letters flooded into ABC headquarters using the same invective and expressing outrage. A small percentage directly addressed the issue of race. More than fifty thousand complaints flooded the Federal Communications Commission. The NFL was particularly troubled because just nine months earlier at the Super Bowl halftime show, Janet Jackson's "wardrobe malfunction" had created all sorts of problems. And ABC executives were concerned, because the FCC had fined CBS $550,000 for broadcasting an indecent act. It was the largest fine ever levied against a television company. *[The FCC action was later overturned and CBS never had to pay the fine.]*

In my position as president of ESPN and ABC Sports, I knew something like this could occur at a moment's notice and we would be in the hot seat. After all, we were always on the air, always visible, and we never knew when something or somebody was going to become a lightning rod. Because it came with the job, we had to be prepared to take the heat and, in this case, that was primarily my role.

The next day, I dealt with all of our constituents—either personally or on the phone. During those conversations, I could have pointed to the *Monday Night Football* production crew and said it was not my fault, but I would never do that. Rather, I spoke with my boss, Disney President Bob Iger, and simply explained the circumstances. Being a veteran of ABC Sports, he said he completely understood the situation and expected me to manage through it. I also spoke with ABC executives, team owners, NFL Commissioner Paul Tagliabue, and Disney's Washington lobbyists. Subsequently, on the communications front, later that day we (ABC Sports) issued a formal public apology stating that the intro video was "inappropriate and unsuitable for our *Monday Night Football* audience."

After the firestorm died down, I knew I had to do something to prevent a similar incident in the future. But I didn't want to get into the habit of overseeing the production elements of any program. I just didn't have time for it. And I certainly didn't want to stifle the creativity of Fred Gaudelli, who had assembled for *Monday Night Football* one of the best teams in the business. In the end, Fred and I simply increased our communications prior to Monday nights, and that did the trick. Sometimes our conversation was as short as Fred saying, "George, there's nothing this week that is even remotely controversial." And I trusted his judgment.

The Terrell Owens–Nicollette Sheridan–*Monday Night Football* skit turned out to be a tempest in a teapot. It was a big story for a week, but it did not have any long-lasting business significance. After an in-depth investigation, the FCC concluded "the material in question [was] not patently offensive, and thus, not indecent." There were no fines levied against ABC.

By the way, I didn't get to watch the game at all that night. But it turned out to be quite entertaining as the Eagles beat the Cowboys 49–21. Terrell Owens caught a fifty-nine-yard pass for a touchdown on the second play of the game. He scored three touchdowns that night.

Season of the Fan

I t was quite a party. Four full floors at the ESPN Zone restaurant in the heart of Times Square. A band, the Dallas Cowboys Cheerleaders, and a red carpet welcomed some of the biggest names in sports—athletes and coaches like Carl Lewis, Nancy Kerrigan, Franco Harris, Richard Petty, Amanda Beard, Sarah Hughes, Bill Walsh, and Scotty Bowman, to name just a few. There were fifteen hundred VIP guests among the thousands of people who attended. We invited executives from all the major sports leagues, cable companies, and our advertising partners. ESPN people were there en masse, including founder Bill Rasmussen, and former presidents Chet Simmons, Bill Grimes, Roger Werner, and Steve Bornstein. Earlier that day, we rang the opening bell on the New York Stock Exchange. For that honor, accompanying me were Bob Ley, Chris LaPlaca, and ESPN's longest-tenured employee, Cheryl Therriault. In Bristol, we broke out the champagne, shot off fireworks, and gave out gifts.

It all happened on September 7, 2004, twenty-five years to the day that ESPN first went on the air.

After a quarter century in operation, ESPN was a presence in ninety million American homes and sitting atop the sports media landscape.

Through ESPN International, we also operated thirty networks in 192 countries and territories around the world. We were a profitable multi-billion-dollar company with one of the most recognizable brands in the world, and it was time to celebrate. After all, having fun was part of our culture.

ESPN twenty-fifth anniversary print advertisement thanking the city of Bristol, CT, 2004. *Rich Arden / ESPN Images*

Even with twenty-five years of growth, ESPN's culture was still intact. Our head of marketing, Lee Ann Daly, who joined the company from the world of New York advertising, was impressed with how different ESPN was from other major companies. As a passionate sports fan, for instance, Lee Ann felt she could be herself at ESPN, in part because she was surrounded by colleagues who were equally or even more passionate about sports. People were respected for being the best in their areas of expertise, and because of that, decisions were pushed down and made at relatively lower levels of the company. "Decision making where the rubber meets the road makes people more accountable for their own work," said Lee Ann. "Ultimately you get a better product." Our marketing leader also pointed out that silos and turf wars were rare at ESPN. "Turf doesn't really exist here," she said, "because we run lean and people have to accept help and work across department lines. That makes us good team players and helps us better serve sports fans."

Anticipating ESPN's twenty-fifth anniversary, Lee Ann came to me in 2003 with an idea that she and the marketing department had developed. They proposed to focus our yearlong marketing efforts very specifically on fans. "After all, that is our mission," said Lee Ann. "They are the ones who have made ESPN successful since day one. So let's dedicate our twenty-fifth anniversary year as the 'Season of the Fan.' We can dream up all kinds of great things with a theme like that. And I think people will pay attention." One of the easiest decisions I ever made at ESPN was to say, "Okay, do it."

Early on, our marketing and advertising sales departments worked with several of our best partners to market the anniversary, including the right to use ESPN's logo. Gatorade manufactured more than a million bottles with an "ESPN The Flavor" drink. And it was appropriate that Anheuser-Busch, with whom we'd had a strong relationship from day one, came on big to celebrate with us. They produced three hundred million cans of Bud Light with the following prominently displayed on each: "ESPN 25: Bud Light salutes ESPN for satisfying our thirst for all things sport. On behalf of fans everywhere, we raise our glasses to the next 25!"

More specific to our "Season of the Fan" initiative was the creation of a Facebook-like social media website. All the sports fans who wanted to participate were given their own page to share photographs, videos, and text back and forth to each other. It sounds old hat now, but when we launched the site, Facebook (which was unknown to us) was in its infancy at Harvard. *[Facebook was founded on February 4, 2004.]* Toyota also donated SUVs for ESPN to travel around the country and shoot videos of fans at all kinds of sporting venues, including high school, college, and professional games, rodeos, pee wee hockey rinks, tailgate parties, and just about anything else you could think of. Each vehicle became a mobile recording unit manned by a producer and a camera operator.

The videos were then uploaded to our "Season of the Fan" website where everybody could click and watch them. Again, this was a full year before YouTube came on the scene and two years before Google snapped it up for $1.6 billion. *[YouTube was founded on February 14, 2005.]* Thinking ahead, ESPN also secured permission from participating fans to use their pictures and videos in the body of our twenty-fifth-anniversary marketing campaign. So we were able to feature ESPN sports fans in just about every venue we had. It was a lot of fun, a true celebration, and it perfectly captured ESPN's relationship with fans.

Additionally, our marketing department wanted to build on the notion that Judy Fearing and Wieden+Kennedy had started fifteen years earlier to remind everybody at ESPN that we were sports fans, too. So a sister program to "Season of the Fan" was instituted that year called "ESPN: World's Biggest Sports Fan." Buttons and T-shirts were handed out, our people began talking it up, and the next thing you knew it had become a mantra of the organization. I even found myself opening just about every address to ESPN employees with a hearty, "Hello, sports fans!"

———

Right about the time we were celebrating our twenty-fifth anniversary birthday bash in Times Square, Artie Bulgrin began talking about the results of a big research study his department had been conducting for some years. It began in the aftermath of the 2001 ratings crisis when we were concerned about the effect of digital media on television (our core business). In a great example of ESPN people working together, the study was initiated after our head of advertising sales, Ed Erhardt, asked Artie for help. "You know, if we could prove that there is incremental audience coming from the emergence of digital," said Ed, "it would be a big deal for us from an advertising perspective."

Essentially, the research department study had predicted high rates of growth in new technology and related digital businesses, including the advent of powerful new media and devices such as smartphones. At that time, the Internet was viable and mobile phones were becoming wildly popular, although it would be several years before Apple released its first iPhone. *[The first-generation iPhone came out on June 29, 2007.]* Artie's study also proved beyond any doubt that the use of digital media was incremental to television rather than at its expense. In other words, media use was *not* the zero-sum game that our industry had originally feared. Actually, we found that people who used ESPN's digital content were by far our heaviest television viewers.

With this critically important study, ESPN became one of the first media companies to understand that the growth of digital media had real potential to *expand* individual interest and, of course, business far beyond television. As soon as our leadership team was fully informed about the research department's study, we took action by implementing three new strategies. First, we made it a business priority to become more aggressive in growing our audience across all platforms, especially Internet and mobile. Second, we charged Ed Erhardt and his sales management team to educate our sales staff about, and begin selling, multimedia. Third, and perhaps most important, we decided to formally update ESPN's mission.

Marketing led the charge to revise our current mission statement, which had been written in 1993 before Disney bought us. For an initial draft, the marketing department built on the momentum they had created from "Season of the Fan," and also employed wording that was originally contained in Wieden+Kennedy's 1994 white paper. Once a good draft statement was generated, it was then reviewed and discussed by our senior management team.

Over the course of a month, we met to share ideas, debate, and reach a consensus. It wasn't a hard decision to adopt the revised mission. After all, we knew that media habits were changing rapidly, and ESPN needed to change right along with them. At the end of the process, ESPN's new 2005 mission read:

To serve sports fans wherever sports are watched, listened to, discussed, debated, read about or played.

While we were at it, we also updated our ESPN values and separated them from the previous longer-worded mission statement:

People are our most valuable resource, and care and respect for employees and each other will always be at the heart of our operations. We embrace diversity to best serve all sports fans worldwide, and we are passionately committed to teamwork, quality, creativity, integrity, the aggressive pursuit of new ideas, audience growth and building shareholder value.

Six years later, when the world witnessed an explosion of handheld devices, we chose to revise our mission statement once again—largely because we didn't want anybody in the company to be confused. When a new technological device was released, one that had the potential to be a useful product for sports fans, we didn't want anybody sitting around saying, "Gee, I wonder if we're going to serve that new device. I hope our manager calls a meeting soon and tells us what to do."

Rather, we wanted everybody at ESPN to know that our goal was *always* to produce a great product for every new device that came out—and that we wanted to do so rapidly. In other words, we wanted our employees to feel enabled to act on their own initiative. That's power for a company. So in July 2011, ESPN's mission was revised again to read very succinctly:

To Serve Sports Fans. Anytime. Anywhere.

That year, we began putting the ESPN mission and values on the backs of the annual priority cards. And we continued to produce them with the holes already punched so people could wear them with the ID/security badges, if they wished to do so.

After ESPN wrote our first mission statement back in the early 1990s, I sometimes had the impression that people viewed it as just another piece of paper to put in their drawers and forget about. That was unacceptable to me. And now that I was president of the company, I intended to see that our revised mission was driven home with every constituent we had—our distributors, our advertisers, our customers, and, most important, our people. My dream was to make sure that every one of our employees, all seven thousand of them, understood what they were charged with doing every day *and* that they were empowered to take action. I can't imagine anything more valuable to a business leader.

Along those lines, we didn't just hand out the mission statement and say, "Okay, we're done." Over a couple of years, we also set several priorities to get everybody in the company moving. For instance, after our success with "Season of the Fan," the marketing department kept working on brand expansion and developed a set of "brand values." So we added the priority "Integrate ESPN brand values into our decision-making process."

Disney had drilled into us that developing and nurturing your brand is never over. But that idea was really brought home to me when we invited Rishad Tobaccowala to speak at one of our priority-setting meetings. Among the many important things Rishad said to us, as a pioneer in the field of digital marketing and sales, was the simple yet powerful statement, "Brand is the ultimate navigator." When I heard that for the first time, I immediately related it to the technological changes our industry was witnessing. It was not just about television anymore. People were now surfing the web, the competition was only a click away, and sports fans are drawn to brands they like and trust. So the ESPN brand had to be strong to attract people as they navigated their way through a sea of digital choices.

In its ongoing quest to strengthen ESPN's brand, our marketing department (led by Lee Ann Daly and Aaron Taylor in consultation with Wieden+Kennedy) came up with a very creative idea to support our priority of integrating ESPN's brand values into our decision-making process. They decided to print them on a baseball and give one to every employee. By 2005, you couldn't go anywhere on the Bristol campus without seeing one of those baseballs. They were very effective. Our advertising people even took them on sales calls and gave them out to clients. Here, in part, is what was printed on the ball:

The ESPN Brand isn't kept in a box, or a safe, or owned by some crazy sports collector.

Like this ball, it's owned by you and is in your hands.

Respect a sports fan's knowledge.

Surprise them, entertain them, and always give them something to talk about.

Our brand is the FAN's perception of us—

It's what they think or feel when they see the letters ESPN—

Everything we do—whether it's a program, a movie, a commercial, a product, a service, a press release—can alter or reinforce the FAN's perception of who we are.

ESPN: The world's biggest sports FAN.

A company's brand is critical in an environment with rapid technological innovation, because such change constantly alters how fans can access the product. That sentiment drove two more collaborations between ESPN's research and marketing departments not long after the Brand Baseball was distributed. In the first effort, Artie Bulgrin and Katie Lacey (who had succeeded Lee Ann Daly as head of marketing) assembled a group of people from across the company to define what our brand stood for and articulate it in one sentence. They rolled it out at the priorities meeting in May 2006 and, shortly thereafter, to the entire company. I was particularly proud of their work, because this one statement served to remind everybody about what truly was the core of our company. And it simplified for our employees the sometimes confusing topic of just what a brand really is. ESPN's "Brand Promise" read:

Sports (what we do) with Authority (how we do it) and Personality (what sets us apart).

What that meant was immediately understandable to every ESPN employee. If it happens in sports, whether it's in Brazil, the United States, Beijing, London, or wherever we operate, ESPN is all over it.

More specifically, *Authority* means that fans value and rely on ESPN's expertise and knowledge; that they trust ESPN's integrity as an independent, objective source; and that ESPN is authentic and true to sports in a way that cannot be imitated. *Personality* conveys several important facts about our company. First, ESPN is known for its humor, wit, and originality. Second, ESPN's passion for sports is apparent in the energy and enthusiasm displayed on all our platforms. And third, ESPN cares about the community of sports fans (regardless of age, gender, or nationality) and the social bond that sports enables.

The brand promise simplified things for our employees.

The next collaboration between research and marketing involved what we called a "Deprivation" study, which, I must admit, yielded some amazing revelations about ESPN and our fans. We selected sixty avid fans (ethnically diverse, and across different age groups) and took away their ESPN for two weeks. We had three objectives for the study: (1) to get a vivid illustration of consumer connection to our brand; (2) to identify "blind spots" (where fans go in place of ESPN); and (3) to learn how to entice viewers to use our other media platforms (additional to television). Each fan filled out periodic online surveys and kept video, photo, and audio journals throughout the two weeks.

In general, they all missed ESPN. We were not just a media outlet to them, but an ingrained part of their everyday lives. In place of ESPN, our selected fans turned to a variety of alternatives. "I have to go to four or five different websites to get the same amount of in-depth coverage," noted one person. Actually, for part of the study, we exposed half of the participants to ESPN platforms *other* than television. One enthusiastic fan summed up the group's consensus by saying, "These new ways of experiencing ESPN that you're having me try are really great!" Our conclusion was that consumers weren't using our additional platforms, in part, because they hadn't been exposed to them enough.

Perhaps the most striking outcome of being without ESPN for two weeks was the personal impact it had on the fans. "This is incredibly difficult," said one person after only a few days. "I am simply dying without my ESPN." The most acute pain points were live events, such as *Monday Night Football* and college football games. "You mean I can't watch the Texas Tech game? Oh, my God!" Some of the participants actually experienced withdrawal symptoms much like someone quitting an addiction.

Artie Bulgrin studied the psychology of deprivation to see if what he was seeing was normal. *Deprivation*, he learned, is defined as: "the act or process of removing something normally present and usually essential for mental or physical well-being." Moreover, the four faces of "deprivation" had emerged among our ESPN study participants: Irritability: "*I am used to having my information at my fingertips. Now I don't, and it's like cutting out a part of my brain.*" Depression: "*I've been sleeping to avoid the agony of not being able to watch* Mike and Mike." Desperation: "*I am sweating and getting light-headed.*" and Hallucination: "*This is the final week and I've been seeing floating ESPN logos everywhere!*"

"Being without ESPN on TV is torture to the nth degree," said one of the fans. "It's like having your right arm removed with a pair of pliers. I'm taking it one day at a time."

Al Michaels for Oswald
the Lucky Rabbit

In June 2004, I took a couple of days off so my wife and I could go out of town for a long weekend. When I sat down for breakfast that Monday morning and opened the sports section of the newspaper, there was an article about ABC's television coverage of a three-way sudden-death play-off during Sunday's final round of the Buick Open golf tournament. At 7 p.m., the network had cut away in the middle of the first play-off hole between Sergio García, Padraig Harrington, and Rory Sabbatini to air a rerun of *America's Funniest Home Videos*. Fortunately, ESPN interrupted *Baseball Tonight* to show live shots on the greens at the second and third play-off holes, including Sergio García's winning putt. As president of ABC Sports, I would have been directly involved in that breakaway decision had I not been out of town. "Uh-oh," I thought. "What a day to take off!"

When I called into the office, I was told we were getting tons of negative feedback from golf fans. Then I received a call from PGA Commissioner Tim Finchem, who was understandably upset about what had happened. But Tim was a cool customer and, because of our good relationship, we were able to talk things out. I apologized for what had happened and promised to call him back with a more detailed explanation after speaking with the producers and programmers involved. It turned out that as 7 p.m. approached and it was clear the tournament was going to continue beyond that time, ABC network people were on the phone pressing the ABC Sports staff to agree to the switch. Unfortunately, the incorrect decision was reached and we switched to *America's Funniest Home Videos*.

Sports fans had invested time in that golfing event and wanted to see who would win the play-off. After many years at ESPN, I had learned that we needed to respect their wishes. But I wasn't in town that day and I had delegated the decision, so I had to suck it up and assume responsibility and protect our people with Finchem, my boss, and the public. But in the end, I made sure we never cut away from a live ABC sporting event again.

Back then, it was a bit tricky wearing dual hats as president of both ESPN and ABC Sports. I had to pay much more attention to ABC Sports programming on the weekend than I ever did at ESPN. If something ran long on ESPN, we'd just start *SportsCenter* late or put the scheduled game on ESPN2 for a while. But at ABC, there was always pressure to get off the air on time to make way for the regularly scheduled programming. And for good reason, because local network affiliates had a lot of advertising revenue at stake, and the network wanted to keep their prime-time schedule in place.

That dual role also put me in the middle of a string of major decisions that happened in rapid-fire succession between 2005 and 2006. It all began shortly after a major corporate shuffle at The Walt Disney Company. On March 13, 2005, it was announced that Bob Iger would succeed Michael Eisner as CEO in the wake of a shareholder revolt led by Walt's nephew Roy Disney. *[Iger would also later become chairman of the board.]*

Within a month, Bob and I were sitting together at the table with the National Football League for negotiations about *Monday Night*

Football, which was currently being broadcast by ABC, and *Sunday Night Football*, by ESPN. In the end, we chose to purchase *Monday Night Football* (the crown jewel of sports broadcasting since it was created in 1970) for ESPN, rather than for ABC.

It was a difficult decision to take that program off ABC after such a storied thirty-six years and nearly six hundred broadcasts. However, Iger (who had worked his way up through ABC Sports) really believed it was the right thing to do, because ESPN had emerged as the strongest brand in sports programming. We were able to secure an eight-year contract for $8.8 billion (averaging $1.1 billion per year). After NBC purchased *Sunday Night Football*, ESPN no longer had the right to broadcast *NFL Primetime*, our award-winning program that had preceded every Sunday night football game. We all took that loss hard, but it was especially difficult for Chris Berman and Tom Jackson, who hosted the show and had turned it into one of the highest-rated programs in the history of cable television.

Things were swiftly changing with Bob Iger now in charge at The Walt Disney Company. He was setting a new direction not only for the entire company, but for ESPN in particular. It was a wonderful benefit that my boss was always accessible, an avid sports fan, and very familiar with the sports television business. He also believed in decentralized management and was extremely supportive of my leadership at ESPN. The two of us talked by phone almost every morning. The first several minutes were about our families, and then the latest in sports (Bob is a fan of the Yankees, Packers, Clippers, and New York Rangers). He would then ask me about what was going on at the company. If there were important topics, I would give him an update, and he would offer his thoughts. If there wasn't anything major to report, I'd often respond by saying, "Business is good and morale is high." And then Bob would thank me and that would end the call.

One day, not long after the NFL negotiations had concluded, Iger called and said, "We've been talking about this for a while, George.

Having two separate sports organizations doesn't make much sense anymore. I think we need to consolidate ABC Sports and ESPN into one division. Disney is going to focus on one sports brand, and it has to be ESPN. Make it happen, will you, George?"

With that direction, my team and I began developing an action plan. I knew it was going to be difficult given the illustrious past of ABC Sports. There were a lot of good people there and a lot of tradition.

One of my first actions was to call Frank Bennack, Hearst's CEO. Frank had spearheaded their acquisition of 20 percent of ESPN in 1990 from RJR Nabisco. *[When ABC acquired ESPN in 1984, it retained 80 percent and sold 20 percent to Nabisco.]* As both the largest ABC network affiliate through its major market broadcast stations and, as cofounders with ABC of leading cable networks A&E, Lifetime, and History Channel, Frank had extensive experience on both sides of the broadcast/cable aisle. As such, he was in a unique position to offer me advice. Frank had been a mentor to me for years, always offering steady, straightforward counsel. Integrity and the value of a handshake were paramount to Frank Bennack's leadership style, and I felt like I learned something every time I talked to him. Frank understood the benefits of what we were proposing. He also offered some sage advice on how to handle the people situation, because I wanted to do the right thing for the personnel at ABC Sports.

Back in March 2003 when I was named president, I knew very few people at ABC Sports, so I met personally with the staff. In a packed conference room on the thirteenth floor of ABC corporate headquarters in New York, I introduced myself and took questions. Now two years later, in June 2005, I found myself in the same conference room in front of the same people to tell them that going forward, our sports operations were going to be run under the ESPN banner.

I wanted to be honest and straightforward with everybody and was especially intent on telling them face-to-face. There was a lot of anxiety in the room, because rumors had been circulating in the days leading up to this meeting. I did my best to address concerns and reassure people. Some were clearly bitter, and there didn't seem to be much I could say to assuage their feelings. But I simply told it like it was. "It's a new day and we are now one company," I said. "I hope you will get on board with the new direction, because our company is growing and you can continue to have great careers." As it turned out, some people did leave—but others stayed, embraced the change, and continued with successful careers at ESPN.

The next major decision in which I was involved was equally tough because, again, it involved some really wonderful people. When we gained *Monday Night Football* but lost *Sunday Night Football*, all of a sudden we had two very gifted talent and production teams, but only one game to telecast each week. So which team was going to do the new *Monday Night Football* telecast? Do we choose Sunday's Mike Tirico, Joe Theismann, Director Chip Dean, and Producer Jay Rothman? Or do we go with *MNF*'s John Madden, Al Michaels, Director Drew Esocoff, and Producer Fred Gaudelli, or some combination of both?

From the outset, I placed personal phone calls to everybody involved to explain that we were thinking through our options. Unfortunately, several people were very unhappy, especially John Madden, whose contract happened to be up. I later learned that within a day or two of NBC acquiring the NFL rights to televise *Sunday Night Football*, the entire ABC team was being recruited over to NBC. Madden signed with NBC right away (effective with the 2006 season), even though I wrote him a long letter to try to persuade him to stay with us. It didn't work, but I was proud of our efforts to keep him—and to this day I have great respect and admiration for John Madden. For the *MNF* production team, we chose Jay Rothman and Chip Dean and, while we tried to retain Esocoff and Gaudelli with other assignments, they followed Madden over to NBC.

Then, at the 2006 Super Bowl, a colleague informed me that Al Michaels wanted to get out of his ABC contract so he could join

Madden on the *Sunday Night Football* team. If true, this was a big development, as Al had been with ABC for thirty years. Among his many accomplishments was his signature call "Do you believe in miracles? Yes!" at the 1980 Lake Placid Olympics when the U.S. men's hockey team upset the heavily favored Soviet Union.

In any event, I wanted to hear this news directly from Al to confirm that he really did want out of his contract. Sure enough, when we spoke after the game, he told me it was true.

The first thing I did was call Bob Iger to give him the news. A couple of days later, Iger called me back. "George," he said, "I'd be willing to let Al Michaels go if you can get us the rights to Oswald the Lucky Rabbit from NBC."

After a slight pause, I responded, "Who or what is Oswald the Lucky Rabbit?"

"Well, it goes back to the very beginning of Walt Disney's career," Iger explained. "Oswald is a revered figure at Disney and I'd like to get him back."

My next phone call was to my counterpart at NBC, Dick Ebersol. I opened the conversation by saying, "I'm willing to talk to you about letting Al go to NBC, but I gotta have Oswald the Lucky Rabbit back."

"What?"

"Yeah, you heard me right. I gotta have Oswald the Lucky Rabbit back."

"Who or what is Oswald the Lucky Rabbit?"

"Well, here's what I know. You'll have to research it on your end."

It turns out that Oswald was a precursor to Mickey Mouse designed personally by Walt Disney for Universal Pictures back in the 1920s—and Bob Iger knew it was important to the Disney family. Within a week, Ebersol had run the traps at NBC's sister company, Universal, received approval, and the deal was worked out.

So nearly eighty years after Walt Disney first created the priceless precursor to Mickey Mouse, Oswald was back home where he belonged.

Oswald the Lucky Rabbit   *The Walt Disney Company*

At company headquarters in Burbank, California, they celebrated with an "Oswald the Lucky Rabbit Day" complete with a parade, balloons, free lunches, and buttons. It was truly a big deal for The Walt Disney Company. And that's how Al Michaels was traded to NBC for a cartoon character.

[Every year since its debut in 2006, Monday Night Football *on ESPN has been the most watched series on cable television. Over the years, our talent team has consisted of Mike Tirico, Jon Gruden,*

Joe Theismann, Tony Kornheiser, and Ron Jaworski (in the booth), and Michele Tafoya, Suzy Kolber, and Lisa Salters (on the sidelines).]

Monday Night Football (2009) featuring Ron Jaworski, Jon Gruden, and Mike Tirico in the booth.   *Joe Faraoni / ESPN Images*

The last of our string of major decisions in 2005–06 involved finalizing our move to have ESPN become Disney's single sports brand. Bob Iger and I were both very focused on making that happen. To that end, I sent Bob a memo in July 2006 recommending that we change all of our on-air branding for sports that appear on ABC to be presented as "ESPN on ABC." Our research revealed that with all things being equal (the event, the on-air talent, and so on), sports fans believed that *branding* a game as ESPN was a significant improvement in quality. So with this move, Disney would expose ESPN, the number one brand in sports media, to a substantially broader audience on the ABC television network. It would be a boost for both ESPN and ABC.

Our executive team put in a lot of time thinking through how best to execute the change. After working it through with the ABC affiliates, our decision was to launch "ESPN on ABC" in September 2006 with our opening coverage of college football.

Once the consolidation was complete, I took some time to reflect on that change in terms of ESPN's history. In 1979, when we opened our doors, ABC Sports was on top of the world as far as sports media was concerned—and nobody outside the company thought our small start-up had even the remotest chance to be successful. But now, nearly three decades later, not only was ESPN the premier brand in sports, we also carried with us the legacy of ABC Sports. When you look at it that way, it really was an amazing transformation.

Perhaps just as important, our research department proved that moving to one consistent sports brand for Disney actually increased ratings and enhanced the brands of all three companies—ABC, ESPN, and Disney. The move was better for the organization as a whole, and with time even some of the longest-serving people at ABC Sports came to realize it. The fact that some individuals were hurt personally in the transformation was painful to me. But in truth, I just don't believe it could have been avoided.

Everybody Can Be a Leader

Steve Jobs was standing over at the coffee bar. It was about fifteen minutes before the start of The Walt Disney Company's spring board meeting in Orlando in March 2006. Two months earlier, in one of Bob Iger's first initiatives as CEO, Disney had purchased Pixar Animation Studios at a cost of $7.4 billion, which made Jobs (Pixar's CEO and majority owner) Disney's largest shareholder. It was Steve's first meeting as a new member of the board of directors. I was attending, because two years earlier I had been named co-chairman, Disney Media Networks (along with Disney/ABC Television Group President Anne Sweeney), and was often invited to attend board meetings. Of course, I was very familiar with Steve Jobs, but we had never met. So I figured this would be a good time to go up, get a cup of coffee, and introduce myself. "Good morning, Steve. How are you," I said. "I'm George Bodenheimer, with ESPN."

Steve finished stirring his coffee, looked up at me, and said, "I hate your phone." Then he walked away.

ESPN had just launched a mobile phone with a lot of fanfare, including purchasing a thirty-second Super Bowl ad for $2.5 million as part of our massive introductory advertising campaign. We called our phone "The MVP." It was a Sanyo flip model with a retro look (black with red buttons). I didn't know if Steve meant he didn't like the *look* of our phone or the *idea* of it. Maybe he meant both. The *idea* was to create a phone for sports fans with instant access to scores and breaking news. Our business model was both aggressive and creative. Customer contracts, care, and other services were to be managed directly by us. We projected sales on the order of 500,000 phones with a breakeven point of about 250,000. Given the enthusiasm of sports fans and their growing interest in accessing up-to-the-minute sports news and scores, we were confident we could achieve these numbers.

Everything would have been great if the phone had sold, but it didn't. In eight months, we moved only thirty thousand units. Not surprisingly, in October 2006 my boss, Bob Iger, called me. "George, what are we doing here?" he said. "We're really under projections. It's not going to work. Let's cut our losses sooner rather than later."

Both Iger and Jobs were right. So despite all the publicity and all the upfront money we had spent, ESPN pulled the plug on the MVP phone.

Our original intent was to be aggressive about growing ESPN's audience across all platforms. On the heels of Artie Bulgrin's study, we no longer had any trepidation about entering these new "digital" markets. In addition, part of Iger's new direction for Disney and ESPN was to rapidly embrace technology. And I wanted to get out in front of the competition and be the first cable network to truly serve its customers by embracing multimedia. Unfortunately, our strategy and business plan to begin with a mobile phone were flawed.

Despite our success over the years, ESPN had also tried many things that didn't work. For example, ESPN2 played rock music, and that didn't pan out. ESPN retail stores weren't profitable, so we closed them. In 2010, ESPN created the first 3-D television network. We shut it down in 2013.

We had also changed business plans in midstream before. Bill

Rasmussen elected to go with national and twenty-four-hour satellite network instead of his original idea for local and part-time. Bill Grimes and Roger Werner totally flipped ESPN's business model back in 1982 and started charging cable operators a monthly fee, rather than us paying them. And we had created new business models to pay for the NFL, for ESPN2, and for the X Games. Risk taking had always been a part of ESPN's culture, and I believe it had been an important catalyst for our success over the years. But when you take risks, you are sometimes going to have setbacks. It is how a company handles those setbacks that determines whether or not it will be successful in the long run.

Another part of ESPN's culture has always been to take advantage of mistakes by learning from them. Executives sometimes hang on to unsuccessful initiatives too long because they're afraid to admit they were wrong. In the case of the ESPN phone, we tried it, it didn't work out, so we made a quick correction. I heard Bob Iger say it frequently: "Pack light and travel fast."

So I assembled the "MVP" phone group, laid out the facts, thanked everyone for all their hard work, and told them that we had to shift gears and develop a new strategy for entering the mobile market. That effort was led by a large team, which included John Zehr, who had joined ESPN back in 1993 during our partnership with Starwave to create our first Internet site. So, in essence, all the talented people who created the ESPN phone worked together to develop a Plan B for ESPN mobile. And it paid off, too, because between 2006 and 2012, ESPN more than doubled its cross-platform audience.

We began our aggressive expansion by building on the original 2001 launch of ESPN Broadband. Back then, Sean Bratches applied our traditional cable network business model and charged high-speed Internet providers a per-subscriber fee rather than use the Internet industry's approach of giving away content and generating revenue solely on advertisements. In 2007, we placed more emphasis on streaming live sporting events via the Internet. By 2010, we had changed the name of that popular service to ESPN3.com and made it available in the United States, Europe, the Middle East, and major markets in Latin America.

In the wake of the ESPN phone, we also reconcentrated our efforts on serving the mobile market by getting out in front of the rest of the industry with apps for smartphones. Of course, that explosion didn't occur until a year or so after Apple's iPhone appeared on the scene. *[I guess Steve Jobs did have a better idea.]* But ESPN responded by introducing a customizable app named ScoreCenter, which was rapidly downloaded by more than ten million people. ScoreCenter was upgraded and rebranded as SportsCenter in 2013.

In October 2010, ESPN launched the WatchESPN app, first for desktops and laptops and, six months later, for smartphones and tablets. The app included access to live simulcasts of ESPN, ESPN2, ESPNews, ESPN Classic, ESPNU, and ESPN Deportes (our Spanish-language network). We also renamed our online channel ESPN3 and made it accessible on the WatchESPN app. Then, taking a page from our early history, ESPN3 included live streaming of lower-profile sporting events, such as rugby, polo, college gymnastics, and cricket. The WatchESPN app was a significant product for our company, because it meant that sports fans could watch ESPN on virtually any compatible device whenever and wherever they chose. And that ability quite literally met our mission: "To Serve Sports Fans. Anytime. Anywhere."

Looking back on it, I can say that I never really did consider the ESPN phone a failure. Rather, it was our first step on the road to success in the mobile market. ESPN was not bulletproof—and the day we thought we were would be the day our company started a downhill slide. We made a mistake, learned from it, and moved on. Once we revised our strategy and tweaked the business model, everything we employed to create the phone was put to good use. I'm proud to say that, by 2014, ESPN was setting all-time records for the number of sports fans using ESPN mobile, nearly fifty million per month. And that was no accident. It was the result of good, solid teamwork and group leadership.

Through the years, I was often asked to state ESPN's business strategy. My response was pretty simple. "Well, we try a lot of things," I'd reply. "The things that don't work, we stop doing. And the things that do work, we keep improving in order to make them the best we can. That's our strategy."

More specifically, I was also asked how ESPN successfully transformed itself from a television company to a multimedia company. The answer, in part, is that we adhered to three main business principles: (1) be first to market; (2) do not fear cannibalization of your existing business; and (3) stay true to your brand and your mission. The keys to expanding into multimedia are really no more complicated than that. ESPN won the race by being the first company to seamlessly deliver what sports fans wanted.

It's a hard thing to explain, but even when things looked their bleakest for the ESPN phone, I was still optimistic that everything was going to be okay. I don't believe in overnight success. But I do believe in the power of optimism. If we just kept to our knitting, worked hard, and stayed positive, we were going to find ways to grow. As far as I was concerned, that was the only possible outcome. Some people have said my leadership style is overly optimistic. But if you think about it, people do not follow pessimists. One of the key fundamentals in leadership is optimism.

During ESPN's years of rapid growth, a lot of hardworking people were promoted into management positions without much preparation or training for their new roles. Regardless of what area or department of the company a future leader happens to be in, however, it's not good enough to have only mastered the technical aspects of a profession. People skills are necessary to be a good supervisor. So unless those who were promoted all happened to be natural leaders, ESPN was bound to have some problems. Sure enough, in 2004, our annual employee survey was very critical of ESPN's basic management skills, especially among middle managers. In response, we initiated the company's first formal leadership training program, for which we developed multi-level courses and proprietary materials. The basic tenets and principles of leadership are like what blocking and tackling are to football. But what are the fundamentals of leadership?

In order to be specific about what was expected of leaders at ESPN, we defined and published a set of "leadership competencies." They included: vision, strategic thinking, a drive for results, entrepreneurial spirit, embracing diversity, effective communication, teamwork, passion, integrity, trust, and courage. We formally named our new leadership training program the "Bristol School of Management," and we made sure that everybody knew we were serious about the program, and that it was going to be a continuing focus for our company.

By 2008, we had started to focus on *leadership versus management*. The main difference can really be summed up with the well-known maxim, "You *manage* things, but you *lead* people." Leadership is a people business—so we placed a major emphasis on compassion and caring, which are very important for effective leadership. Along the way, we adopted our own definition of *leadership*: "Leaders make other people better." That thought, I believe, came out of looking at great athletes. Back in Michael Jordan's heyday, for instance, the other Chicago Bulls used to say that their star teammate not only made them *look* better, but he inspired them to *perform* better. Jordan's teammates also became leaders, themselves, especially when he wasn't on the court.

Everybody can be a leader, on every team, and in every company. You don't need a lofty position or an impressive title. If you work in the mailroom, you can figure out a better way to deliver the mail. If you're a good salesperson, you can share your ideas with your colleagues. If you become a middle manager, you can inspire the people on your team to be the best they can be. And if you are the chairman of the board, you can help take your company to unimaginable heights. It's all in how individuals inspire the people around them. Individual leadership is the key—and you have to be a leader every day. There is no part-time leadership. That's the message we tried to instill at ESPN.

During the Great Recession of 2008–09, we doubled down on employee spending and people initiatives when most corporations were cutting back on them. I felt strongly that we needed to demonstrate to our employees that we cared about them, especially now that they were worried about possibly losing their jobs. I know it's paradoxical to traditional management thinking, but spending money on employee-related items actually keeps costs down. When people know they are appreciated as valuable members of the team, and if they know the company needs to cut back on spending, then they will find ways to cut back on spending. It's that simple. At our annual priority meeting the first year of the recession, we adopted the theme, "Emerge Stronger."

And in the ensuing difficult years, we purposefully created formal ESPN priorities specifically dedicated to taking care of our employees, including: "Develop, mentor, and measure our current and future leaders," "Support, develop, and empower our people in this challenging environment," and "Focus on employee development." The formal goals at most corporations are money-related rather than specifically about people. But it is *people* who actually achieve those business goals. It is *people* who make things happen, not the goals themselves. That's one reason I have always worked so hard at forging relationships and in making personal connections.

I was heartened one time when a consultant helping out with our diversity initiative told me he had asked several of his ESPN focus groups if they had any personal connection to the president of the company. "You mean George?" they said. "Well, sure we do. Everybody knows George." Of course, it wasn't 100 percent of employees who raised their hands, but the majority certainly did. And that piece of unsolicited feedback let me know that my efforts to reach company employees were working.

Going to the gym in the morning, eating at the cafeteria, walking the grounds, dropping by offices to have a chat, writing personal notes, making phone calls, and caring about their families—all that was making a difference. I wanted ESPN people to *know* me, to know that I really did care about them, to feel like they had a personal connection to the president, and to feel like we were all part of the same team. That's why as much as I possibly could, I used the plural pronouns *we* and *us* rather than *I* or *me*. And that's why I worked hard to spread the credit around to where it was due, just like Scotty Connal and Chet Simmons did in the early days. Back then, we were a family, and I wanted ESPN to be a family no matter how large we grew.

Just before Christmas in 2007, I received word that Dick Vitale was in the hospital for tests that might reveal cancer of the throat. My first thought was for the genuinely good man who had befriended me when I first started at ESPN. And, of course, I knew that Dick's career depended on his voice, so a cancer diagnosis would be especially hard for him. I immediately called Dick to give him some reassurance. "No matter what happens, we're going to be there for you, Dick," I said. "No matter *what* happens. So don't worry about anything."

For the first time in his career, Dick Vitale had to take some time off from work. He underwent successful surgery to have lesions removed from his vocal cords. Fortunately, a biopsy revealed them to be nonmalignant. Dick returned to the announcer's booth on February 6, 2008, for ESPN's coverage of the Duke–North Carolina game. And was it ever good to see him there and hear him say, "It's serendipity, baby! Everything's okay!"

In May 2009, the heart and soul of ESPN's *College GameDay*, Lee Corso, suffered a stroke at his home in Florida. He spent a week in the hospital, three days of it in intensive care. Then he had to go through an arduous rehabilitation process to overcome the partial paralysis he had suffered. During those tough days, Lee didn't know if he would ever be able to return to the job he loved. Fortunately, he came back sooner than expected and ended up not missing a season. When I saw Lee and asked him how he was doing, his response said it all.

"George, when adversity hit, ESPN and all our people stuck with me," he said. "There was never any pressure to return to work. During my recovery, all I received were good wishes and support. No one had to say it, but I knew I was part of a family. And let me tell you, George, that meant everything. Loyalty is a two-way street. You get it back in direct proportion to how much you give. It's far more important than money or prestige. If you support people and give them a chance, which ESPN does, nine times out of ten they'll come through for you. And guess what, you get their loyalty, too. I love this company. I love the people I work with."

Three Strikes

One morning, my longtime assistant, Kitty Bradley, informed me that Keith Olbermann was on the phone and wanted to speak to me. I wasn't surprised, as I had been tipped off that he might call. Still, I hadn't spoken with Keith since 1997 when he left ESPN. "George," he said, "I've called to apologize. I'm very sorry for all that I have said and done in regard to ESPN. I was wrong."

"Well, Keith, it's nice of you to say that," I replied.

"I really regret how I left ESPN," said Keith. "I blew it and I'm very sincere about this apology."

"Thank you, Keith," I responded.

We had been through a lot with Olbermann. As an on-air personality, his brains, style, and sports savvy were both electric and undeniable. But off camera, he was often at odds with management. Basically, I think Olbermann let stardom go to his head, which is not all that uncommon for high-profile media stars. Keith had stormed out of ESPN, and some of our employees expressed relief that he was gone. The most-remembered quote at ESPN was made by Communications Director Mike Soltys, who said of Olbermann, "He didn't just burn bridges here, he napalmed them!" Over the next dozen or so years, Keith came and went with media outlets Fox Sports Net, MSNBC, and Current TV.

I came to find out that in addition to me, Olbermann had called a number of other ESPN executives to deliver his mea culpa. Several years after Keith made his apology calls, he asked if ESPN would consider bringing him back on television. At that point, I was working as ESPN executive chairman and was not directly involved in the company's day-to-day activities, although I was informed of his request. To make a long story short, in August 2013, ESPN gave Keith Olbermann a two-year contract to host a sixty-minute nightly show on ESPN2. Of course, the national media made a lot of hay with the news. The best headline came from *Adweek*, which read: HELL FREEZES OVER, OLBERMANN REJOINS ESPN.

I hadn't really interacted directly with Keith Olbermann while he was at ESPN. I came up through the sales and marketing side of the business and he had left the company by the time I became president. Of course, there were times when I had to sit down with some top people and talk to them about an issue related to performance. Once in a while it included on-air talent, whether it was dealing with salary demands, new contracts, or behavioral issues. But that didn't happen often, largely because I delegated the responsibility to the appropriate executive in the chain of command. I didn't want to take away from their authority and, by the way, once you start interrupting the chain, some people think it's okay to bypass their boss every time there's a problem.

Many corporate executives will avoid serious confrontation with subordinates at all costs. But by not handling such situations, things often just get worse. I really never found it too difficult to sit down with an employee to resolve an issue. When preparing for such a meeting, even though they can be stressful, I always took comfort in the belief that my job was to protect the overall organization. Whatever I had to do with one individual, I had to do.

Discretion, too, is a very important tool in being a successful leader, so such meetings should be kept as private as possible. Nobody wants conversations about performance issues to become public knowledge. And heaven forbid that such an event ever becomes watercooler talk, because that only serves to exacerbate the problem. So whenever I had to have such a conversation, whether it was with a subordinate or one of the stars of our network, I often tried to do it out of the office. In a one-on-one conversation, sometimes over a cocktail, I'd quietly set things straight.

All organizations have problems with people. It's one of the areas of leadership that few people like to talk about, but it's a fact of life. Generally, in large companies, some bad judgment is exercised no matter how much you try to prevent it and ESPN was no different. When these instances happened on my watch as president, I took quick action, in part, because I felt such behavior was both intolerable and counter to our culture, which emphasized respect for people. In July 2002, for example, I felt it necessary to send out a company-wide memo on the subject, and I did not mince words. "Events over the last several months force me to remind everybody of the importance of maintaining compliance with our sexual harassment practice policy," I wrote. "Conduct that violates any of these policies can and will result in significant disciplinary actions, including termination." Things settled down after I sent that out, and we went a number of years without a major incident until all hell broke loose in the fall of our thirtieth anniversary year.

One morning in late October 2009, I arrived at work to find a copy of the *New York Post* lying prominently in the center of my desk. The front-page headline read: STEVE'S LUST: STAR ADMITS SHAME IN ESPN SEX SCANDAL.

The subject of the article was forty-six-year-old Steve Phillips, one of our high-profile on-air talents and a big part of our Major League Baseball coverage. ESPN hired Steve in 2005 after he had worked as general manager of the New York Mets. Unfortunately, a few months before the *New York Post* article appeared, he'd had an affair with a twenty-two-year-old ESPN production assistant, and we were dealing with it internally. But now there were lurid details being splashed all over New York's biggest tabloid newspaper and I knew it would stay on the front page until we addressed the issue publicly.

Norby Williamson had already taken Steve off the air and formally suspended him while an investigation was conducted. As we were gathering information and dealing with it internally, Steve asked for (and received) an extended leave of absence to enter a treatment center. As president of the company, I had been informed of the suspension and was pleased that Williamson had taken the initiative to act. It was the right thing to do.

Unfortunately, what I had hoped would remain an internal issue at ESPN rose to an entirely unexpected level when the *New York Post* got hold of an explosive police report that had everything a tabloid could ever want: a national television personality, married with kids, and an angry ex-lover. I quickly convened a meeting with a few of our top executives to discuss the issue and, predictably, the initial conversation was full of emotion. "We're getting raked over the coals on the biggest tabloid in New York!" somebody said.

"We have to stop this!" said another.

"Well, the worst thing we can do is to stonewall or try to deny the situation," I said. Accordingly, we issued a brief press release.

ESPN PRESS RELEASE

We were aware of this and took appropriate disciplinary action at the time. We have granted
Steve's request for an extended leave of absence
to allow him to address it. We have no further
comment.

Other national news outlets jumped on the bandwagon and began writing about what some termed "ESPN's locker room mentality." One website even suggested that we change our slogan to "Worldwide Leader in Sex." Internally, everybody was talking about it. Quickly, the scandal created a negative effect on our company, and our working environment suffered. Our employees would go home and their spouses would say, "What the heck is going on at that place, anyway?"

It was now glaringly apparent that the behavior of a couple of employees had negatively affected just about everybody else at ESPN— and I really had a problem with that. Because I saw a big part of my job as protecting both our culture and reputation, I knew I had to act quickly to resolve the situation.

Moreover, we now had to ask ourselves if one of our prominent faces for ESPN's coverage of Major League Baseball could continue to effectively represent our company to the public. Clearly, he could not. In my view, Steve Phillips had forfeited his privilege to work at ESPN. So we fired him. It was as simple as that.

After taking that action, we issued another press statement without mentioning the young production assistant.

ESPN PRESS RELEASE

Steve Phillips is no longer working for ESPN. His ability to be an effective representative for ESPN has been significantly and irreparably damaged, and it became evident it was time to part ways.

Some attributed our misfortune to the nature of the sports television business as having a "fraternity house" atmosphere. I never agreed with that assessment. But because we were a high-profile company, these issues tended to get blown out of proportion. It took time for this incident to drop from the papers entirely and a bit longer for it to settle down internally. But shockingly to me, we then experienced another couple of instances of poor behavior, so I told my senior management team "Enough is enough!" and that I was going to address all of ESPN's talent. "But George, that's over seven hundred people," one of them said. "It'll be unprecedented, and it'll be difficult getting them all assembled at one time."

"Yes, I know," I replied. "But I want to speak to everybody. It needs to be done."

ESPN had more on-air talent than any other network by far. No one else even came close. So we had to schedule it in two back-to-back sessions and include videoconferencing for those who could not be there in person.

I was very torn going into this meeting, because I knew the vast majority of our people always conducted themselves professionally, and it was only the improper actions of a few that were hurting everybody else. Nonetheless, I needed to get it across that if people acted this way, they were going to be fired—although I conveyed the message more diplomatically. You could hear a pin drop in the room as I spoke. Here's what I said, in part:

> As the leader of this company, I am committed to addressing these issues in a positive manner that will make us all better. The actions of a few have cast a shadow over the great work of the many. Poor judgment and reckless behavior do not reflect our company values. Rather, they undermine our effort to create a high-performance culture—a culture we have all worked hard to build over thirty years.
>
> Directly or indirectly, all of us are ESPN's most visible ambassadors. So it is incumbent on us to be fully aware of expectations regarding professional conduct and how we can

best carry out our critical roles as the daily face of our company. ESPN leadership will do our part to support you. However, ultimate responsibility and accountability for individual choices reside with each of us.

I see how we should act as a pretty simple formula: Represent ESPN every day with class, dignity, and integrity.

30 for 30

There were no big parties in 2009 marking ESPN's thirtieth anniversary, certainly nothing like the celebration we had in 2004 on our silver jubilee. This time the economy was struggling, so we thought it would be appropriate to tone things down. "Let's do something more meaningful," I said to our executive team during our initial talks. Although it was a simple enough idea, that basic direction generated a series of actions that significantly impacted ESPN.

For starters, Rosa Gatti's corporate outreach team proposed that we boost volunteerism with thirty thousand hours of local community service around the world (which we called the "TEAM ESPN 30K Challenge"). I loved the idea as soon as I heard it. So from March through early September, thousands of ESPN employees participated in all kinds of wonderful projects that ranged from building homes with Habitat for Humanity to events for elders in nursing homes to community-wide cleanups. In Bristol, one of the highlights was our refurbishing of a baseball field for the Cambridge Park Boys & Girls Club. And in Brazil, ESPN (led by vice president and general manager German Hartenstein) introduced "Caravan de Sports," which brought sports equipment to some of the poorest rural areas of Brazil, where many children do not go to school. But when "the caravan" showed up, school attendance rose. The six-month TEAM ESPN 30K Challenge effort took us right up to the day we first went on the air thirty years earlier.

On September 7, 2009, we had a special event on campus to honor the '79ers, as we like to call them—those still on the payroll who had started work in ESPN's first year of existence (1979). During a meaningful ceremony (wonderfully hosted by *SportsCenter* anchor Sage Steele) that included family, friends, and a large crowd of employees, forty-three '79ers were given their own stars on our new ESPN "Walk of Fame." Chris Berman and Bob Ley spoke about the early days when we were working out of a half-finished building and several trailers. Now the ESPN campus was a sprawling 120-plus acres with eighteen buildings. When our founder, Bill Rasmussen, made a brief appearance wearing a VISITOR badge, I made a mental note that we needed to have him back one day as the center of attention.

From a business perspective, 2009 also saw two significant events for ESPN. First, we opened up our new Los Angeles production facility. A few years earlier, we had decided to build a second broadcast center on the West Coast. We chose to construct it in the downtown area next to the Staples Center. It was a prominent location to plant the ESPN flag.

One of our goals in making the new facility a success involved transferring ESPN's culture three thousand miles from Bristol to LA. To achieve that, we chose Executive Vice President Steve Anderson to lead the project. Steve had been with us since 1980 and was a true culture carrier. He carefully selected seventy people to staff the new facility, with over half transferring from Bristol. We immediately took advantage of the plethora of high-profile sports stars in Southern California by having them as guests in the studio, particularly on the new LA-based *SportsCenter*, which was anchored by Bristol transfers Neil Everett and Stan Verrett. The new production facility became an enormous success and complemented ESPN's other offices in Charlotte, Chicago, San Francisco, Miami, and Washington, DC.

The second major business event of 2009 was the launch of the documentary series *30 for 30*. It, too, had its genesis when ESPN's programming department, now under the leadership of John Skipper, responded to my request that we do something more meaningful to mark ESPN's anniversary. The timing was ideal, because the evolution of our programming strategy under Skipper's leadership had made it possible for a whole new product to be created.

After Mark Shapiro resigned from ESPN back in 2005, John called on a Friday afternoon and asked to meet with me. *[Mark left ESPN to become CEO of Six Flags Inc., a major step for his career.]* "Well, I'm planning to take my boat out tomorrow," I replied. "Why don't you come along?" Skipper met me the next day and we took my small fishing boat out on Long Island Sound. After we broke out a couple of beers, John said what was on his mind. "George, I'd like you to consider me for Mark's job. Here are some notes I made outlining why I think I can do it." He then proceeded to pull about a dozen loose sheets of notebook paper that the wind almost blew overboard.

At the time, Skipper had been leading ESPN's advertising sales efforts for only a short while, and I was surprised he was interested in making the move to content. John had come over from Disney, led the effort to create *ESPN The Magazine*, and as such had *print* content experience. However, he had zero experience in producing television content. Looking back on it, though, I had been in the same boat before I became president in 1998. It was part of ESPN's culture to put an individual like John Skipper in a position for which he didn't necessarily have all the "right" experience. He did, however, possess the creativity and intelligence, and I felt he could learn what he needed to know beyond that. After hearing him out and thinking about it for a while, I decided to give John the job.

During Skipper's first few years as head of programming, ESPN shifted our strategy away from scripted dramas, reality shows, and made-for-television films more toward live sporting events and the programs that led into them. As such, we dissolved ESPN Original Entertainment in 2007. EOE, which had a good six-year run, was formed, in part, to help solve our 2001 ratings crisis. It had produced six made-for-TV movies and had started our company's creative juices flowing by experimenting with a very innovative content mix. Under John Skipper's leadership, EOE evolved into a producer of "one-off" documentaries (films that are stand-alone projects, not part of a series). That process began when documentary filmmaker Dan Klores approached ESPN with an idea to make a documentary about the history of basketball, similar to Ken Burns's PBS project on baseball.

While Skipper's team determined that we weren't prepared to take on the entire history of the sport, they did start talking to Klores about producing a documentary on basketball played at black colleges prior to the civil rights movement. That idea turned into a spectacular two-part film called *Black Magic*, which aired over two days in March 2008. The reviews and reactions were very good, so we decided to dive headfirst into the documentary business. Over the next eighteen months, ESPN produced six altogether, including *The Greatest Game Ever Played*, to commemorate the fiftieth anniversary of the 1958 NFL Championship Game between the Baltimore Colts and New York Giants (won by the Colts 23–17 in overtime). Executive produced by ESPN's John Dahl in association with the NFL, the film movingly linked players from that game with current players from the Colts and Giants.

It was while these six documentaries were being produced that I suggested we do something meaningful to mark ESPN's thirtieth anniversary. Once that seed was planted, John Skipper's content group began discussing the possibilities. The original idea for *30 for 30* came from the creative mind of the most popular writer on ESPN.com, Bill Simmons ("The Sports Guy"). Bill, a former writer for Jimmy Kimmel, initially suggested producing ten documentaries about individual athletes, ten about events, and ten about teams—thirty documentaries over the thirty years of ESPN's existence. He also voiced the opinion that, as the Worldwide Leader in Sports, we should not concede the sports documentary space to HBO, which at that time was the clear leader in that genre. Simmons then huddled with producer Connor Schell, who loved the idea, but suggested that well-known filmmakers from outside ESPN should be recruited to do all thirty of the documentaries. Connor also suggested that each director could choose a subject for which *they* had a passion or a personal interest.

That way, in contrast to the same-style HBO documentaries, every *30 for 30* would look and feel different. And finally, in order to handle the volume of projects being considered, ESPN Business Affairs Executive Marie Donoghue devised a one-page template so that all essential contract terms (fees, future rights, and so on) would be consistent. After a big meeting where the entire team discussed the pros and cons of the plan, Skipper gave the go-ahead.

ESPN's first *30 for 30* film, *Kings Ransom* (directed by Peter Berg), debuted in October 2009. It was about hockey legend Wayne Gretzky's momentous trade from the Edmonton Oilers to the Los Angeles Kings in 1988. Other documentaries that ran during the first full year included *Unmatched*, about the personal friendship of Martina Navratilova and Chris Evert and their rivalry on the court (produced by ESPN's Hannah Storm and directed by Lisa Lax and Nancy Stern); *The 16th Man*, chronicling the 1995 Rugby World Cup and Nelson Mandela's support for his South Africa team, which helped unite the post-apartheid nation (directed by Cliff Bestall); and *Jordan Rides the Bus*, about Michael Jordan's brief career in minor league baseball (directed by Ron Shelton). Also in the first thirty were documentaries made by the director of *Diner*, Barry Levinson (*The Band That Wouldn't Die*); and by Ice Cube, about his love for the Los Angeles Raiders (*Straight Outta LA*).

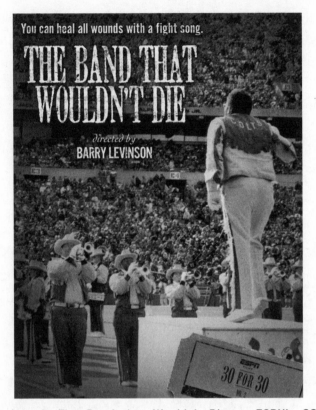

Barry Levinson's *The Band that Wouldn't Die* **on ESPN's** *30 for 30*.
Baltimore Ravens

The entire *30 for 30* series soon turned into a monster success. Of particular note was that our under-thirty audience soared, because young sports fans loved the education about sports history that the programs provided. Another unforeseen bonus was how rewatchable the individual films in the series were. Every time we re-aired any of the documentaries, they received good ratings. In that regard, *30 for 30* is a classic example of "evergreen" programming. Each documentary is timeless, and it soon became evident that our grandchildren are one day going to be watching them on their wireless tablets and smartphones.

Early in the production process, Simmons and Schell had to seek out well-known directors, find out what sports stories they wanted to tell, and then persuade them to do the work. But after the first thirty came out, a lot of filmmakers contacted us to ask if they, too, could do a documentary. So we expanded the series to include more great stories. One of those included 2013's *Survive and Advance*, a film produced by Jim Valvano's former player Dereck Whittenburg about NC State's magical postseason road to the NCAA National Championship in 1983.

Eventually, we had so many good ideas popping up for documentaries that our producers (Simmons, Schell, Dahl, Donoghue, and Dan Silver) realized that many of the possible subjects didn't require an hour or more to tell the story. As a matter of fact, Silver realized that a lot of them only needed seven or eight minutes. So ESPN also began creating *30 for 30* "shorts" designed especially for our online and mobile platform—and *they* performed very well, too. The entire concept just kept growing and evolving.

In general, there were three big reasons ESPN's *30 for 30* series was successful. First, we produced so many documentaries at one time, we were able to garner a lot of attention in the marketplace. Second, each documentary was a great story told by a director whose own passion and interest drove the production. Not only was storytelling one of the central tenets to ESPN's early success, so was letting people do their own thing—like Chris Berman's baseball nicknames or George Grande assigning *SportsCenter* reporters to cover the sports they enjoyed most. Third, the series redefined the art, innovation, and style of producing sports documentaries—to the point where even the expression *30 for 30* became synonymous with a quality sports production, not just internally at ESPN, but also in the overall sports vernacular. That fact, alone, strengthened the ESPN brand significantly. Actually, *30 for 30* created its own brand, which is very hard to do in the media business. In turn, that changed the conversation about ESPN. It gave us credibility in the Hollywood film community and established our leadership role in the production of sports documentaries.

It all started when, looking ahead to ESPN's thirtieth anniversary, we simply agreed "to do something more meaningful." From there, our team developed two major initiatives that had a significant impact on both the self-esteem of our employees and on our company's bottom line.

ESPN's *30 for 30* story reinforces the importance of idea generation in leadership. A good idea sparks the creative process, which can lead to all kinds of new things. And that good idea can come from any person anywhere in the organization.

[In 2010, ESPN's 30 for 30 *series earned a Peabody Award, a Producers Guild Award, an IDA Documentary Award, and was nominated for an Emmy. And in 2014, Dereck Whittenburg's* Survive and Advance *won an Emmy as part of the* 30 for 30 *series. That year the* 30 for 30 *shorts also took home a prime-time Emmy for Outstanding Short Format Nonfiction Program.]*

The Worldwide Leader in Sports

H ey, George, I believe soccer is growing in the United States. The World Cup is one of the great events in sports and I'd like to take a small team over to Switzerland and see if we can secure rights to the next two World Cups."

"Okay, John," I replied. "That would be great. You have my complete support. Keep me informed and good luck."

John Skipper was in his first week as head of content, and part of the ESPN culture was to let people pursue what they're passionate about. So when Skipper wanted to chase his passion for soccer and the World Cup, I immediately gave him the go-ahead. ESPN had broadcast the event a number of times in the past, but rights generally had to be renegotiated with FIFA (soccer's international governing body) every eight years—and it was that time again. After two transatlantic trips over the next ten days, Skipper and his team had secured rights to the nineteenth World Cup games in South Africa (2010) *and* the twentieth games in Brazil (2014). It's safe to say that without John Skipper's passion, ESPN would not have ended up with those two world-class events.

Ever since I got the top position at ESPN, I had emphasized that one of our main goals as a company was going to be to increase our focus on obtaining world-class programming. To continue that effort, we elevated John Wildhack to executive vice president of programming acquisition and strategy so he could be directly involved in all of those critical negotiations. This new arrangement suited Skipper (who had a massive learning curve on his hands), it suited Wildhack (who got a promotion out of the deal), and it suited me, because I knew they would make a great team. Actually, John Wildhack and I had grown up together at ESPN. I'll never forget pulling cable for him in Totowa, New Jersey, when he produced *Top Rank Boxing*, one of ESPN's early staples. Over the years, John had developed into one of the company's best executives, and it made perfect sense to take full advantage of his skills and the many personal relationships he had developed throughout the sports world.

On the top of ESPN's wish list was televising golf's premier major, the Masters, in the United States. Of course we knew that was not going to be an easy acquisition, as the Augusta National Golf Club is known for loyalty to its existing business partners. *[CBS had been televising the tournament's third and fourth rounds since 1956, and the USA Network the first and second rounds since 1982.]* Fortunately, ESPN's international strength paved the way for our first formal relationship when, in 1994, we acquired rights to televise the Masters in Latin America, Africa, and the Middle East on our networks in those regions.

Back then, neither CBS nor any of the other major broadcast networks had the kind of international reach ESPN did, so we were a natural choice when the Masters wanted to expand around the world. *[ESPN did the same for other major sports leagues, including the NBA, the NFL, the NHL, and Major League Baseball, among others.]* In 1995, under the leadership of producer Mike McQuade, *SportsCenter* advanced the ball with Augusta National by building a stellar team of anchors and reporters (such as Scott Van Pelt, Tom Rinaldi, Mike Tirico, and major winners Andy North, Paul Azinger, and Curtis Strange) to provide live on-site reports while the Masters was in progress. Mike had started in the ESPN mailroom as a driver back in 1987 and had worked his way up the production ranks. I guess his bosses felt if he could find John Walsh in a convention of albinos (which he did on his first day of work), he could handle just about anything they threw at him.

In 1999, I wrote a letter to Jim Armstrong, the general manager of Augusta National Golf Club, expressing our ongoing interest in the Masters. In response, John Wildhack and I were invited down to Georgia for an introductory meeting with Armstrong and Senior Director of Business Affairs Will Jones. As passionate golf fans, John and I were both thrilled to make that trip, and it turned out to be a very productive meeting. To continue to be visible and to tangibly demonstrate our interest, we then attended the tournament every subsequent year.

Eight years later, in early 2007, we were invited back to meet Augusta National's new chairman, Billy Payne, who had engineered Atlanta's successful bidding and staging of the 1996 Olympics. At that meeting, we began talking seriously about ESPN televising the Masters. Billy was very interested in new thinking to achieve his long-term goals for the Masters, two of which were to grow the audience and attract younger fans.

After showing him my eight-year-old letter to Jim Armstrong, Wildhack and I made a presentation titled "Innovation with Respect for Tradition." Artie Bulgrin and his research team had armed us with the facts to demonstrate that ESPN had the largest and youngest audience among America's golf fans. As a matter of fact, we pointed out that nearly 70 percent of them watched ESPN every week. No other network even came close. John and I also emphasized our respect for the Masters' tradition, which we felt had been demonstrated both personally and professionally since 1993. By the time we concluded our presentation, I felt we had made a very good case of showing that partnering with ESPN would help Billy Payne achieve his goals. We were on the verge of a breakthrough, and both John and I knew it.

In one of my proudest moments at ESPN, the Augusta National Golf Club announced in October 2007 that ESPN had earned the right to cover the first and second rounds of the Masters beginning with the 2008 tournament. In addition, we were granted rights to the first television coverage of the popular Par 3 tournament held on Wednesday before the opening round, and ESPN Deportes gained Spanish-language rights in the United States. Our Spanish-speaking announcers really came in handy, too, when Argentine Angel Cabrera won the Masters in 2009. Because Cabrera does not speak English, and CBS did not have a Spanish-speaking announcer on staff that day, ESPN's John Sutcliffe was pressed into service to translate for Angel during the champion's interview.

From 1993, when we began our international relationship with Augusta National, it took ESPN a full fifteen years to secure rights to televise the Masters in America, and it took John Wildhack and me nine years of personal effort. We were patient, persistent, and focused on our goal—and our passion for world-class programming never waned. The strength of our company worldwide and the power of the ESPN brand certainly helped us. But in the end, I firmly believe that once again, the personal relationships we had developed played a very big part, as well. *[Two years later, in 2009, ESPN was able to report to Billy Payne that the Masters' audience among young fans in the United States had more than doubled.]*

The Masters was one element of the world-class programming that helped ESPN earn our moniker *The Worldwide Leader in Sports*. The truth is that the amount of valuable sports programming we had produced over the years virtually dwarfed that of any other sports network. Acquiring top-tier sports was an expensive proposition, and once in a while John Wildhack and I would justify the sizable rights fees we paid by saying, "You never go wrong buying world-class product." And in the long run, that became an undeniable fact. Having programming that fans loved and cable and satellite operators couldn't live without was the main reason we were able to grow profits on a regular basis. By 2014, there weren't a lot of publicly held companies that were worth more than ESPN. Actually, *Forbes* valued ESPN at $50 billion, which was exceeded by only three media companies (Time Warner, 21st Century Fox, and Comcast) that traded on Wall Street. *[Forbes, April 29, 2014.]*

Between 2005 and 2014, in addition to the Masters, we added four world-class properties that I believe represented ESPN's growth, creativity, and commitment to sports fans: (1) <u>*Monday Night Football*</u>, (2) the <u>2010 and 2014 World Cups</u>, (3) <u>Wimbledon</u>, and (4) <u>college football's National Championship Game</u>.

1. It was a big deal when ESPN acquired the rights to <u>*Monday Night Football*</u> in 2005. Because *MNF* was the crown jewel of sports programming and history's longest-running prime-time television series, the conservative approach would have been to leave the program alone and not tinker with it. But our production team wanted to put our stamp on it. So we came up with the idea to provide twenty-four hours of "Full Circle" coverage revolving around every aspect of the game, including features on the venue, the teams, the players, the matchups, and of course pregame and postgame analysis. Ed Erhardt developed a new advertising strategy of selling *Monday Night Football* spots for the complete twenty-four hours. We promoted it as "the game around the game," and it became an immediate success with our sponsors and marketing partners. We also took the opportunity to redefine how a network covers a big event from a multimedia standpoint. For the first time, *MNF* was covered on all media across all ESPN platforms in order to reach football fans wherever they happened to be. We were living out our mission to serve fans anytime, anywhere. And the television audience soared to the point where our seventh regular-season broadcast between the New York Giants and the Dallas Cowboys (October 23, 2006) set the record for the largest audience in the history of cable television. *[In 2011, the NFL awarded ESPN a $15.2 billion eight-year*

extension for Monday Night Football. *ESPN also earned the right to telecast its first NFL Wild Card play-off game in January 2015.]*

2. In 2005, John Skipper had the vision to obtain rights to televise both the <u>2010 and 2014 World Cups</u>, some of the most watched sporting events in the world. And when the first rolled around five years later, we were ready. For the 2009–10 year, we had a formal company priority that simply read, "World Cup 2010 South Africa." Everybody at ESPN knew what that meant and did all they could to make it one of the most successful events in the thirty-one-year history of our company. Our television ratings for the 2010 World Cup jumped 41 percent over those for the 2006 World Cup. But the event's success wasn't only about TV. One in every three viewers watched the games on a device other than television. The 2010 World Cup proved that big events can transform companies. It verified in stunning fashion that our multimedia approach caused a rising tide that floated all ESPN boats. It also set the stage for ESPN's coverage of the 2014 World Cup from Brazil, which turned out to be the most viewed World Cup ever.

ESPN covers the 2014 World Cup from Brazil with (L to R) Bob Ley, Taylor Twellman, Rudd van Nisterlrooy, and Gilberto Silva.   *Phil Ellsworth / ESPN Images*

3. In July 2011, ESPN signed a twelve-year deal to expand our coverage of the revered <u>Wimbledon Championships</u>, the oldest and most prestigious tennis tournament in the world. Of particular note about this acquisition was that a good deal of the tournament, including the men's and women's finals, had been televised by NBC for more than forty years. Similar to the Masters, the strength of ESPN's brand, our multiplatform showcase, and our long-term strategy helped us win the day. And in the first few years of our coverage, I was particularly proud of how hard our team worked to validate the trust placed in us by the All England Lawn Tennis and Croquet Club. A 150-member production crew (led by ESPN veterans Jed Drake and Jamie Reynolds) worked as hard as can be imagined for the "fortnight" (as it is referred to at Wimbledon) to cover matches on fourteen separate courts. Virtually living and working together for the entire event, they become a one-for-all-and-all-for-one family, leaving no stone unturned to produce the finest tennis coverage possible. And sitting at Center Court to anchor the Wimbledon matches for ESPN was none other than *College GameDay*'s Chris Fowler, who as a young reporter in 1985 had been mistaken for a high school student while he worked on *Scholastic Sports America*. Fowler was joined by ESPN veterans Cliff Drysdale, Patrick McEnroe, Pam Shriver, and Mary Joe Fernandez, among many others. *[In May 2013, ESPN signed an eleven-year deal to broadcast the U.S. Open tennis tournament on all its platforms (effective in 2015). CBS had held television rights for the previous forty-six years.]*

4. In January 2014, I attended the <u>Bowl Championship Series (BCS) National Championship Game</u> (pitting the number one Florida State Seminoles versus the number two Auburn Tigers) at the Rose Bowl in Pasadena, California, the preeminent site for college football in the United States. ESPN's coverage was part of a multiyear agreement that began in 2011 and included telecasts of the Fiesta, Orange, Sugar, and

Rose Bowls and, of course, the National Championship Game. Calling our coverage the BCS Megacast, we offered six different ways to watch the game. While ESPN aired traditional television game coverage (called by Brent Musburger and Kirk Herbstreit), ESPN2 simultaneously broadcast *BCS Title Talk*, which included commentary from analysts, college players, celebrities, and guest hosts. ESPN Classic ran the game without any announcers at all. Only the public address system and other natural sounds could be heard. We also carried the game with various unique features and presentations on ESPN Radio, ESPNews, and ESPN3. Also, ESPN2 featured live Twitter comments from celebrities (like LeBron James and Deion Sanders) who were watching the game. Sitting with Ann and my sons George and James at the Rose Bowl in the midst of that crowd of one-hundred-thousand-plus screaming college football fans, with all the pageantry around us, and with ESPN covering the game from every conceivable angle, I couldn't help but think back to the days when I'd drive to the Hartford airport to pick up Saturday's games and hustle back to Bristol so they could be shown on tape delay. Both ESPN and college football had come a long way since then. As John Wildhack and I often said to each other, "It's a long way from Totowa."

[Responding to the fans, a new play-off was instituted (effective with the 2014 season), and ESPN was right there in setting the stage for a new era in college football. In November 2012, ESPN signed a twelve-year, eighty-four-game, $7.3 billion contract to provide coverage of all play-offs (including the championship game) through January 2026 on all of our ESPN platforms.]

In the late spring of 2007, ESPN's *College GameDay* team held a planning meeting for the upcoming football season. Looking at the full schedule, there was some discussion about the first telecast going to Berkeley for the University of California's home game against Tennessee. After all, both teams were probably going to be ranked in the Top 25, and at first glance no other games seemed obvious to merit a *GameDay* appearance. But then the show's producer, Lee Fitting, piped up. "Virginia Tech has a home game the first week of the season," he said.

"Who do they play?"

"East Carolina."

There was silence around the room. Everybody knew that a horrendous tragedy had just taken place at Virginia Tech. *[On April 16, 2007, thirty-two people were killed and seventeen wounded when a gunman senselessly opened fire on campus.]* They also knew that the game, itself, would probably be no contest, because the Atlantic Coast Conference's Virginia Tech Hokies were ranked number nine in the nation and the East Carolina Pirates, out of Conference USA, were unranked.

"This will be the first big opportunity for the campus to come together after the tragedy for something other than grieving," continued Lee. "It'll be a new semester, a new academic year, and the school's first football game."

"It'll be risky," someone said.

"Yes, it will. But it'll also be the right thing to do. By being there, we can help them heal. I want to go. I know it won't be the biggest game that week, but it'll certainly be the biggest story."

Everybody agreed. "Okay, we're going to Virginia Tech."

Planning for the event began early. The teams for *GameDay* and game production sat down together beforehand to make sure ESPN's effort was seamless. The game would be telecast on ESPN right behind *GameDay*. Mike Tirico and Todd Blackledge would call it, and Tim Corrigan would produce it. Cameras, event trucks, and all other resources would be shared so that the sights and sounds inside the stadium could be captured during the entire five- or six-hour production. These two ESPN production units (that normally worked independently) were going to be one and the same on that day.

On September 1, 2007, *College GameDay* was set up just outside Lane Stadium for the first hour of the show (to be among the students, as usual). But at 11 a.m., an hour before game time, part of the set was moved inside the stadium near the edge of the field. As the football players amassed in the stadium tunnel, a special video tribute to Virginia Tech and the victims of the tragedy played on the Jumbotron. The scene then shifted to Chris Fowler, Lee Corso, and Kirk Herbstreit at the *GameDay* desk. Corso put on the Virginia Tech Hokie mascot head and said, "I don't know what a Hokie is, but... God bless Virginia Tech."

And then, in a show of unity, both teams emerged from the dark tunnel into the light of the stadium carrying an American flag. When they ran out onto that football field, I thought it was symbolic of Virginia Tech trying to put the past behind them and usher in the brightness of a new day. The entire occasion was not a lament, it was a celebration. The loudspeakers blared Virginia Tech football's unofficial theme song, "Enter Sandman" by Metallica. The crowd roared. The cheerleaders cheered. And then it was time to play the game.

I was there and saw the whole thing. During an early commercial game break, I walked into the production truck to congratulate Lee Fitting and the crew. Tears were still in their eyes. There was no mistaking how much everybody cared about what they were doing. But on that day, their passion was not about the game being played. College football was merely the vehicle that provided an opportunity for ESPN to help play a small part in the healing process by showcasing the game and bringing the people of Blacksburg, Virginia, together.

I'm not sure if we will ever be able to sufficiently explain the beautiful bond between sports and people. But by any measure, it was at Virginia Tech on that day.

Thank You for Our Playground

When you're in the mud in ninety-degree heat, you get to know people. We put together swing sets and Jungle Gyms, mixed a lot of cement, and spread several tons of ground cover from one big pile to the rest of the play area. It was sweaty and messy and heavy. I was there with members of the community, kids (lots of kids), and thirty of ESPN's top executives—Rosa Gatti, Christine Driessen, Chuck Pagano, John Wildhack, and Artie Bulgrin, to name a few. We were at the Boys & Girls Club in Slidell, Louisiana, just across Lake Pontchartrain from New Orleans. Eighteen months earlier, the entire area had been hard hit by Hurricane Katrina. The club had been devastated, its playground destroyed. We were working with KaBOOM!, an American nonprofit organization that helps communities build playgrounds for children. By the end of the day, these kids had a new playground.

In the immediate aftermath of Katrina (in 2005), ESPN did our part to help out. We provided immediate help for our employees and their relatives along the Gulf Coast, contributed relief funds, and ran on-air spots supporting the American Red Cross and its efforts. With the kind of devastation everybody saw on television, I felt it was a moral imperative for ESPN to help out. That fall, ESPN partnered with the NFL for a fund-raising telethon that culminated in a special *Monday Night Football* doubleheader. And a year later, on September 25, 2006, the first game in the rebuilt New Orleans Superdome was on *Monday Night Football*. In our twenty-four-hour coverage of the event, we featured the people of New Orleans and their ongoing courage to recover from Katrina.

At the very beginning of the game between the Saints and Atlanta Falcons, the home team blocked a Falcons punt and recovered it in the end zone for a touchdown. I happened to be down on the sidelines and had never heard louder cheering at a sporting event. The Saints never looked back and went on to win 23–3. That game was a cathartic experience for the city of New Orleans, and our company was proud to have been part of it. NFL Commissioner Roger Goodell even sent us a congratulatory letter mentioning that ESPN's "pregame and game production teams deftly balanced an exciting sporting event with sensitivity to capture the emotions of the reopening of the Superdome and the Saints' return to New Orleans."

ESPN's efforts to help the Gulf Coast get back on its feet continued periodically and included reconstruction of the Slidell playground. That particular mission was undertaken by our MAX group and coordinated by Laura Gentile, my chief of staff at the time. In 2006, she and I had conceived the idea to assemble ESPN's top executives to meet regularly, discuss important topics, and, generally, reinforce our team. We had chosen the name *MAX* as an acronym for "Movement" and "Action" to send a signal to everybody involved that this was not going to be a do-nothing group and that they were all expected to actively participate. We formed MAX in early 2006 on the heels of both Mark Shapiro and Lee Ann Daly leaving the company. Amid those executive changes and some reorganization, it was a significant transitional time for ESPN. But we could not just switch on the automatic pilot and expect everything to keep moving at the same rapid pace. So I decided to create something new to pull together the members of the team and empower them in running the company. To me, it was kind of like an NCAA basketball team that had to regroup after the graduation of three or four seniors. It was a new year and we needed to draw together.

We held six to eight MAX meetings each year. They were scheduled well in advance, thoughtfully planned out, and if somebody couldn't attend I wanted to know why. I opened each meeting with general comments that included an overview of the financial performance of ESPN. Bottom-line numbers are not always shared with the executives of a major corporation. But I wanted every member of my team to know exactly where we stood in that regard all the time.

After my opening remarks, we selected three or four topics to be discussed. Very candid dialogue was encouraged and everybody expected to hear opinions from their fellow executives. It became a unique opportunity to learn how our departments could better interact with each other, and from our very first meetings, the MAX group really gelled as a team.

Sometimes, rather than meeting in Bristol, we took road trips, which further served to help us bond. We went to the Texas Motor Speedway in Fort Worth to immerse ourselves in the world of NAS-CAR, for example. Afterward, I took everybody out to a couple of the favorite places I'd frequented twenty-five years before when I was an account executive working in Arlington, Texas. We went to Angelo's in Fort Worth for a frosty beer and some of the best barbecue in the world. Then we went to Billy Bob's, "The World's Largest Honky Tonk," located in the stockyards section of town, where everybody got into the Texas spirit.

I liked getting our executives out in the field. Sometimes we get so focused on our day-to-day work that we forget what life is really all about, and that there are plenty of people out there who are less fortunate. Everybody should step back once in a while to see what's going on in the world around us and lend a helping hand. Giving back is not only the right thing to do, it helps build the culture of your company.

Over the years, ESPN has supported many charitable efforts large and small. While we have been sponsors for the Special Olympics, the Make-A-Wish Foundation, AmeriCares, and many others, we have perhaps been best known for our efforts in the areas of fighting cancer and honoring America's veterans. Back in 1993, ESPN partnered with Jim Valvano to create the V Foundation for Cancer Research, which was announced at the very first ESPY Awards. Ever since then, the ESPYS have grown strong under the leadership of longtime producer Maura Mandt. After many years in New York City and a few years in Las Vegas, the show settled in Los Angeles, where it has thrived.

At the first ESPY Awards, Robin Roberts was waiting in the wings when Jimmy V gave his historic "Don't Ever Give Up" speech while accepting the Arthur Ashe Award for Courage. She was the very next person on stage and summed up the feeling of everybody in our company when she said, "I've never been more proud of ESPN than I am tonight." As a matter of fact, Robin was present at the press conference with Arthur Ashe, Steve Bornstein, and Chris Berman when the award was first announced. At that time, she had not been touched by cancer and did not know how important Jim Valvano's words would one day be to her. In 2007 Robin was diagnosed with breast cancer, underwent treatment, and beat it into remission. Then in 2012, the doctors found she had a type of bone marrow cancer called myelodysplastic syndrome. In October of that year, Robin fought back hard by undergoing a risky but successful bone marrow transplant.

Less than a year later, at the twentieth ESPY Awards in 2013, Robin Roberts, herself, was given the Arthur Ashe Award for Courage. Introducing her that night were First Lady Michelle Obama (via video) and LeBron James. In accepting the award, Robin couldn't help but wonder who might be watching at that moment, just like she was watching Jim Valvano twenty years earlier. She offered advice from her beloved mother, Lucimarian: "When fear knocks, let faith answer the door." And then Robin remembered Valvano:

> That night, in establishing the V Foundation for Cancer Research, Jim said: "We need your help. *I* need your help. We need money for research. It may not save my life, it may save my children's, it may save someone you love." I never imagined that I'd be standing here twenty years after Jimmy V's speech and say that, because of everyone who has responded to his challenge, because of all the donations, research, and support—*mine* is one of the lives that has been saved.

Robin Roberts with the Arthur Ashe Award for Courage at the 2013 ESPYS. *ESPN Images*

The V Foundation for Cancer Research has awarded more than $130 million in research grants. One hundred percent of direct cash contributions goes straight to doctors for their studies. In 2014, Jim Valvano's former teammate Bob Lloyd stepped down as chairman of the V Foundation and turned the reins over to Steve Bornstein. Ever since ESPN and Jim agreed to move forward, the V Foundation has been fully enmeshed in the DNA of ESPN and its people. We think a lot about it and we do things for it—like the Jimmy V Week for Cancer Research, Dick Vitale's Annual Gala, and the ESPY Celebrity Golf Classic. Every year before the ESPYS, *SportsCenter* anchor Stuart Scott, who tragically passed away in January 2015, represented the many ESPN people who have been touched by cancer. He participated in our ESPY golf tournament, often kicking off the event with moving words of encouragement and hope. In accepting the Jimmy V Perseverance Award at the 2014 ESPYS, Stuart eloquently summed it up for a lot of people. "You beat cancer by *how* you live, *why* you live, and *the manner in which* you live," he said.

ESPN's Stuart Scott addresses participants at the ESPY Celebrity Golf Classic, 2007. *Phil Ellsworth / ESPN Images*

In addition to being a great basketball coach, Jim Valvano's legacy is the millions of people who have been and will be affected by the work of the V Foundation. His message (and the foundation's motto) is important for all aspects of life, whether it's fighting cancer or waging an uphill battle to build something of value. "Don't give up," said Jimmy V. "Don't ever give up."

⸻

In all my years as a manager at ESPN, I never once turned down an employee who asked to see me. In 2003, one gentleman made the request and I could tell as soon as he walked into my office that he had a chip on his shoulder. After a few pleasantries were exchanged, he got right to the point: "Why doesn't this company do anything to recognize and honor veterans of the armed forces?"

I looked him in the eye and said, "I am sure that I do not have a good answer for that question. Why don't you form a group and make some recommendations?" He did and that's how the ESPN Veterans Committee started. It began with only eight or ten people, but once word spread we cobbled together a list of about forty veterans who were working at ESPN, most of whom had served in the Vietnam War. Our first effort to recognize them was at an early-evening cocktail party with a retired general from Connecticut as speaker. *[I learned very early in my tenure that if you really want to get a group of ESPN people together, you announce an open bar.]* A few days later, we delivered to each veteran customized ESPN athletic jackets (embroidered with their names and the branches of the military in which they served), accompanied by a special letter thanking them for their service to our country. Their response moved me deeply. Many broke down and wept at their desks, saying that nobody had ever thanked them before.

Over the next few years, we held more luncheons and brought in a variety of speakers. Then we began going on trips, usually in conjunction with Veterans Day. We went to the U.S. Military Academy at West Point and to the Intrepid Sea, Air & Space Museum in Manhattan, for instance. With time, ESPN's veterans began marching in Veterans Day parades to represent our company and, before you knew it, we were honoring them and all American veterans on the air. In September 2004, *SportsCenter* went on the road for the first time to broadcast live from Camp Arifjan in Kuwait, where U.S. troops gathered before and after heading into combat in Iraq. For a week, the ESPN crew (led by Norby Williamson, and including Steve Levy, Stuart Scott, Kenny Mayne, and Lisa Salters) mixed and mingled with the soldiers in 120-degree heat, interviewed them live on camera, and most important let them know that Americans back home appreciated what they were doing.

Soon, our Veterans Day celebration morphed into Veterans Week and included many of our programs and all of our platforms. From 2009 to 2014, *SportsCenter* continued their road show with programs from such military installations as the U.S. Naval Academy in Annapolis, Maryland; Ramstein Air Base in Germany; and the Marine Corps Air Station in Jacksonville, North Carolina, to name a few. *College GameDay* went to the U.S. Air Force Academy in Colorado Springs, Colorado. *Mike and Mike in the Morning* broadcast live from the U.S. Coast Guard Academy in New London, Connecticut, and from the Coast Guard Cutter *Mohawk* in Key West, Florida.

Bob Ley hosted *Outside the Lines* from the USS *Arizona* in Pearl Harbor and the National World War II Museum in New Orleans, Louisiana. ESPN also often partnered with various athletic organizations and leagues to telecast sporting events during Veterans Week. In 2011, we covered the Carrier Classic NCAA men's basketball game between Michigan State and North Carolina live aboard the USS *Carl Vinson* in San Diego Harbor. And in 2013, when Veterans Day coincided with a *Monday Night Football* game between the Miami Dolphins and the Tampa Bay Buccaneers, ESPN's entire twenty-four-hour "game-around-the-game" was interspersed with features, interviews, and salutes to our veterans from all wars and all branches of the military.

Veterans Day 2010 on the ESPN campus. *Joe Faraoni*

In the wake of the Great Recession (post-2009), one story making national headlines reported that veterans from the Iraq and Afghanistan wars were having a difficult time finding jobs when they returned home. When I sat down to discuss the issue with Paul Richardson, ESPN's head of human resources (and later The Walt Disney Company's chief diversity officer, as well), it became clear that if we were really going to make a serious impact on hiring veterans, it would have to be accomplished at the Disney level. After all, ESPN employed seven thousand people, but Disney had more than one hundred thousand. To his everlasting credit, Bob Iger immediately embraced the idea and then personally spearheaded a company-wide initiative to hire, train, and support American's returning veterans. At the 2012 shareholder meeting, Bob announced the new project, called Heroes Work Here, which included Disney Career Expos and veteran outreach programs being conducted across the nation. And within a few years, Disney had added more than three thousand veterans to the ranks of America's employed.

In 2009 we placed a plaque by the flagpole in "Veterans Circle" at the front entrance of the Bristol campus. It is a permanent reminder that veterans of all U.S. military services should be honored and thanked for their service to our country. After all, through their hard-fought efforts to preserve freedom around the world, they have made it possible for companies such as ESPN to succeed and prosper in the free enterprise system we all enjoy today. The plaque reads:

> VETERANS MEMORIAL
> Dedicated to
> All men and women of the United States Armed Forces
> whose sacrifices and deeds shall be written in
> history and forever remain in our memory.

ESPN's efforts to honor America's veterans began when that one disgruntled Vietnam veteran had the courage to walk into my office to tell me we needed to do more. And he was right.

About a week after completing work on the playground at the Boys & Girls Club in Slidell, Louisiana, every member of the MAX group received a construction paper "thank you" from the children who played there. Mine was from a seven-year-old girl who drew a smiley face and simply wrote, "Thank you for our playground." Then she signed her name. I was so proud of it, I had it framed and hung it on my wall. It will always mean as much to me as any trophy or award I will ever receive.

A playground is an important part of a child's life. It's often where they first learn social skills and how to get along with other children. On a playground, imagination runs wild as kids constantly experiment and try new things. These are seeds that eventually grow into such skills as creativity, innovation, and thinking outside the lines. Perhaps most important, kids try new things while they're enjoying themselves.

Thank-you poster from a seven-year-old girl at the Boys & Girls Club in Slidell, Louisiana.

Having fun is important for children. It's also important for adults.

Darell Hammond, founder of KaBOOM! (with which ESPN partnered to build the Slidell playground), has said that his nonprofit organization strives to make playgrounds better so that kids want to stay longer and come back more often. That makes sense to me. So why wouldn't business leaders strive to make corporations more fun so that employees enjoy being there? Well, I believe that's what people like Bill Rasmussen, Scotty Connal, and Chet Simmons had in mind all along.

When I started at ESPN in 1981, we were pinching ourselves that we actually got paid to work at a start-up that focused solely on sports. We loved working at ESPN because sports are enjoyable—whether you're watching or participating. You *play* the game. You *play* your position. You have *fun*. In that sense, ESPN was the ultimate adult playground. Our corporate culture allowed people to use their imaginations, which resulted in unparalleled creativity, innovation, and thinking outside the lines.

As president of ESPN, I thought a lot about the old days when we had only a couple hundred employees. When I worked in the mailroom, when I drove Dick Vitale to and from the airport, and when I supplied videotapes to Chris Berman in the middle of the night, I loved every minute of it. I truly did. ESPN was our playground back then. And now that we numbered more than seven thousand employees, I viewed it as part of my job to keep that spirit alive.

To mark our thirty-first anniversary, we invited ESPN's founder, Bill Rasmussen, back to Bristol to honor him. September 7, 2010, was going to be his day.

Bill traveled all the way from his home in Seattle to be with us. He brought along his family, including his wife, Mickey, and young granddaughters. After a casual welcoming in my office, I escorted them to a large employee function we had planned. Everywhere we walked, Bill was the big celebrity on campus. Our employees mobbed him, asked for his autograph, and wanted to shake his hand. After lunch, we set up a table for him to do a book signing and people waited in line for an hour just to speak to him. Bill told me later that many employees made a point of telling him how much they really enjoyed being at ESPN. "I've been here for twelve years and I love it," said one person. "I've been at ESPN for twenty years and I'm going to retire here," said another. "I've never worked at a place this great. Thank you, Mr. Rasmussen, for founding ESPN. Thank you."

Later that day, Bill and his family were genuinely moved when, outside at the foot of the main flagpole on the Bristol campus, we dedicated a permanent plaque to him. It read:

> DEDICATED TO ESPN FOUNDER
> BILL RASMUSSEN
> In honor of his entrepreneurial spirit and passion for sports
> * ESPN hallmarks today *
> September 7, 2010—ESPN'S 31st anniversary

That was a proud day for all of us at ESPN. Essentially, we were saying thank you to Bill Rasmussen. Thank you for your idea. Thank you for ESPN. Thank you for our playground.

The Best Is Yet to Be

On any given morning, a car pulls up in the circular driveway at ESPN's main entrance and some prominent athlete or celebrity steps out to run through the "Bristol Car Wash"—our series of interviews on multiple programs and media. We may start with *Mike and Mike in the Morning*, ESPN Radio's *The Herd with Colin Cowherd*, and then move on to a live chat on ESPN.com, *SportsCenter*, *ESPN The Magazine*, *Outside the Lines*, or any one of our many offerings. In most media companies, individuals will do an interview on television or radio and then leave for their next appointment. But at ESPN, they stay the entire day, from 8:30 a.m. to 4 p.m.

One morning, Bob Ley (who coined the phrase *Bristol Car Wash*) ran into Billy Crystal in the makeup room and was surprised to find him nervous. "Billy Crystal was nervous about being on *SportsCenter*?" thought Bob. "Well, he *is* a big sports fan." Actually, everybody who comes to ESPN is a sports fan—and virtually everybody who works at ESPN is a sports fan.

From the very first broadcast with George Grande at the desk saying we were going to be here every day to serve fans, *SportsCenter* has continued to grow. In the old days, we produced three live shows at

6 p.m., 11 p.m., and 2:30 a.m. Over the years the individual shows grew in length, and during the early 1990s we began re-airing the late show in the mornings, eventually from 6 a.m. to 1 p.m. A few years later, both to serve fans and report on the growing amount of sports news breaking in the morning, we began live *SportsCenter* cut-ins. In 2008, we determined that our signature show needed to go fully live beginning at 9 a.m. and continuing right through to 3 p.m. By 2014, we were producing more than eighteen hours of live *SportsCenter* each and every day. As a matter of fact, if *SportsCenter* were its own television network, it would rank as the fifth most watched among men aged eighteen to thirty-four.

According to John Walsh, there were five stages in *SportsCenter*'s history. First, there were the early years when we scrambled just to stay on the air. Then the personalities of our anchors took over when, for instance, Chris Berman with his baseball player nicknames started putting his own stamp on the show. The "journalism" years came next as *SportsCenter* led the way in "flooding the zone" and creating a new way of reporting sports news. The fourth stage could be called the "opinion" period as our anchors began infusing more debate into the broadcasts, which in turn led to such new ESPN programs as *Around the Horn* and *Pardon the Interruption*. And finally, the fifth stage of *SportsCenter* revolved around the Internet and new technology, which provided many new opportunities for us to serve sports fans. So we placed our flagship program on mobile phones, tablets, and every other available platform that fans might be using. And in June 2014, *SportsCenter* reinvented itself again, with the debut of its new studio in the state-of-the-art Digital Center II.

It was no accident that ESPN led the way not only on TV, but also with multimedia. We planned for it years in advance by investing billions of dollars in programming and new technology to relentlessly drive innovation across every screen. Essentially, for thirty-five years, we delivered on our promise to cable and satellite operators that we would provide the highest-value sports programming in the market-place. That's one reason the ESPN brand became a household name, in the same league with Coca-Cola, IBM, Google, and, of course, our parent company, Disney. Not bad for a twenty-four-hour sports channel that was widely ridiculed in the beginning.

In the process of building that brand, ESPN changed the American landscape from both an enterprise and a social perspective. Our business model transformed cable TV into a highly desired consumer product, which then became the foundation for the TV/phone/broadband business that we know today. And in a reciprocal relationship, sports leagues grew right along with ESPN, because our coverage elevated their national and international profiles. That list is impressive, and includes college football, college basketball, the NFL, Major League Baseball, the NBA, the NHL, NASCAR, and professional golf and tennis, to name some of the big ones. Moreover, there's no question we helped grow interest in sports leagues beyond their regular seasons to a year-round dialogue.

Socially, ESPN has become a part of American culture. There was a time not too long ago when ESPN just didn't exist. Today, adults often have ESPN on their television sets when they're doing projects at home. Kids watch *SportsCenter* in the morning so they can know how their favorite teams fared before they get on the school bus. An interesting trivia note is that more than thirty babies have been named after ESPN (Espen or some similar derivation). And think about how many restaurants, taverns, and bars have multiple television screens with various ESPN channels running all the time. *[Now that I'm not in the president's office, I'm going to do a lot more research on ESPN in those bars.]*

Any curious person might be interested in how ESPN grew from a laughingstock to a household name. If I had to choose just one key to ESPN's success, I'd say that ESPN's culture was our strategic advantage. And over the years, we managed to perpetuate that entrepreneurial, underdog, never-stop-innovating mentality that went right along with it. From the very beginning, ESPN's strategy was to hire young people, put them in a team environment, and let them do what they did best. There was a reason, for example, that Chet Simmons and Scotty Connal started me in the mailroom as a driver. Their idea was to bring in young people who were not encumbered by the old ways of doing things. And then, in their "Monday Morning Quarterback" meetings, they identified the hard workers and gave them even more responsibility to see how they'd do. *["Okay, time to give young George the true test. Put him on Vitale."]*

Once at ESPN, employees worked in a team-oriented environment. Every department, every small group tried to capture the bond and the chemistry that exists among great sports teams. We cared about and supported each other. We started our sentences with "we," not "I." It was about "us," not "me." *[The whole is bigger than any of its individual parts.]* And just like on any sports team, we put people in positions they liked to play, and played best. George Grande, for instance, let the young reporters on *SportsCenter* cover the sports they were passionate about—Tom Mees on hockey, Lou Palmer on golf, Chris Berman on football, and Bob Ley on basketball. And it didn't necessarily matter how much seniority a person had. If they were good at what they did, and they really wanted to try something, we gave them the opportunity to do so. *[Do not stand on ceremony and title.]*

Then as careers progressed, we often stretched our employees by moving them into new positions, whether they had the "right" qualifications or not. You can do that when you have competent, creative, energetic, and smart people. New challenges breathe new life into employees and that, in turn, often results in new thinking. *[Creative people will be creative wherever they are.]* That's the way it was at ESPN in the 1980s and that's the way it still is today. *Outside the Lines*, for instance, keeps our young staffers involved by encouraging them to use their imaginations and to be outspoken. At weekly team meetings, whoever has the best idea will carry the day. "Hey, that young PA just had a terrific idea! Let's flesh that out! Let's talk about it! We can do that!" *[One good idea can lead to all kinds of new things.]*

Some new ideas affected only individual departments or programs. Some affected the entire company. For most, we took time to dot all the *i*'s and cross all the *t*'s. For many, we took a risk, often implementing action without a formal business plan, such as when we launched ESPNews or first sent *College GameDay* on the road. And if circumstances and events required people to act on their own initiative, they had the green light to do so. That's what happened during the San Francisco earthquake when our on-site team turned on a dime and did what they needed to do without waiting for permission. *[Empowered people exceed expectations.]*

From day one, hard work was part of the ESPN culture, in part, I think, because we hired passionate people. Passion drives hard work. The two are almost inseparable. And passion not only drove our company, it sustained the longstanding bond between ESPN and sports fans. You never see "passion" as a line item in any business plan, but I have yet to see a business plan succeed without it. *[Passionate people over-deliver.]*

As president of ESPN, I was always being asked questions. "George, what are we going to do about this?" "George, what are we going to do about that?" The questions never stopped, nor should they have, because we were a business and decisions had to be made. But I never professed to have all the answers, nor did I pretend to be an expert in every field important to ESPN. Rather, I surrounded myself with smart, passionate, and motivated people who had expertise in a wide variety of areas (technology, production, communication, finance, you name it). So when somebody asked me, "George, what are we going to do about this," my response was usually, "Well, I'm not sure I know.

But I *will* tell you what I *do* know. We've got seven thousand diverse people at ESPN and, collectively, we'll find the answer."

My job was not to tell those seven thousand people what to do. My job was to lead them. Leadership was a part of our culture—perhaps the most important part. At ESPN, we were all judged on how we made other people better, and that lifted the entire organization to unimaginable heights.

Leadership is about people. And if there's one skill I think I do have, it's getting along with others. I got that from my parents, Julian and Vivian Bodenheimer. "Often, the help you need comes from other people," my dad used to say. "Don't forget the Golden Rule," Mom said more times than I can count. One question repeatedly posed to me over the years was, "George, how did you get those hard-core cable CEOs to agree to a 20 percent increase for six years in a row?" Well, part of the answer to that question is that I developed personal relationships with them. "George, we hate the price," they'd say, "but we like you."

I also credit my parents with instilling in me the value of respect, which is directly related to leadership. It's a belief that *every* person should be treated fairly, civilly, and with dignity. I also believe that a good leader can be tactful, polite, and down-to-earth. You don't have to scream, yell, drop an F-bomb, or be threatening to get your point across. In fact, I think it takes a lot more strength not to berate people in such a manner. Furthermore, people can tell a phony a mile off. They know if you really care about them or not. And if you really do care, you're halfway home in becoming a leader.

Caring about people—that's leadership. Achieving great things for your organization—that's also leadership. You can grow your company economically. You can also grow your company culturally, spiritually, and emotionally. Great leadership does both.

I have often been asked, what are the most important things a leader can do for an organization? Here's the answer: You define the mission, you work with employees to set priorities, you live the culture, and you support everybody in doing their thing. That's it. That's my message.

━━━━━━━━

In March 2011, I informed my boss, Bob Iger, that I was not going to renew my contract as president of ESPN when it expired at the end of the year. After thirteen years as president, I was simply ready for a change, and I felt it was time to give other people a chance to move up and run the company. I also wanted to care for and spend more time with my parents, who had recently entered a retirement home only a short drive from my house. Although surprised, Bob respected my decision and suggested I stay on in a higher-level role that did not include day-to-day operations. I agreed to that, and we began the process of determining who was going to become the next president of ESPN. Meanwhile, I went about my normal everyday duties.

In the summer of that year, I attended my final annual priorities meeting, although no one else knew it would be my last. During our discussions, someone suggested that we make the affiliate department a priority. But David Preschlack (the department leader at the time) surprised everybody. "Guys, we were a priority last year and it worked great," he said. "We are getting all the help we need. Please give the priority to somebody else."

I was very proud to hear that. First of all, I had hired David as an intern back in 1995 from Denison University (my alma mater), and I was proud of his career at ESPN and of his selflessness in that instance. Second, it was clear from David's comment that the priority system was working well. We had started it ten years before during the ratings crisis of 2001 as a way to solve the problem and to give every employee a voice in how ESPN was run. The process had grown every year, steadily increasing the number of suggestions from thousands of our employees. So it was very clear to me from that meeting that our culture was being perpetuated. The priorities were working great, the affiliate sales department (where I had grown up) was working great, and young people were progressing to become leaders. I couldn't have been more proud at that moment.

In the late fall of 2011, I recommended to Bob Iger that John Skipper be promoted to the presidency of ESPN. Bob readily agreed to the move and John took over on January 1, 2012. My new title was executive chairman of ESPN. I continued a busy schedule, but Skipper ran the day-to-day operations of the business. Two years later, in May 2014, after thirty-three fantastic years, I left the greatest company in the world.

It means a lot to me to know that ESPN is going to thrive in the future. And for a variety of reasons, I have no doubt that will happen.

Shortly before leaving, I asked John Skipper about where ESPN goes from here. "George, we have a compass that has true north on it," he said. "We serve sports fans, anytime, anywhere. We're going to achieve our mission by galvanizing the people of ESPN. They'll come out of the locker room and run onto the field. They'll be ready to play."

ESPN's Mission prominently displayed in Digital Center II, 2014. *Rich Arden / ESPN Images*

ESPN was built on hard work, passion, integrity, and persevering when the odds were against us. That's our history. That's our tradition. And as long as the people of ESPN remember that history and continue that tradition, I really believe the best is yet to be.

ESPN will also be okay as long as there are sports. And there will always be sports.

When life brings us down, sports can pick us up. One highlight, one play, or one game can inspire us and make us smile. Whether you're a kid on the school bus or an octogenarian in a retirement community, whether you like the Yankees or the Seahawks or the Pacers or the Stars, if you're a sports fan, you can make a connection.

Sports brings people together. And that's beautiful. That's everything.

Epilogue

Every summer, my family and I spend some time in the tiny hamlet of Weekapaug, Rhode Island. The favorite part of my day is when I go to the local coffee shop every morning to pick up a newspaper and a cup of coffee. One morning as I was walking in, George Grande was coming out. It turned out that his mother had lived there for many years and we were staying less than a mile apart. George and I hadn't seen each other in years, but we immediately reconnected, picking up our relationship as though no time had passed at all. I think Chris Berman said it best when he noted that whenever any of us runs into ESPN guys from the old days, it's always with a big smile and a "hearty hello." We all share a bond that will never be broken.

The coffee shop is run by a fellow named Sprock and his wife, Ann. Ann handles the books and the food; Sprock stands behind the counter, takes care of the coffee, and talks to everybody. There are only about four or five stools at the bar, and usually I get there before the regulars come in. Sometimes when I walk in, Sprock will say, "George, you just missed George!"

"Yeah, we ran into each other," I'll respond. Most of the time the first thing we do is discuss yesterday's baseball scores. Weekapaug is only a couple of hours from Boston and the Red Sox are a big part of the summer conversation. The only problem is that Sprock is a die-hard Yankee fan.

"George, I know the Yanks lost last night, but the Sox played on the West Coast. Did they win or lose?"

"Let me check, Sprock," I respond as I look up the score on my phone. "Sorry, buddy. They won 5–4 on Big Papi's ninth-inning homer."

"Oh, man, I'm going to get it when Tom and the boys come in. Uh-oh, here they come now."

"Hey, Sprock, the Sox won last night," says Tom, walking through the door. "How'd the Yanks do? Ha, ha, ha."

"Yeah, yeah, I know, I know. Ortiz hit one out. Yanks lost a tough one. We'll get 'em tomorrow."

Tom and the guys then grab their coffees and belly up to the bar with Sprock and me.

Every town is a sports town.

Acknowledgments

I'd like to thank Rick Wolff, former vice president and executive editor at Grand Central Publishing, for his guidance and support of this project from the beginning. Bob Barnett served as literary representative for this book and did a great job. Harry Rhoads Jr. of the Washington Speakers Bureau and Ben Sherwood of Disney/ABC Television were instrumental in providing initial encouragement to write this book.

The following people participated in discussions and interviews, for which I am most grateful: Jim Allegro, Frank Bennack, Chris Berman, Ann Bodenheimer, Steve Bornstein, Kitty Bradley, Arthur Bulgrin, Don Colantonio, Lee Corso, Lee Ann Daly, Judy Fearing, Lee Fitting, Chris Fowler, George Grande, Bob Iger, Katie Lacey, Bill Lamb, Chris LaPlaca, Bob Ley, Tom Odjakjian, Chuck Pagano, Bill Rasmussen, Robin Roberts, Stuart Scott, Ron Semiao, Bill Simmons, Mark Shapiro, John Skipper, Pam Valvano, Dick Vitale, John Walsh, Roger Werner, Dereck Whittenburg, John Wildhack, and Russell Wolff.

Ed Durso, Chris LaPlaca, Mike Soltys, the excellent communications staff at ESPN, John Walsh, Barbara Blake, Laurel Daggett, Rich Arden, Joe Faraoni, and Arthur Bulgrin provided valuable assistance along the way, for which I am very appreciative.

I'd also like to thank Michael O'Connor of Williams & Connolly, Gretchen Young and the staff at Grand Central Publishing, and Jamie Raab, president and publisher at Hachette Book Group USA.

In covering thirty-five years of ESPN history along with my own personal experiences, I've mentioned many ESPN people by name. There are many more friends and colleagues who are not mentioned only because they did not come up specifically in the stories I wrote about. That does not lessen their contribution to ESPN in any way. I would like to acknowledge *everyone* who has ever worked for our company. Collectively, they deserve the credit for building ESPN into the great organization it is today.

Index

Note: Page numbers in *italics* indicate photos/illustrations.

About the Authors

George Bodenheimer is an ESPN and cable industry pioneer and was the company's longest-tenured president, a position he held from 1998 to 2011, overseeing all multimedia sports assets of The Walt Disney Company, including ABC Sports, from 2003 to 2011 and serving as co-chairman, Disney Media Networks, from 2004 to 2011. He served as executive chairman of ESPN, Inc., from 2012 to 2014. Mr. Bodenheimer graduated from Denison University with a degree in economics. He is married with three children. He also continues to serve on a number of commercial and nonprofit boards, and speaks frequently through the Washington Speakers Bureau.

Donald T. Phillips is the bestselling author of more than twenty books, including *Lincoln on Leadership*.